MznLnx

Missing Links Exam Preps

Exam Prep for

International Economics: Theory and Policy

Krugman & Obstfeld, 7th Edition

The MznLnx Exam Prep is your link from the texbook and lecture to your exams.
The MznLnx Exam Preps are unauthorized and comprehensive reviews of your textbooks.

All material provided by MznLnx and Rico Publications (c) 2010
Textbook publishers and textbook authors do not particpate in or contribute to these reviews.

MznLnx

Rico
Publications

Exam Prep for International Economics: Theory and Policy
7th Edition
Krugman & Obstfeld

Publisher: Raymond Houge
Assistant Editor: Michael Rouger
Text and Cover Designer: Lisa Buckner
Marketing Manager: Sara Swagger
Project Manager, Editorial Production: Jerry Emerson
Art Director: Vernon Lowerui

Product Manager: Dave Mason
Editorial Assitant: Rachel Guzmanji
Pedagogy: Debra Long
Cover Image: Jim Reed/Getty Images
Text and Cover Printer: City Printing, Inc.
Compositor: Media Mix, Inc.

(c) 2010 Rico Publications
ALL RIGHTS RESERVED. No part of this work covered by the copyright may be reproduced or used in any form or by an means--graphic, electronic, or mechanical, including photocopying, recording, taping, Web distribution, information storage, and retrieval systems, or in any other manner--without the written permission of the publisher.

For more information about our products, contact us at:
Dave.Mason@RicoPublications.com

For permission to use material from this text or product, submit a request online to:
Dave.Mason@RicoPublications.com

Printed in the United States
ISBN:

Contents

CHAPTER 1
Introduction — 1

CHAPTER 2
World Trade: An Overview — 7

CHAPTER 3
Labor Productivity and Comparative Advantage: The Ricardian Model — 11

CHAPTER 4
Resources, Comparative Advantage, and Income Distribution — 17

CHAPTER 5
The Standard Trade Model — 24

CHAPTER 6
Economies of Scale, Imperfect Competition, and International Trade — 32

CHAPTER 7
International Factor Movements — 41

CHAPTER 8
The Instruments of Trade Policy — 47

CHAPTER 9
The Political Economy of Trade Policy — 53

CHAPTER 10
Trade Policy in Developing Countries — 62

CHAPTER 11
Controversies in Trade Policy — 66

CHAPTER 12
National Income Accounting and the Balance of Payments — 71

CHAPTER 13
Exchange Rates and the Foreign Exchange Market: An Asset Approach — 82

CHAPTER 14
Money, Interest Rates, and Exchange Rates — 92

CHAPTER 15
Price Levels and the Exchange Rate in the Long Run — 104

CHAPTER 16
Output and the Exchange Rate in the Short Run — 112

CHAPTER 17
Fixed Exchange Rates and Foreign Exchange Intervention — 120

CHAPTER 18
The International Monetary System, 1870-1973 — 130

CHAPTER 19
Macroeconomic Policy and Coordination Under Floating Exchange Rates — 145

CHAPTER 20
Optimum Currency Areas and the European Experience — 154

Contents (Cont.)

CHAPTER 21
   The Global Capital Market: Performance and Policy Problems   163
CHAPTER 22
   Developing Countries: Growth, Crisis, and Reform   172
ANSWER KEY   184

TO THE STUDENT

COMPREHENSIVE

The *MznLnx* Exam Prep series is designed to help you pass your exams. Editors at MznLnx review your textbooks and then prepare these practice exams to help you master the textbook material. Unlike study guides, workbooks, and practice tests provided by the texbook publisher and textbook authors, *MznLnx* gives you **all** of the material in each chapter in exam form, not just samples, so you can be sure to nail your exam.

MECHANICAL

The MznLnx Exam Prep series creates exams that will help you learn the subject matter as well as test you on your understanding. Each question is designed to help you master the concept. Just working through the exams, you gain an understanding of the subject--its a simple mechanical process that produces success.

INTEGRATED STUDY GUIDE AND REVIEW

MznLnx is not just a set of exams designed to test you, its also a comprehensive review of the subject content. Each exam question is also a review of the concept, making sure that you will get the answer correct without having to go to other sources of material. You learn as you go! Its the easiest way to pass an exam.

HUMOR

Studying can be tedious and dry. MznLnx's instructional design includes moderate humor within the exam questions on occassion, to break the tedium and revitalize the brain

Chapter 1. Introduction

1. _____ was a survey conducted by the U.S. Department of Justice to gauge the prevalence of alcohol and illegal drug use among prior arrestees. It was a reformulation of the prior Drug Use Forecasting (DUF) program, focused on five drugs in particular: cocaine, marijuana, methamphetamine, opiates, and PCP.

Participants were randomly selected from arrest records in major metropolitan areas; because no personally identifying information is taken from each record chosen, the resulting data can be correlated to arrest rates, but not to the total population of persons charged.

   a. ACEA agreement   b. AD-IA Model
   c. ACCRA Cost of Living Index   d. Arrestee Drug Abuse Monitoring

2. In economics, an _____ is any good or commodity, transported from one country to another country in a legitimate fashion, typically for use in trade. _____ goods or services are provided to foreign consumers by domestic producers. _____ is an important part of international trade.

   a. ACCRA Cost of Living Index   b. ACEA agreement
   c. AD-IA Model   d. Export

3. In economics, an _____ is any good (e.g. a commodity) or service brought into one country from another country in a legitimate fashion, typically for use in trade. It is a good that is brought in from another country for sale. _____ goods or services are provided to domestic consumers by foreign producers. An _____ in the receiving country is an export to the sending country.

   a. Incoterms   b. Import quota
   c. Economic integration   d. Import

4. _____ was a Scottish moral philosopher and a pioneer of political economy. One of the key figures of the Scottish Enlightenment, Smith is the author of The Theory of Moral Sentiments and An Inquiry into the Nature and Causes of the Wealth of Nations. The latter, usually abbreviated as The Wealth of Nations, is considered his magnum opus and the first modern work of economics.

   a. Alan Greenspan   b. Adolph Fischer
   c. Adolf Hitler   d. Adam Smith

5. _____s is the social science that studies the production, distribution, and consumption of goods and services. The term _____s comes from the Ancient Greek οἰκονομῖα from οἶκος (oikos, 'house') + νόμος (nomos, 'custom' or 'law'), hence 'rules of the house(hold)'. Current _____ models developed out of the broader field of political economy in the late 19th century, owing to a desire to use an empirical approach more akin to the physical sciences.

   a. Energy economics   b. Inflation
   c. Economic   d. Opportunity cost

6. The _____ was a period of financial crisis that gripped much of Asia beginning in July 1997, and raised fears of a worldwide economic meltdown (financial contagion.)

The crisis started in Thailand with the financial collapse of the Thai baht caused by the decision of the Thai government to float the baht, cutting its peg to the USD, after exhaustive efforts to support it in the face of a severe financial overextension that was in part real estate driven. At the time, Thailand had acquired a burden of foreign debt that made the country effectively bankrupt even before the collapse of its currency.

a. Asian financial crisis
b. ACEA agreement
c. ACCRA Cost of Living Index
d. AD-IA Model

7. _____ in its literal sense is the process of transformation of local or regional phenomena into global ones. It can be described as a process by which the people of the world are unified into a single society and function together.

This process is a combination of economic, technological, sociocultural and political forces.

a. Global Cosmopolitanism
b. Helsinki Process on Globalisation and Democracy
c. Globalization
d. Globally Integrated Enterprise

8. _____ is a branch of economics with three main subdisciplines international trade, monetary economics and international finance.

- International trade studies goods-and-services flows across international boundaries from supply-and-demand factors, economic integration, and policy variables such as tariff rates and trade quotas.
- International finance studies the flow of capital across international financial markets, and the effects of these movements on exchange rates.
- International monetary economics and macroeconomics studies money and macro flows across countries.

- Stanley W. Black (2008.) 'international monetary institutions,' The New Palgrave Dictionary of Economics. 2nd Edition.

a. Economic depreciation
b. International economics
c. Index number
d. ACCRA Cost of Living Index

9. _____ is exchange of capital, goods, and services across international borders or territories. In most countries, it represents a significant share of gross domestic product (GDP.) While _____ has been present throughout much of history, its economic, social, and political importance has been on the rise in recent centuries.

a. Intra-industry trade
b. International trade
c. Import license
d. Incoterms

10. The term _____ is applied broadly to a variety of situations in which some financial institutions or assets suddenly lose a large part of their value. In the 19th and early 20th centuries, many financial crises were associated with banking panics, and many recessions coincided with these panics. Other situations that are often called financial crises include stock market crashes and the bursting of other financial bubbles, currency crises, and sovereign defaults.

a. Co-operative economics
b. Macroeconomics
c. Market failure
d. Financial crisis

11. _____ is a type of trade policy that allows traders to act and transact without interference from government. Thus, the policy permits trading partners mutual gains from trade, with goods and services produced according to the theory of comparative advantage.

Under a _____ policy, prices are a reflection of true supply and demand, and are the sole determinant of resource allocation.

Chapter 1. Introduction 3

    a. 100-year flood
    b. 130-30 fund
    c. Free Trade
    d. 1921 recession

12. The _____ is a trilateral trade bloc in North America created by the governments of the United States, Canada, and Mexico. The agreement creating the trade bloc came into force on January 1, 1994. It superseded the Canada-United States Free Trade Agreement between the U.S. and Canada.
    a. Federal Reserve Bank Notes
    b. Case-Shiller Home Price Indices
    c. North American Free Trade Agreement
    d. Demand-side technologies

13. The _____ commenced in September 1986 and continued until April 1994. The round, based on the General Agreement on Tariffs and Trade (GATT) ministerial meeting in Geneva (1982), was launched in Punta del Este in Uruguay (hence the name), followed by negotiations in Montreal, Geneva, Brussels, Washington, D.C., and Tokyo, with the 20 agreements finally being signed in Marrakech - the Marrakesh Agreement. The Round transformed the GATT into the World Trade Organization.
    a. ACEA agreement
    b. ACCRA Cost of Living Index
    c. AD-IA Model
    d. Uruguay Round

14. The _____ is an important selective, mainly private, international organization designed by its founders to supervise and liberalize international trade. The organization officially commenced on 1 January 1995, under the Marrakesh Agreement, succeeding the 1947 General Agreement on Tariffs and Trade (GATT.)

The _____ deals with regulation of trade between participating countries; it provides a framework for negotiating and formalising trade agreements, and a dispute resolution process aimed at enforcing participants' adherence to _____ agreements which are signed by representatives of member governments and ratified by their parliaments.

    a. Bio-energy village
    b. World Trade Organization
    c. 2009 G-20 London summit protests
    d. Backus-Kehoe-Kydland consumption correlation puzzle

15. In economics, the _____ measures the payments that flow between any individual country and all other countries. It is used to summarize all international economic transactions for that country during a specific time period, usually a year. The _____ is determined by the country's exports and imports of goods, services, and financial capital, as well as financial transfers.
    a. Gross world product
    b. Skyscraper Index
    c. Gross domestic product per barrel
    d. Balance of payments

16. The _____ is the official currency of 16 of the 27 member states of the European Union (EU.) The states, known collectively as the Eurozone, are Austria, Belgium, Cyprus, Finland, France, Germany, Greece, Ireland, Italy, Luxembourg, Malta, the Netherlands, Portugal, Slovakia, Slovenia, and Spain. The currency is also used in a further five European countries, with and without formal agreements and is consequently used daily by some 327 million Europeans.
    a. Euro
    b. Import and Export Price Indices
    c. IRS Code 3401
    d. Equity capital market

17. In finance, the _____s between two currencies specifies how much one currency is worth in terms of the other. It is the value of a foreign natione;s currency in terms of the home natione;s currency. For example an _____ of 102 Japanese yen to the United States dollar means that JPY 102 is worth the same as USD 1.
   a. Interbank market
   b. ACCRA Cost of Living Index
   c. ACEA agreement
   d. Exchange rate

18. The balance of trade (or net exports, sometimes symbolized as NX) is the difference between the monetary value of exports and imports in an economy over a certain period of time. It is the relationship between a nation's imports and exports. A favorable balance of trade is known as a _____ and consists of exporting more than is imported; an unfavorable balance of trade is known as a trade deficit or, informally, a trade gap.
   a. Trade surplus
   b. Business valuation standards
   c. Black-Scholes
   d. Dividend unit

19. In economics, the _____ is one of the two primary components of the balance of payments, the other being the capital account. It is the sum of the balance of trade (exports minus imports of goods and services), net factor income (such as interest and dividends) and net transfer payments (such as foreign aid.)

$$\text{Current account} = \text{Balance of trade} \\ + \text{Net factor income from abroad} \\ + \text{Net unilateral transfers from abroad}$$

The _____ balance is one of two major metrics of the nature of a country's foreign trade (the other being the net capital outflow.)

   a. Compensation of employees
   b. National Income and Product Accounts
   c. Gross private domestic investment
   d. Current account

20. A _____ is the transfer of wealth from one party (such as a person or company) to another. A _____ is usually made in exchange for the provision of goods, services or both, or to fulfill a legal obligation.

The simplest and oldest form of _____ is barter, the exchange of one good or service for another.

   a. Social gravity
   b. Payment
   c. Soft count
   d. Going concern

21. The _____ is the market for securities, where companies and governments can raise longterm funds. It is a market in which money is lent for periods longer than a year. The _____ includes the stock market and the bond market.
   a. Financial instrument
   b. Performance attribution
   c. Multi-family office
   d. Capital market

22. _____ is that which is owed; usually referencing assets owed, but the term can also cover moral obligations and other interactions not requiring money. In the case of assets, _____ is a means of using future purchasing power in the present before a summation has been earned. Some companies and corporations use _____ as a part of their overall corporate finance strategy.
   a. Hard money loan
   b. Collateral Management
   c. Debenture
   d. Debt

23. The term _____ is used to describe a nation's social or business activity in the process of rapid growth and industrialization. Currently, there are approximately 28 _____ in the world, with the economies of China and India considered to be two of the largest. According to The Economist many people find the term dated, but a new term has yet to gain much traction.
- a. Affinity diagram
- b. Occupational welfare
- c. Asymmetric price transmission
- d. Emerging markets

24. The _____ or gross domestic income (GDI), a basic measure of an economy's economic performance, is the market value of all final goods and services produced within the borders of a nation in a year. _____ can be defined in three ways, all of which are conceptually identical. First, it is equal to the total expenditures for all final goods and services produced within the country in a stipulated period of time (usually a 365-day year.)
- a. Countercyclical
- b. Market structure
- c. Monopolistic competition
- d. Gross domestic product

25. The _____ is a region that spans southwestern Asia and northeastern Africa. It has no clear boundaries, often used as a synonym to Near East, in opposition to Far East. The term '_____' was popularized around 1900 in the United Kingdom.
- a. Middle East
- b. 1921 recession
- c. 100-year flood
- d. 130-30 fund

26. _____s are deposits denominated in US dollars at banks outside the United States, and thus are not under the jurisdiction of the Federal Reserve. Consequently, such deposits are subject to much less regulation than similar deposits within the United States, allowing for higher margins. There is nothing 'European' about _____ deposits; a US dollar-denominated deposit in Tokyo or Caracas would likewise be deemed _____ deposits.
- a. AD-IA Model
- b. ACCRA Cost of Living Index
- c. ACEA agreement
- d. Eurodollar

27. In economics, _____ is the total demand for final goods and services in the economy (Y) at a given time and price level. It is the amount of goods and services in the economy that will be purchased at all possible price levels. This is the demand for the gross domestic product of a country when inventory levels are static.
- a. Aggregate demand
- b. Aggregation problem
- c. Aggregate expenditure
- d. Aggregate supply

28. Economics:

- _____,the desire to own something and the ability to pay for it
- _____ curve,a graphic representation of a _____ schedule
- _____ deposit, the money in checking accounts
- _____ pull theory,the theory that inflation occurs when _____ for goods and services exceeds existing supplies
- _____ schedule,a table that lists the quantity of a good a person will buy it each different price
- _____ side economics,the school of economics at believes government spending and tax cuts open economy by raising _____

a. McKesson ' Robbins scandal
b. Production
c. Variability
d. Demand

Chapter 2. World Trade: An Overview

1. In economics, economic output is divided into physical goods and intangible services. Consumption of _____ is assumed to produce utility. It is often used when referring to a _____ Tax.
   - a. Private good
   - b. Manufactured goods
   - c. Composite good
   - d. Goods and services

2. _____ are goods that have been processed by way of machinery. As such, they are the opposite of raw materials, but include intermediate goods as well as final goods.
   - a. Search good
   - b. Pie method
   - c. Manufactured goods
   - d. Superior goods

3. In economics, _____ refers to the ability of a person or a country to produce a particular good at a lower marginal cost and opportunity cost than another person or country. It is the ability to produce a product most efficiently given all the other products that could be produced. It can be contrasted with absolute advantage which refers to the ability of a person or a country to produce a particular good at a lower absolute cost than another.
   - a. Hot money
   - b. Triffin dilemma
   - c. Comparative advantage
   - d. Gravity model of trade

4. A _____ is an object whose consumption increases the utility of the consumer, for which the quantity demanded exceeds the quantity supplied at zero price. _____s are usually modeled as having diminishing marginal utility. The first individual purchase has high utility; the second has less.
   - a. Composite good
   - b. Merit good
   - c. Pie method
   - d. Good

5. In microeconomics, _____ is quite simply the conversion of inputs into outputs. It is an economic process that uses resources to create a good or service that is suitable for exchange. This can include manufacturing, storing, shipping, and packaging.
   - a. Red Guards
   - b. Solved
   - c. MET
   - d. Production

6. The _____ or gross domestic income (GDI), a basic measure of an economy's economic performance, is the market value of all final goods and services produced within the borders of a nation in a year. _____ can be defined in three ways, all of which are conceptually identical. First, it is equal to the total expenditures for all final goods and services produced within the country in a stipulated period of time (usually a 365-day year.)
   - a. Monopolistic competition
   - b. Countercyclical
   - c. Market structure
   - d. Gross domestic product

7. _____ is exchange of capital, goods, and services across international borders or territories. In most countries, it represents a significant share of gross domestic product (GDP.) While _____ has been present throughout much of history, its economic, social, and political importance has been on the rise in recent centuries.
   - a. Intra-industry trade
   - b. Import license
   - c. International trade
   - d. Incoterms

8. In finance, _____ is investment originating from other countries. See Foreign direct investment.
   - a. Preclusive purchasing
   - b. Horizontal merger
   - c. Demand side economics
   - d. Foreign investment

Chapter 2. World Trade: An Overview

9. A _____ is a general term that describes any government policy or regulation that restricts international trade. The barriers can take many forms, including the following terms that include many restrictions in international trade within multiple countries that import and export any items of trade.

- Import duty
- Import licenses
- Export licenses
- Import quotas
- Tariffs
- Subsidies
- Non-tariff barriers to trade
- Voluntary Export Restraints
- Local Content Requirements
- Embargo

Most _____s work on the same principle: the imposition of some sort of cost on trade that raises the price of the traded products. If two or more nations repeatedly use _____s against each other, then a trade war results.

a. Trade barrier
c. Certificate of origin
b. Global financial system
d. National Foreign Trade Council

10. _____ is a type of trade policy that allows traders to act and transact without interference from government. Thus, the policy permits trading partners mutual gains from trade, with goods and services produced according to the theory of comparative advantage.

Under a _____ policy, prices are a reflection of true supply and demand, and are the sole determinant of resource allocation.

a. 130-30 fund
c. 1921 recession
b. Free Trade
d. 100-year flood

11. The _____ is a trilateral trade bloc in North America created by the governments of the United States, Canada, and Mexico. The agreement creating the trade bloc came into force on January 1, 1994. It superseded the Canada-United States Free Trade Agreement between the U.S. and Canada.

a. Demand-side technologies
c. Federal Reserve Bank Notes
b. Case-Shiller Home Price Indices
d. North American Free Trade Agreement

12. The _____ is an economic and political union of 27 member states, located primarily in Europe. It was established by the Treaty of Maastricht on 1 November 1993, upon the foundations of the pre-existing European Economic Community. With a population of almost 500 million, the _____ generates an estimated 30% share (US$18.4 trillion in 2008) of the nominal gross world product.

a. European Court of Justice
c. ACEA agreement
b. European Union
d. ACCRA Cost of Living Index

13. _____, 1st Baron Keynes was a renowned economist from Britain whose many ideas on economic and political theories as well as on many governments' monetary policies influenced America. He advocated a government that played an active role in the lives of people regarding business, economy, etc. In this role, the government would use fiscal measures to reduce the consequences of recessions, economic depressions and booms.
   a. John Maynard Keynes
   b. Adolph Fischer
   c. Adolf Hitler
   d. Adam Smith

14. In economics, an _____ is any good or commodity, transported from one country to another country in a legitimate fashion, typically for use in trade. _____ goods or services are provided to foreign consumers by domestic producers. _____ is an important part of international trade.
   a. ACCRA Cost of Living Index
   b. Export
   c. AD-IA Model
   d. ACEA agreement

15. _____ is subcontracting a process, such as product design or manufacturing, to a third-party company. The decision to outsource is often made in the interest of lowering cost or making better use of time and energy costs, redirecting or conserving energy directed at the competencies of a particular business, or to make more efficient use of land, labor, capital, (information) technology and resources. _____ became part of the business lexicon during the 1980s.
   a. Averch-Johnson effect
   b. Electronic business
   c. Outsourcing
   d. Additional Funds Needed

16. _____ is a categorical label used to describe states that are considered to be underdeveloped in terms of their economy or level of industrialization, globalization, standard of living, health, education or other criteria for 'advancements'.

_____ was a reference to the 'the Third Estate, the commoners of France before and during the French Revolution, opposed to the priests and nobles who composed the First Estate and the Second Estate.

   a. 2008 budget crisis
   b. Bulgarian-American trade
   c. Developed markets
   d. Third world

17. _____ is that which is owed; usually referencing assets owed, but the term can also cover moral obligations and other interactions not requiring money. In the case of assets, _____ is a means of using future purchasing power in the present before a summation has been earned. Some companies and corporations use _____ as a part of their overall corporate finance strategy.
   a. Debenture
   b. Hard money loan
   c. Collateral Management
   d. Debt

18. Economics:

    - _____, the desire to own something and the ability to pay for it
    - _____ curve, a graphic representation of a _____ schedule
    - _____ deposit, the money in checking accounts
    - _____ pull theory, the theory that inflation occurs when _____ for goods and services exceeds existing supplies
    - _____ schedule, a table that lists the quantity of a good a person will buy it each different price
    - _____ side economics, the school of economics at believes government spending and tax cuts open economy by raising _____

a. Variability
c. Production

b. McKesson ' Robbins scandal
d. Demand

Chapter 3. Labor Productivity and Comparative Advantage: The Ricardian Model

1. In economics, _____ refers to the ability of a person or a country to produce a particular good at a lower marginal cost and opportunity cost than another person or country. It is the ability to produce a product most efficiently given all the other products that could be produced. It can be contrasted with absolute advantage which refers to the ability of a person or a country to produce a particular good at a lower absolute cost than another.
   - a. Gravity model of trade
   - b. Hot money
   - c. Triffin dilemma
   - d. Comparative advantage

2. _____s is the social science that studies the production, distribution, and consumption of goods and services. The term _____s comes from the Ancient Greek οἰκονομῖα from οἶκος (oikos, 'house') + νόμος (nomos, 'custom' or 'law'), hence 'rules of the house(hold)'. Current _____ models developed out of the broader field of political economy in the late 19th century, owing to a desire to use an empirical approach more akin to the physical sciences.
   - a. Energy economics
   - b. Opportunity cost
   - c. Inflation
   - d. Economic

3. _____, in microeconomics, are the cost advantages that a business obtains due to expansion. They are factors that cause a producere;s average cost per unit to fall as scale is increased. _____ is a long run concept and refers to reductions in unit cost as the size of a facility, or scale, increases.
   - a. Economies of scale
   - b. Isoquant
   - c. Economic production quantity
   - d. Underinvestment employment relationship

4. _____ is a type of trade policy that allows traders to act and transact without interference from government. Thus, the policy permits trading partners mutual gains from trade, with goods and services produced according to the theory of comparative advantage.

   Under a _____ policy, prices are a reflection of true supply and demand, and are the sole determinant of resource allocation.
   - a. 130-30 fund
   - b. Free trade
   - c. 1921 recession
   - d. 100-year flood

5. The _____ is a general equilibrium mathematical model of international trade, developed by Eli Heckscher and Bertil Ohlin at the Stockholm School of Economics. It builds on David Ricardo's theory of comparative advantage by predicting patterns of commerce and production based on the factor endowments of a trading region. The model essentially says that countries will export products that utilize their abundant and cheap factor(s) of production and import products that utilize the countries' scarce factor(s.)
   - a. Jamaican Free Zones
   - b. Free trade zone
   - c. Linder hypothesis
   - d. Heckscher-Ohlin model

6. _____ is exchange of capital, goods, and services across international borders or territories. In most countries, it represents a significant share of gross domestic product (GDP.) While _____ has been present throughout much of history, its economic, social, and political importance has been on the rise in recent centuries.
   - a. Incoterms
   - b. Import license
   - c. Intra-industry trade
   - d. International trade

7. _____ in economics refers to metrics and measures of output from production processes, per unit of input. Labor _____, for example, is typically measured as a ratio of output per labor-hour, an input. _____ may be conceived of as a metrics of the technical or engineering efficiency of production.

a. Fordism
b. Piece work
c. Production-possibility frontier
d. Productivity

8. _____ or economic opportunity loss is the value of the next best alternative foregone as the result of making a decision. _____ analysis is an important part of a company's decision-making processes but is not treated as an actual cost in any financial statement. The next best thing that a person can engage in is referred to as the _____ of doing the best thing and ignoring the next best thing to be done.
   a. Economic ideology
   b. Economic
   c. Opportunity cost
   d. Industrial organization

9. In microeconomics, _____ is quite simply the conversion of inputs into outputs. It is an economic process that uses resources to create a good or service that is suitable for exchange. This can include manufacturing, storing, shipping, and packaging.
   a. MET
   b. Production
   c. Solved
   d. Red Guards

10. _____ is an online peer-reviewed magazine published by the Agricultural ' Applied Economics Association (AAEA) for readers interested in the policy and management of agriculture, the food industry, natural resources, rural communities, and the environment. _____ is published quarterly and is available free online. It is currently one of three outreach products offered by AAEA, along with the more timely Policy Issues and the forthcoming Shared Materials section of the AAEA Web site.
   a. 1921 recession
   b. 130-30 fund
   c. 100-year flood
   d. Choices

11. _____ is a common concept in economics, and gives rise to derived concepts such as consumer debt. Generally _____ is defined by opposition to production. But the precise definition can vary because different schools of economists define production quite differently.
   a. Cash or share options
   b. Consumption
   c. Foreclosure data providers
   d. Federal Reserve Bank Notes

12. _____ is the price of a commodity such as a good or service in terms of another; ie, the ratio of two prices. A _____ may be expressed in terms of a ratio between any two prices or the ratio between the price of one particular good and a weighted average of all other goods available in the market. A _____ is an opportunity cost.
   a. False economy
   b. Relative price
   c. False shortage
   d. Food cooperative

Chapter 3. Labor Productivity and Comparative Advantage: The Ricardian Model

13. Economics:

    - _____, the desire to own something and the ability to pay for it
    - _____ curve, a graphic representation of a _____ schedule
    - _____ deposit, the money in checking accounts
    - _____ pull theory, the theory that inflation occurs when _____ for goods and services exceeds existing supplies
    - _____ schedule, a table that lists the quantity of a good a person will buy it each different price
    - _____ side economics, the school of economics at believes government spending and tax cuts open economy by raising _____

    a. Demand
    b. Production
    c. McKesson ' Robbins scandal
    d. Variability

14. In finance, the _____s between two currencies specifies how much one currency is worth in terms of the other. It is the value of a foreign natione;s currency in terms of the home natione;s currency. For example an _____ of 102 Japanese yen to the United States dollar means that JPY 102 is worth the same as USD 1.

    a. ACEA agreement
    b. ACCRA Cost of Living Index
    c. Interbank market
    d. Exchange rate

15. In economic models, the _____ time frame assumes no fixed factors of production. Firms can enter or leave the marketplace, and the cost (and availability) of land, labor, raw materials, and capital goods can be assumed to vary. In contrast, in the short-run time frame, certain factors are assumed to be fixed, because there is not sufficient time for them to change.

    a. Diseconomies of scale
    b. Price/performance ratio
    c. Productivity world
    d. Long-run

16. _____ in economics and business is the result of an exchange and from that trade we assign a numerical monetary value to a good, service or asset. If Alice trades Bob 4 apples for an orange, the _____ of an orange is 4 apples. Inversely, the _____ of an apple is 1/4 oranges.

    a. Price book
    b. Price
    c. Premium pricing
    d. Price war

17. In economics, _____ is when quantity demanded is more than quantity supplied. See Economic shortage.

    a. ACCRA Cost of Living Index
    b. AD-IA Model
    c. ACEA agreement
    d. Excess demand

18. In economics, _____ refers to the ability of a party to produce a good or service using fewer real resources than another entity producing the same good or service..A party has an _____ when using the same input as another party, it can produce a greater output. Since _____ is determined by a simple comparison of labor productivities, it is possible for a a party to have no _____ in anything. It can be contrasted with the concept of comparative advantage which refers to the ability to produce a particular good at a lower opportunity cost.

    a. Index number
    b. ACCRA Cost of Living Index
    c. Absolute advantage
    d. International economics

14 **Chapter 3. Labor Productivity and Comparative Advantage: The Ricardian Model**

19. _____ theory is a branch of theoretical economics. It seeks to explain the behavior of supply, demand and prices in a whole economy with several or many markets. It is often assumed that agents are price takers and in that setting two common notions of equilibrium exist: Walrasian (or competitive) equilibrium, and its generalization; a price equilibrium with transfers.
   a. Human capital
   b. Rational choice theory
   c. New Keynesian economics
   d. General equilibrium

20. A _____ is a type of economic equilibrium, where the clearance on the market of some specific goods is obtained independently from prices and quantities demanded and supplied in other markets. In other words, the prices of all substitutes and complements, as well as income levels of consumers are constant. Here the dynamic process is that prices adjust until supply equals demand.
   a. Partial equilibrium
   b. Horizontal market
   c. Market depth
   d. Market system

21. In economics, the _____ can be defined as the graph depicting the relationship between the price of a certain commodity, and the amount of it that consumers are willing and able to purchase at that given price. It is a graphic representation of a demand schedule. The _____ for all consumers together follows from the _____ of every individual consumer: the individual demands at each price are added together.
   a. Kuznets curve
   b. Wage curve
   c. Cost curve
   d. Demand curve

22. The _____ movement is movement of movements which are critical of the globalization of capitalism. Participants base their criticisms on a number of related ideas. What is shared is that participants stand in opposition to the unregulated political power of large, multi-national corporations and to the powers exercised through trade agreements.
   a. Overcapitalisation
   b. Anti-consumerism
   c. Asset price inflation
   d. Anti-globalization

23. In international commerce and politics, an _____ is the prohibition of commerce (division of trade) and trade with a certain country, in order to isolate it and to put its government into a difficult internal situation, given that the effects of the _____ are often able to make its economy suffer from the initiative.

The _____ is usually used as a political punishment for some previous disagreed policies or acts, but its economic nature frequently raises doubts about the real interests that the prohibition serves.

One of the most comprehensive attempts at an _____ happened during the Napoleonic Wars.

   a. Overshooting model
   b. Optimum currency area
   c. International finance
   d. Embargo

24. _____ is a comparative concept of the ability and performance of a firm, sub-sector or country to sell and supply goods and/or services in a given market. Although widely used in economics and business management, the usefulness of the concept, particularly in the context of national _____, is vigorously disputed by economists, such as Paul Krugman .

The term may also be applied to markets, where it is used to refer to the extent to which the market structure may be regarded as perfectly competitive.

Chapter 3. Labor Productivity and Comparative Advantage: The Ricardian Model   15

a. Competitiveness
b. Countervailing duties
c. Quota share
d. Debt moratorium

25. _____ or worker mobility is the socioeconomic ease with which an individual or groups of individuals who are currently receiving remuneration in the form of wages can take advantage of various economic opportunities.

Worker mobility is best gauged by the lack of impediments to such mobility. Impediments to mobility are easily divided into two distinct classes with one being personal and the other being systemic.

a. Labor mobility
b. Genuine progress indicator
c. Purchasing power
d. Physical quality-of-life index

26. In economics, economic output is divided into physical goods and intangible services. Consumption of _____ is assumed to produce utility. It is often used when referring to a _____ Tax.
a. Manufactured goods
b. Private good
c. Composite good
d. Goods and services

27. _____ are goods that have been processed by way of machinery. As such, they are the opposite of raw materials, but include intermediate goods as well as final goods.
a. Pie method
b. Manufactured goods
c. Superior goods
d. Search good

28. A _____ is an object whose consumption increases the utility of the consumer, for which the quantity demanded exceeds the quantity supplied at zero price. _____s are usually modeled as having diminishing marginal utility. The first individual purchase has high utility; the second has less.
a. Composite good
b. Pie method
c. Good
d. Merit good

29. _____ is a term in economics, where demand for one good or service occurs as a result of demand for another. This may occur as the former is a part of production of the second. For example, demand for coal leads to _____ for mining, as coal must be mined for coal to be consumed.
a. Leontief production function
b. Rate risk
c. Days Sales Outstanding
d. Derived demand

30. In finance, _____ rate of profit or sometimes just return, is the ratio of money gained or lost on an investment relative to the amount of money invested. The amount of money gained or lost may be referred to as interest, profit/loss, gain/loss, or net income/loss. The money invested may be referred to as the asset, capital, principal, or the cost basis of the investment.
a. Rate of return
b. Sortino ratio
c. Current ratio
d. Cost accrual ratio

31. A variety of measures of _____ and output are used in economics to estimate total economic activity in a country or region, including gross domestic product (GDP), gross national product (GNP), and net _____

There are three main ways of calculating these numbers; the output approach, the income approach and the expenditure approach. In theory, the three must yield the same, because total expenditures on goods and services must equal the total income paid to the producers (Gnational income), and that must also equal the total value of the output of goods and services (GNP.)

   a. Gross world product
   b. National income
   c. GNI per capita
   d. Volume index

32. A _____ is an expression that compares quantities relative to each other. The most common examples involve two quantities, but any number of quantities can be compared. _____s are represented mathematically by separating each quantity with a colon, for example the _____ 2:3, which is read as the _____ 'two to three'.
   a. 130-30 fund
   b. Y-intercept
   c. Ratio
   d. 100-year flood

33. In economics, an _____ is any good or commodity, transported from one country to another country in a legitimate fashion, typically for use in trade. _____ goods or services are provided to foreign consumers by domestic producers. _____ is an important part of international trade.
   a. ACCRA Cost of Living Index
   b. ACEA agreement
   c. AD-IA Model
   d. Export

Chapter 4. Resources, Comparative Advantage, and Income Distribution 17

1. _____ is a type of trade policy that allows traders to act and transact without interference from government. Thus, the policy permits trading partners mutual gains from trade, with goods and services produced according to the theory of comparative advantage.

Under a _____ policy, prices are a reflection of true supply and demand, and are the sole determinant of resource allocation.

   a. 130-30 fund
   b. 100-year flood
   c. 1921 recession
   d. Free trade

2. _____ is exchange of capital, goods, and services across international borders or territories. In most countries, it represents a significant share of gross domestic product (GDP.) While _____ has been present throughout much of history , its economic, social, and political importance has been on the rise in recent centuries.
   a. Intra-industry trade
   b. Incoterms
   c. Import license
   d. International trade

3. In economics, _____ are the resources employed to produce goods and services. They facilitate production but do not become part of the product (as with raw materials) or significantly transformed by the production process (as with fuel used to power machinery.) To 19th century economists, the _____ were land (natural resources, gifts from nature), labor (the ability to work), and capital goods (human-made tools and equipment.)
   a. Factors of production
   b. Product Pipeline
   c. Long-run
   d. Hicks-neutral technical change

4. In microeconomics, _____ is quite simply the conversion of inputs into outputs. It is an economic process that uses resources to create a good or service that is suitable for exchange. This can include manufacturing, storing, shipping, and packaging.
   a. MET
   b. Red Guards
   c. Solved
   d. Production

5. The _____ is a general equilibrium mathematical model of international trade, developed by Eli Heckscher and Bertil Ohlin at the Stockholm School of Economics. It builds on David Ricardo's theory of comparative advantage by predicting patterns of commerce and production based on the factor endowments of a trading region. The model essentially says that countries will export products that utilize their abundant and cheap factor(s) of production and import products that utilize the countries' scarce factor(s.)
   a. Free trade zone
   b. Jamaican Free Zones
   c. Linder hypothesis
   d. Heckscher-Ohlin model

6. _____ is the price of a commodity such as a good or service in terms of another; ie, the ratio of two prices. A _____ may be expressed in terms of a ratio between any two prices or the ratio between the price of one particular good and a weighted average of all other goods available in the market. A _____ is an opportunity cost.
   a. Food cooperative
   b. False economy
   c. False shortage
   d. Relative price

Chapter 4. Resources, Comparative Advantage, and Income Distribution

7. _____ is an online peer-reviewed magazine published by the Agricultural ' Applied Economics Association (AAEA) for readers interested in the policy and management of agriculture, the food industry, natural resources, rural communities, and the environment. _____ is published quarterly and is available free online. It is currently one of three outreach products offered by AAEA, along with the more timely Policy Issues and the forthcoming Shared Materials section of the AAEA Web site.
   a. 100-year flood
   b. 130-30 fund
   c. 1921 recession
   d. Choices

8. _____ is a common concept in economics, and gives rise to derived concepts such as consumer debt. Generally _____ is defined by opposition to production. But the precise definition can vary because different schools of economists define production quite differently.
   a. Cash or share options
   b. Foreclosure data providers
   c. Federal Reserve Bank Notes
   d. Consumption

9. _____ in economics and business is the result of an exchange and from that trade we assign a numerical monetary value to a good, service or asset. If Alice trades Bob 4 apples for an orange, the _____ of an orange is 4 apples. Inversely, the _____ of an apple is 1/4 oranges.
   a. Premium pricing
   b. Price war
   c. Price book
   d. Price

10. _____ are the prices that the factors of production of a finished item attract.

There has been some economic debate as to what determines these prices. Classical and Marxist economists argued that the _____ decided the value of a product and so value was intrinsic within the product.

   a. Marginal product of labor
   b. Factor prices
   c. Productivity model
   d. Marginal product

11. _____ is the term denoting either an entrance or changes which are inserted into a system and which activate/modify a process. It is an abstract concept, used in the modeling, system(s) design and system(s) exploitation. It is usually connected with other terms, e.g., _____ field, _____ variable, _____ parameter, _____ value, _____ signal, _____ device and _____ file.
   a. ACEA agreement
   b. ACCRA Cost of Living Index
   c. AD-IA Model
   d. Input

12. A _____ is an object whose consumption increases the utility of the consumer, for which the quantity demanded exceeds the quantity supplied at zero price. _____s are usually modeled as having diminishing marginal utility. The first individual purchase has high utility; the second has less.
   a. Composite good
   b. Pie method
   c. Merit good
   d. Good

13. _____ is money accepted for exchange of goods in an economy. The prevalence of one money over another arises, usually, when a government designates through decrees that the government shall accept only particular notes and coins in payment for taxes. Typically, money of _____ consists of stamped coins and minted paper bills.

Chapter 4. Resources, Comparative Advantage, and Income Distribution

   a. Totnes pound
   b. Local currency
   c. Currency
   d. Security thread

14. _____ is the loss of value of a country's currency with respect to one or more foreign reference currencies, typically in a floating exchange rate system. It is most often used for the unofficial increase of the exchange rate due to market forces, though sometimes it appears interchangeably with devaluation. Its opposite is called appreciation.
   a. Fed Shreds
   b. Quote currency
   c. Currency depreciation
   d. Hero Card

15. _____ is a term used in accounting, economics and finance to spread the cost of an asset over the span of several years.

In simple words we can say that _____ is the reduction in the value of an asset due to usage, passage of time, wear and tear, technological outdating or obsolescence, depletion, inadequacy, rot, rust, decay or other such factors.

In accounting, _____ is a term used to describe any method of attributing the historical or purchase cost of an asset across its useful life, roughly corresponding to normal wear and tear.

   a. Depreciation
   b. Historical cost
   c. Net income per employee
   d. Salvage value

16. _____ is a phrase used in Indian English to mean that no bargaining is allowed over the price of a good or, less commonly, a service. As bargaining is very common in many parts of the world outside of Europe and North America, this term expresses an exception from the norm.

In the United Kingdom _____ has a similar meaning, and commonly indicates that an external party has set a price level, which may not be varied by individual sellers of a good or service.

   a. Fixed price
   b. Merchant
   c. Contingent payment sales
   d. Customer not present

17. In finance, _____ rate of profit or sometimes just return, is the ratio of money gained or lost on an investment relative to the amount of money invested. The amount of money gained or lost may be referred to as interest, profit/loss, gain/loss, or net income/loss. The money invested may be referred to as the asset, capital, principal, or the cost basis of the investment.
   a. Sortino ratio
   b. Cost accrual ratio
   c. Current ratio
   d. Rate of return

18. A _____ is an expression that compares quantities relative to each other. The most common examples involve two quantities, but any number of quantities can be compared. _____s are represented mathematically by separating each quantity with a colon, for example the _____ 2:3, which is read as the _____ 'two to three'.
   a. Y-intercept
   b. 100-year flood
   c. Ratio
   d. 130-30 fund

Chapter 4. Resources, Comparative Advantage, and Income Distribution

19. Economics:

- _____, the desire to own something and the ability to pay for it
- _____ curve, a graphic representation of a _____ schedule
- _____ deposit, the money in checking accounts
- _____ pull theory, the theory that inflation occurs when _____ for goods and services exceeds existing supplies
- _____ schedule, a table that lists the quantity of a good a person will buy it each different price
- _____ side economics, the school of economics at believes government spending and tax cuts open economy by raising _____

a. Variability
b. McKesson ' Robbins scandal
c. Production
d. Demand

20. The _____ is the official currency of 16 of the 27 member states of the European Union (EU.) The states, known collectively as the Eurozone, are Austria, Belgium, Cyprus, Finland, France, Germany, Greece, Ireland, Italy, Luxembourg, Malta, the Netherlands, Portugal, Slovakia, Slovenia, and Spain. The currency is also used in a further five European countries, with and without formal agreements and is consequently used daily by some 327 million Europeans.

a. IRS Code 3401
b. Equity capital market
c. Euro
d. Import and Export Price Indices

21. A _____ represents the combinations of goods and services that a consumer can purchase given current prices and his income. Consumer theory uses the concepts of a _____ and a preference map to analyze consumer choices. Both concepts have a ready graphical representation in the two-good case.

a. Budget constraint
b. Quality bias
c. Revealed preference
d. Joint demand

22. In economics, _____ is how a natione;s total economy is distributed among its population. . _____ has always been a central concern of economic theory and economic policy. Classical economists such as Adam Smith, Thomas Malthus and David Ricardo were mainly concerned with factor _____, that is, the distribution of income between the main factors of production, land, labour and capital.

a. Authorised capital
b. Equipment trust certificate
c. Income distribution
d. Eco commerce

23. _____ is an economic theory, which states that the relative prices for two identical factors of production in the same market will eventually equal each other because of competition. The price for each single factor need not become equal, but relative factors will. Whichever factor receives the lowest price before two countries integrate economically and effectively become one market will therefore tend to become more expensive relative to other factors in the economy, while those with the highest price will tend to become cheaper.

a. Price book
b. Premium pricing
c. Big ticket item
d. Factor price equalization

Chapter 4. Resources, Comparative Advantage, and Income Distribution   21

24.   In mathematics, an _____ is a statement about the relative size or order of two objects, or about whether they are the same or not

- The notation a < b means that a is less than b.
- The notation a > b means that a is greater than b.
- The notation a ≠ b means that a is not equal to b, but does not say that one is greater than the other or even that they can be compared in size.

In each statement above, a is not equal to b. These relations are known as strict inequalities. The notation a < b may also be read as 'a is strictly less than b'.

   a. AD-IA Model   b. Inequality
   c. ACCRA Cost of Living Index   d. ACEA agreement

25.   A _____ is a duty imposed on goods when they are moved across a political boundary. They are usually associated with protectionism, the economic policy of restraining trade between nations. For political reasons, _____s are usually imposed on imported goods, although they may also be imposed on exported goods.

   a. Tariff   b. 130-30 fund
   c. 1921 recession   d. 100-year flood

26.   _____ originally was the term for studying production, buying and selling, and their relations with law, custom, and government. _____ originated in moral philosophy. It developed in the 18th century as the study of the economies of states -- polities, hence _____.

   a. Political economy   b. Productive and unproductive labour
   c. Dirigisme   d. Geoeconomics

27.   In economics, an _____ is any good (e.g. a commodity) or service brought into one country from another country in a legitimate fashion, typically for use in trade. It is a good that is brought in from another country for sale. _____ goods or services are provided to domestic consumers by foreign producers. An _____ in the receiving country is an export to the sending country.

   a. Incoterms   b. Economic integration
   c. Import quota   d. Import

28.   An _____ is a type of protectionist trade restriction that sets a physical limit on the quantity of a good that can be imported into a country in a given period of time. Quotas, like other trade restrictions, are used to benefit the producers of a good in a domestic economy at the expense of all consumers of the good in that economy.

Critics say quotas often lead to corruption (bribes to get a quota allocation), smuggling (circumventing a quota), and higher prices for consumers.

   a. Import quota   b. Economic integration
   c. Agreement on Agriculture   d. International Monetary Systems

Chapter 4. Resources, Comparative Advantage, and Income Distribution

29. The _____ were import tariffs designed to support domestic British corn prices against competition from less expensive foreign imports between 1815 and 1846. The tariffs were introduced by the Importation Act 1815 (55 Geo. 3 c. 26) and repealed by the Importation Act 1846 (9 ' 10 Vict. c. 22). These laws are often viewed as examples of British mercantilism, and their abolition marked a significant step towards free trade.

   a. Nexus of contracts   b. Corn Laws
   c. Holder in due course   d. Federal Reserve Police

30. In economics, the _____ is one of the two primary components of the balance of payments, the other being the capital account. It is the sum of the balance of trade (exports minus imports of goods and services), net factor income (such as interest and dividends) and net transfer payments (such as foreign aid.)

$$\text{Current account} = \text{Balance of trade} \\ + \text{Net factor income from abroad} \\ + \text{Net unilateral transfers from abroad}$$

The _____ balance is one of two major metrics of the nature of a country's foreign trade (the other being the net capital outflow.)

   a. Gross private domestic investment   b. National Income and Product Accounts
   c. Compensation of employees   d. Current account

31. The _____ is the apparent contradiction that although water is on the whole more useful, in terms of survival, than diamonds, diamonds command a higher price in the market. The economist Adam Smith is often considered to be the classic presenter of this paradox. Nicolaus Copernicus, John Locke, John Law and others had previously tried to explain the disparity.

   a. 130-30 fund   b. Paradox of value
   c. 100-year flood   d. St. Petersburg paradox

32. The _____ was a period of financial crisis that gripped much of Asia beginning in July 1997, and raised fears of a worldwide economic meltdown (financial contagion.)

The crisis started in Thailand with the financial collapse of the Thai baht caused by the decision of the Thai government to float the baht, cutting its peg to the USD, after exhaustive efforts to support it in the face of a severe financial overextension that was in part real estate driven. At the time, Thailand had acquired a burden of foreign debt that made the country effectively bankrupt even before the collapse of its currency.

   a. ACEA agreement   b. ACCRA Cost of Living Index
   c. AD-IA Model   d. Asian financial crisis

33. The term _____ is applied broadly to a variety of situations in which some financial institutions or assets suddenly lose a large part of their value. In the 19th and early 20th centuries, many financial crises were associated with banking panics, and many recessions coincided with these panics. Other situations that are often called financial crises include stock market crashes and the bursting of other financial bubbles, currency crises, and sovereign defaults.

Chapter 4. Resources, Comparative Advantage, and Income Distribution

    a. Market failure
    b. Macroeconomics
    c. Financial crisis
    d. Co-operative economics

34. The _____ is a trilateral trade bloc in North America created by the governments of the United States, Canada, and Mexico. The agreement creating the trade bloc came into force on January 1, 1994. It superseded the Canada-United States Free Trade Agreement between the U.S. and Canada.
    a. Case-Shiller Home Price Indices
    b. Federal Reserve Bank Notes
    c. North American Free Trade Agreement
    d. Demand-side technologies

35. In economics an _____ line represents a combination of inputs which all cost the same amount. Although similar to the budget constraint in consumer theory, the use of the _____ pertains to cost-minimization in production, as opposed to utility-maximization. The typical _____ line represents the ratio of costs of labour and capital, so the formula is often written as:

$$rK + wL = C$$

Where w represents the wage of labour, and r represents the rental rate of capital.

    a. Epstein-Zin preferences
    b. Inventory analysis
    c. Isocost
    d. Incentive

36. In economics, an _____ is a contour line drawn through the set of points at which the same quantity of output is produced while changing the quantities of two or more inputs. While an indifference curve helps to answer the utility-maximizing problem of consumers, the _____ deals with the cost-minimization problem of producers. _____s are typically drawn on capital-labor graphs, showing the tradeoff between capital and labor in the production function, and the decreasing marginal returns of both inputs.
    a. Economic production quantity
    b. Economies of scale
    c. Underinvestment employment relationship
    d. Isoquant

Chapter 5. The Standard Trade Model

1. In microeconomics, _____s define a relationship between the production of two products in which the total market value is constant.

   For example: In a market that produces bread and wine, the market is willing to trade one bottle of wine for three breads. If this relationship is constant, we would have an _____ that sloped less than 45° downward.

   a. Economic principle of satiation
   b. ASSA AIDS models
   c. Isovalue line
   d. Engineering economic

2. In microeconomics, _____ is quite simply the conversion of inputs into outputs. It is an economic process that uses resources to create a good or service that is suitable for exchange. This can include manufacturing, storing, shipping, and packaging.

   a. Red Guards
   b. MET
   c. Solved
   d. Production

3. In international economics and international trade, _____ or _____ is the relative prices of a country's export to import. '_____' are sometimes used as a proxy for the relative social welfare of a country, but this heuristic is technically questionable and should be used with extreme caution. An improvement in a nation's _____ is good for that country in the sense that it has to pay less for the products it import.

   a. Commercial invoice
   b. Terms of trade
   c. Kennedy Round
   d. Common market

4. _____ is a common concept in economics, and gives rise to derived concepts such as consumer debt. Generally _____ is defined by opposition to production. But the precise definition can vary because different schools of economists define production quite differently.

   a. Foreclosure data providers
   b. Federal Reserve Bank Notes
   c. Consumption
   d. Cash or share options

5. Economics:

   - _____,the desire to own something and the ability to pay for it
   - _____ curve,a graphic representation of a _____ schedule
   - _____ deposit, the money in checking accounts
   - _____ pull theory,the theory that inflation occurs when _____ for goods and services exceeds existing supplies
   - _____ schedule,a table that lists the quantity of a good a person will buy it each different price
   - _____ side economics,the school of economics at believes government spending and tax cuts open economy by raising _____

   a. Variability
   b. Production
   c. McKesson ' Robbins scandal
   d. Demand

6. _____ is the price of a commodity such as a good or service in terms of another; ie, the ratio of two prices. A _____ may be expressed in terms of a ratio between any two prices or the ratio between the price of one particular good and a weighted average of all other goods available in the market. A _____ is an opportunity cost.

Chapter 5. The Standard Trade Model

a. Food cooperative
b. False shortage
c. False economy
d. Relative price

7. _____ in economics and business is the result of an exchange and from that trade we assign a numerical monetary value to a good, service or asset. If Alice trades Bob 4 apples for an orange, the _____ of an orange is 4 apples. Inversely, the _____ of an apple is 1/4 oranges.
   a. Price
   b. Price war
   c. Premium pricing
   d. Price book

8. In microeconomic theory, an _____ is a graph showing different bundles of goods, each measured as to quantity, between which a consumer is indifferent. That is, at each point on the curve, the consumer has no preference for one bundle over another. In other words, they are all equally preferred.
   a. Expenditure minimization problem
   b. Indifference map
   c. Indifference curve
   d. Engel curve

9. _____s is the social science that studies the production, distribution, and consumption of goods and services. The term _____s comes from the Ancient Greek οἰκονομία from οἶκος (oikos, 'house') + νόμος (nomos, 'custom' or 'law'), hence 'rules of the house(hold)'. Current _____ models developed out of the broader field of political economy in the late 19th century, owing to a desire to use an empirical approach more akin to the physical sciences.
   a. Energy economics
   b. Inflation
   c. Opportunity cost
   d. Economic

10. _____ is the increase in the amount of the goods and services produced by an economy over time. It is conventionally measured as the percent rate of increase in real gross domestic product, or real GDP. Growth is usually calculated in real terms, i.e. inflation-adjusted terms, in order to net out the effect of inflation on the price of the goods and services produced.
    a. ACCRA Cost of Living Index
    b. ACEA agreement
    c. AD-IA Model
    d. Economic growth

11. In economics, the _____ is the change in consumption resulting from a change in real income.

Another important item that can change is the money income of the consumer. The _____ is the phenomenon observed through changes in purchasing power.

   a. Inflation hedge
   b. Export subsidy
   c. Income effect
   d. Equilibrium wage

12. _____ is a decrease in the rate of inflation. This phase of the business cycle, in which retailers can no longer pass on higher prices to their customers, often occurs during a recession. In contrast, deflation occurs when prices are actually dropping.
    a. Reflation
    b. Stealth inflation
    c. Mundell-Tobin effect
    d. Disinflation

Chapter 5. The Standard Trade Model

13. In economics, a _____ is a general slowdown in economic activity over a sustained period of time, or a business cycle contraction. During _____s, many macroeconomic indicators vary in a similar way. Production as measured by Gross Domestic Product (GDP), employment, investment spending, capacity utilization, household incomes and business profits all fall during _____s.
   a. Treasury View
   b. Monetary economics
   c. Recession
   d. Leading indicators

14. In economics, an _____ is any good or commodity, transported from one country to another country in a legitimate fashion, typically for use in trade. _____ goods or services are provided to foreign consumers by domestic producers. _____ is an important part of international trade.
   a. ACCRA Cost of Living Index
   b. AD-IA Model
   c. Export
   d. ACEA agreement

15. In economics, an _____ is any good (e.g. a commodity) or service brought into one country from another country in a legitimate fashion, typically for use in trade.It is a good that is brought in from another country for sale. _____ goods or services are provided to domestic consumers by foreign producers. An _____ in the receiving country is an export to the sending country.
   a. Import quota
   b. Economic integration
   c. Incoterms
   d. Import

16. A variety of measures of _____ and output are used in economics to estimate total economic activity in a country or region, including gross domestic product (GDP), gross national product (GNP), and net _____

There are three main ways of calculating these numbers; the output approach, the income approach and the expenditure approach. In theory, the three must yield the same, because total expenditures on goods and services must equal the total income paid to the producers (Gnational income), and that must also equal the total value of the output of goods and services (GNP.)

   a. Volume index
   b. Gross world product
   c. GNI per capita
   d. National income

17. _____ is the a method of technical and economic research of the systems for purpose to optimize a parity between system's consumer functions or properties and expenses to achieve those functions or properties.

This methodology for continuous perfection of production, industrial technologies, organizational structures was developed by Juryj Sobolev in 1948 at the 'Perm telephone factory'

- 1948 Juryj Sobolev - the first success in application of a method analysis at the 'Perm telephone factory' .
- 1949 - the first application for the invention as result of use of the new method.

Chapter 5. The Standard Trade Model

Today in economically developed countries practically each enterprise or the company use methodology of the kind of functional-cost analysis as a practice of the quality management, most full satisfying to principles of standards of series ISO 9000.

- Interest of consumer not in products itself, but the advantage which it will receive from its usage.
- The consumer aspires to reduce his expenses
- Functions needed by consumer can be executed in the various ways, and, hence, with various efficiency and expenses. Among possible alternatives of realization of functions exist such in which the parity of quality and the price is the optimal for the consumer.

The goal of _____ is achievement of the highest consumer satisfaction of production at simultaneous decrease in all kinds of industrial expenses Classical _____ has three English synonyms - Value Engineering, Value Management, Value Analysis.

a. Function cost analysis
b. Staple financing
c. Willingness to pay
d. Monopoly wage

18. The _____ is a general equilibrium mathematical model of international trade, developed by Eli Heckscher and Bertil Ohlin at the Stockholm School of Economics. It builds on David Ricardo's theory of comparative advantage by predicting patterns of commerce and production based on the factor endowments of a trading region. The model essentially says that countries will export products that utilize their abundant and cheap factor(s) of production and import products that utilize the countries' scarce factor(s.)

a. Heckscher-Ohlin model
b. Linder hypothesis
c. Jamaican Free Zones
d. Free trade zone

19. _____ is a situation first proposed by Jagdish Bhagwati, in 1958, where economic growth could result in a country being worse off than before the growth. If growth is heavily export biased it will lead to a fall in the terms of trade of the exporting country, in rare circumstances this fall in the terms of trade may be so large as to outweigh the gains from growth, this situation would cause a country to be worse off after growth than before. This result is only valid if the growing country is able to influence world prices.

a. Uneconomic growth
b. Austerity
c. Investment-specific technological progress
d. Immiserizing growth

20. The category of _____ is a socioeconomic classification applied to several countries around the world by political scientists and economists.

_____s are countries whose economies have not yet reached first world status but have, in a macroeconomic sense, outpaced their developing counterparts. Another characterization of _____s is that of nations undergoing rapid economic growth (usually export-oriented.)

a. Least Developed Countries
b. 100-year flood
c. Trillion dollar club
d. Newly industrialized country

Chapter 5. The Standard Trade Model

21. _____ is that which is owed; usually referencing assets owed, but the term can also cover moral obligations and other interactions not requiring money. In the case of assets, _____ is a means of using future purchasing power in the present before a summation has been earned. Some companies and corporations use _____ as a part of their overall corporate finance strategy.
   a. Collateral Management
   b. Debenture
   c. Hard money loan
   d. Debt

22. _____, 1st Baron Keynes was a renowned economist from Britain whose many ideas on economic and political theories as well as on many governments' monetary policies influenced America. He advocated a government that played an active role in the lives of people regarding business, economy, etc. In this role, the government would use fiscal measures to reduce the consequences of recessions, economic depressions and booms.
   a. Adam Smith
   b. John Maynard Keynes
   c. Adolph Fischer
   d. Adolf Hitler

23. _____ was a Swedish economist and politician. He was a professor of economics at the Stockholm School of Economics from 1929 to 1965. He was also leader of the People's Party, a social-liberal party which at the time was the largest party in opposition to the governing Social Democratic Party, from 1944 to 1967.
   a. Martin Luther
   b. Nicholas II
   c. Maximilian Carl Emil Weber
   d. Bertil Gotthard Ohlin

24. In economics, the _____ can be defined as the graph depicting the relationship between the price of a certain commodity, and the amount of it that consumers are willing and able to purchase at that given price. It is a graphic representation of a demand schedule. The _____ for all consumers together follows from the _____ of every individual consumer: the individual demands at each price are added together.
   a. Wage curve
   b. Cost curve
   c. Kuznets curve
   d. Demand curve

25. A _____ product is a product designed for cheapness and short-term convenience rather than medium to long-term durability, with most products only intended for single use. The term is also sometimes used for products that may last several months (ex. _____ air filters) to distinguish from similar products that last indefinitely (ex.
   a. Disposable
   b. 1921 recession
   c. 100-year flood
   d. 130-30 fund

26. In economics, _____ is a rise in the general level of prices of goods and services in an economy over a period of time. When the general price level rises, each unit of currency buys fewer goods and services; consequently, _____ is also a decline in the real value of money--a loss of purchasing power in the medium of exchange which is also the monetary unit of account in the economy. A chief measure of general price-level _____ is the general _____ rate, which is the percentage change in a general price index (normally the Consumer Price Index) over time.
   a. Energy economics
   b. Economic
   c. Inflation
   d. Opportunity cost

27. A _____ is a duty imposed on goods when they are moved across a political boundary. They are usually associated with protectionism, the economic policy of restraining trade between nations. For political reasons, _____s are usually imposed on imported goods, although they may also be imposed on exported goods.

Chapter 5. The Standard Trade Model

    a. Tariff
    b. 100-year flood
    c. 1921 recession
    d. 130-30 fund

28. An _____ is a type of protectionist trade restriction that sets a physical limit on the quantity of a good that can be imported into a country in a given period of time. Quotas, like other trade restrictions, are used to benefit the producers of a good in a domestic economy at the expense of all consumers of the good in that economy.

Critics say quotas often lead to corruption (bribes to get a quota allocation), smuggling (circumventing a quota), and higher prices for consumers.

    a. Agreement on Agriculture
    b. International Monetary Systems
    c. Economic integration
    d. Import quota

29. The term _____ is applied broadly to a variety of situations in which some financial institutions or assets suddenly lose a large part of their value. In the 19th and early 20th centuries, many financial crises were associated with banking panics, and many recessions coincided with these panics. Other situations that are often called financial crises include stock market crashes and the bursting of other financial bubbles, currency crises, and sovereign defaults.

    a. Market failure
    b. Financial crisis
    c. Macroeconomics
    d. Co-operative economics

30. A _____ is an object whose consumption increases the utility of the consumer, for which the quantity demanded exceeds the quantity supplied at zero price. _____s are usually modeled as having diminishing marginal utility. The first individual purchase has high utility; the second has less.

    a. Pie method
    b. Merit good
    c. Composite good
    d. Good

31. _____ describes a set of laws relating to domestic agriculture and imports of foreign agricultural products. Governments usually implement agricultural policies with the goal of achieving a specific outcome in the domestic agricultural product markets. Outcomes can involve, for example, a guaranteed supply level, price stability, product quality, product selection, land use or employment.

    a. ACEA agreement
    b. Intercropping
    c. ACCRA Cost of Living Index
    d. Agricultural Policy

32. _____ is a government policy to encourage export of goods and discourage sale of goods on the domestic market through low-cost loans or tax relief for exporters, or government financed international advertising or R'D. An _____ reduces the price paid by foreign importers, which means domestic consumers pay more than foreign consumers. The WTO prohibits most subsidies directly linked to the volume of exports.

    a. Illicit financial flows
    b. Economic activity rate
    c. Economic repression
    d. Export subsidy

33. In finance, the _____s between two currencies specifies how much one currency is worth in terms of the other. It is the value of a foreign natione;s currency in terms of the home natione;s currency. For example an _____ of 102 Japanese yen to the United States dollar means that JPY 102 is worth the same as USD 1.

    a. ACEA agreement
    b. ACCRA Cost of Living Index
    c. Interbank market
    d. Exchange rate

Chapter 5. The Standard Trade Model

34. In economics, _____ is how a natione;s total economy is distributed among its population. _____ has always been a central concern of economic theory and economic policy. Classical economists such as Adam Smith, Thomas Malthus and David Ricardo were mainly concerned with factor _____, that is, the distribution of income between the main factors of production, land, labour and capital.
    a. Equipment trust certificate
    b. Authorised capital
    c. Eco commerce
    d. Income distribution

35. In economics, the _____ is the theoretical possibility that the imposition of a tariff on imports may reduce the relative internal price of that good. It was proposed by Lloyd Metzler in 1949 upon examination of tariffs within the Heckscher-Ohlin model.

    The strange result could occur if the exporting country's offer curve is very inelastic.

    a. National Foreign Trade Council
    b. Linder hypothesis
    c. Customs union
    d. Metzler paradox

36. The _____ is the apparent contradiction that although water is on the whole more useful, in terms of survival, than diamonds, diamonds command a higher price in the market. The economist Adam Smith is often considered to be the classic presenter of this paradox. Nicolaus Copernicus, John Locke, John Law and others had previously tried to explain the disparity.
    a. Paradox of value
    b. 100-year flood
    c. St. Petersburg paradox
    d. 130-30 fund

37. In economics, economic equilibrium is simply a state of the world where economic forces are balanced and in the absence of external influences the (equilibrium) values of economic variables will not change. It is the point at which quantity demanded and quantity supplied are equal. _____, for example, refers to a condition where a market price is established through competition such that the amount of goods or services sought by buyers is equal to the amount of goods or services produced by sellers.
    a. Regulated market
    b. Market equilibrium
    c. Marketization
    d. Product-Market Growth Matrix

38. In economics and particularly in international trade, an _____ shows the quantity of one type of product that an agent will export ('offer') for each quantity of another type of product that it imports. The _____ was first derived by English economists Edgeworth and Marshall to help explain international trade.

    The _____ is derived from the country's PPF.

    a. ACCRA Cost of Living Index
    b. Offer curve
    c. AD-IA Model
    d. ACEA agreement

39. In economics, the concept of the _____ refers to the decision-making time frame of a firm in which at least one factor of production is fixed. Costs which are fixed in the _____ have no impact on a firms decisions. For example a firm can raise output by increasing the amount of labour through overtime.
    a. Product Pipeline
    b. Productivity model
    c. Hicks-neutral technical change
    d. Short-run

Chapter 5. The Standard Trade Model

40. In economics, the _____ measures the payments that flow between any individual country and all other countries. It is used to summarize all international economic transactions for that country during a specific time period, usually a year. The _____ is determined by the country's exports and imports of goods, services, and financial capital, as well as financial transfers.

   a. Skyscraper Index
   b. Gross domestic product per barrel
   c. Gross world product
   d. Balance of payments

41. A _____ is the transfer of wealth from one party (such as a person or company) to another. A _____ is usually made in exchange for the provision of goods, services or both, or to fulfill a legal obligation.

The simplest and oldest form of _____ is barter, the exchange of one good or service for another.

   a. Going concern
   b. Social gravity
   c. Payment
   d. Soft count

Chapter 6. Economies of Scale, Imperfect Competition, and International Trade

1. _____s is the social science that studies the production, distribution, and consumption of goods and services. The term _____s comes from the Ancient Greek οá¼°κονομῖα from οá¼¶κος (oikos, 'house') + vÏŒμος (nomos, 'custom' or 'law'), hence 'rules of the house(hold)'. Current _____ models developed out of the broader field of political economy in the late 19th century, owing to a desire to use an empirical approach more akin to the physical sciences.

   a. Opportunity cost
   b. Inflation
   c. Energy economics
   d. Economic

2. _____, in microeconomics, are the cost advantages that a business obtains due to expansion. They are factors that cause a producere;s average cost per unit to fall as scale is increased. _____ is a long run concept and refers to reductions in unit cost as the size of a facility, or scale, increases.

   a. Economies of scale
   b. Underinvestment employment relationship
   c. Economic production quantity
   d. Isoquant

3. _____ is a type of trade policy that allows traders to act and transact without interference from government. Thus, the policy permits trading partners mutual gains from trade, with goods and services produced according to the theory of comparative advantage.

Under a _____ policy, prices are a reflection of true supply and demand, and are the sole determinant of resource allocation.

   a. 1921 recession
   b. 100-year flood
   c. 130-30 fund
   d. Free trade

4. In economic theory, _____ is the competitive situation in any market where the conditions necessary for perfect competition are not satisfied. It is a market structure that does not meet the conditions of perfect competition.

Forms of _____ include:

- Monopoly, in which there is only one seller of a good.
- Oligopoly, in which there is a small number of sellers.
- Monopolistic competition, in which there are many sellers producing highly differentiated goods.
- Monopsony, in which there is only one buyer of a good.
- Oligopsony, in which there is a small number of buyers.

There may also be _____ in markets due to buyers or sellers lacking information about prices and the goods being traded.

There may also be _____ due to a time lag in a market.

   a. AD-IA Model
   b. Imperfect competition
   c. ACCRA Cost of Living Index
   d. ACEA agreement

5. _____ is exchange of capital, goods, and services across international borders or territories. In most countries, it represents a significant share of gross domestic product (GDP.) While _____ has been present throughout much of history , its economic, social, and political importance has been on the rise in recent centuries.

Chapter 6. Economies of Scale, Imperfect Competition, and International Trade

a. Incoterms
b. International trade
c. Import license
d. Intra-industry trade

6. In economics, _____ refers to the ability of a person or a country to produce a particular good at a lower marginal cost and opportunity cost than another person or country. It is the ability to produce a product most efficiently given all the other products that could be produced. It can be contrasted with absolute advantage which refers to the ability of a person or a country to produce a particular good at a lower absolute cost than another.

a. Comparative advantage
b. Hot money
c. Triffin dilemma
d. Gravity model of trade

7. In economics and sociology, an _____ is any factor (financial or non-financial) that enables or motivates a particular course of action, or counts as a reason for preferring one choice to the alternatives. It is an expectation that encourages people to behave in a certain way. Since human beings are purposeful creatures, the study of _____ structures is central to the study of all economic activity (both in terms of individual decision-making and in terms of co-operation and competition within a larger institutional structure.)

a. Isocost
b. Economic reform
c. Epstein-Zin preferences
d. Incentive

8. The _____ of monetary management established the rules for commercial and financial relations among the world's major industrial states in the mid 20th Century. The _____ was the first example of a fully negotiated monetary order intended to govern monetary relations among independent nation-states.

Preparing to rebuild the international economic system as World War II was still raging, 730 delegates from all 44 Allied nations gathered at the Mount Washington Hotel in Bretton Woods, New Hampshire, United States, for the United Nations Monetary and Financial Conference.

a. 100-year flood
b. 1921 recession
c. Bretton Woods system
d. 130-30 fund

9. _____ in economics is a state in which a country maintains full employment and price level stability. It is a function of a country's total output,

II = C (Yf - T) + I + G + CA (E x P*/P, Yf-T; Yf* - T*)

_____ = Consumption [determined by disposable income] + Investment + Government Spending + Current Account (determined by the real exchange rate, disposable income of home country and disposable income of the foreign country.)

External balance signifies a condition in which the country's current account, its exports minus imports, is neither too far in surplus nor in deficit.

a. Uneconomic growth
b. Internal balance
c. Autonomous consumption
d. Energy intensity

Chapter 6. Economies of Scale, Imperfect Competition, and International Trade

10. An example of _____ is when a company is cut in size but the remaining firms still hold the same amount of final output. Therefore the company has become more efficient in production and has experienced _____.the internal part of the business expands enabling the business to make higher profits.

Six main types of _____ can be defined.

   a. AD-IA Model
   b. ACCRA Cost of Living Index
   c. ACEA agreement
   d. Internal economies of scale

11. In economics, _____ describes the state of a market with respect to competition.

   - Perfect competition, in which the market consists of a very large number of firms producing a homogeneous product.
   - Monopolistic competition where there are a large number of independent firms which have a very small proportion of the market share.
   - Oligopoly, in which a market is dominated by a small number of firms which own more than 40% of the market share.
   - Oligopsony, a market dominated by many sellers and a few buyers.
   - Monopoly, where there is only one provider of a product or service.
   - Natural monopoly, a monopoly in which economies of scale cause efficiency to increase continuously with the size of the firm. A firm is a natural monopoly if it is able to serve the entire market demand at a lower cost than any combination of two or more smaller, more specialized firms.
   - Monopsony, when there is only one buyer in a market.

The imperfectly competitive structure is quite identical to the realistic market conditions where some monopolistic competitors, monopolists, oligopolists, and duopolists exist and dominate the market conditions. The elements of _____ include the number and size distribution of firms, entry conditions, and the extent of differentiation.

These somewhat abstract concerns tend to determine some but not all details of a specific concrete market system where buyers and sellers actually meet and commit to trade.

   a. Labour economics
   b. Human capital
   c. Market structure
   d. Monopolistic competition

12. _____ in economics and business is the result of an exchange and from that trade we assign a numerical monetary value to a good, service or asset. If Alice trades Bob 4 apples for an orange, the _____ of an orange is 4 apples. Inversely, the _____ of an apple is 1/4 oranges.

   a. Price war
   b. Premium pricing
   c. Price book
   d. Price

13. In microeconomics, _____ is the extra revenue that an additional unit of product will bring. It is the additional income from selling one more unit of a good; sometimes equal to price. It can also be described as the change in total revenue/change in number of units sold.

   a. Reservation price
   b. Marginal revenue
   c. Long term
   d. Market demand schedule

Chapter 6. Economies of Scale, Imperfect Competition, and International Trade

14. In economics, a _____ exists when a specific individual or enterprise has sufficient control over a particular product or service to determine significantly the terms on which other individuals shall have access to it. Monopolies are thus characterized by a lack of economic competition for the good or service that they provide and a lack of viable substitute goods. The verb 'monopolize' refers to the process by which a firm gains persistently greater market share than what is expected under perfect competition.
    a. 100-year flood
    b. Monopoly
    c. 1921 recession
    d. 130-30 fund

15. Monopoly power is an example of market failure which occurs when one or more of the participants has the ability to influence the price or other outcomes in some general or specialized market. The most commonly discussed form of market power is that of a monopoly, but other forms such as monopsony, and more moderate versions of these two extremes, exist. Market participants that have market power are sometimes referred to as 'price makers', while those without are sometimes called '_____'.
    a. Market power
    b. Monopolization
    c. Price takers
    d. Market concentration

16. _____ is the price of a commodity such as a good or service in terms of another; ie, the ratio of two prices. A _____ may be expressed in terms of a ratio between any two prices or the ratio between the price of one particular good and a weighted average of all other goods available in the market. A _____ is an opportunity cost.
    a. Food cooperative
    b. False economy
    c. False shortage
    d. Relative price

17. _____ is a concept found in moral, political, and bioethical philosophy. Within these contexts, it refers to the capacity of a rational individual to make an informed, un-coerced decision. In moral and political philosophy, _____ is often used as the basis for determining moral responsibility for one's actions.
    a. ACEA agreement
    b. AD-IA Model
    c. ACCRA Cost of Living Index
    d. Autonomy

18. In microeconomics, _____ is quite simply the conversion of inputs into outputs. It is an economic process that uses resources to create a good or service that is suitable for exchange. This can include manufacturing, storing, shipping, and packaging.
    a. Red Guards
    b. MET
    c. Solved
    d. Production

19. In economics, _____ is equal to total cost divided by the number of goods produced (the output quantity, Q.) It is also equal to the sum of average variable costs (total variable costs divided by Q) plus average fixed costs (total fixed costs divided by Q.) _____s may be dependent on the time period considered (increasing production may be expensive or impossible in the short term, for example.)
    a. Average variable cost
    b. Average fixed cost
    c. Explicit cost
    d. Average cost

20. _____ is a common concept in economics, and gives rise to derived concepts such as consumer debt. Generally _____ is defined by opposition to production. But the precise definition can vary because different schools of economists define production quite differently.

Chapter 6. Economies of Scale, Imperfect Competition, and International Trade

    a. Cash or share options
    b. Foreclosure data providers
    c. Federal Reserve Bank Notes
    d. Consumption

21. In finance, the _____s between two currencies specifies how much one currency is worth in terms of the other. It is the value of a foreign natione;s currency in terms of the home natione;s currency. For example an _____ of 102 Japanese yen to the United States dollar means that JPY 102 is worth the same as USD 1.
    a. Interbank market
    b. ACEA agreement
    c. ACCRA Cost of Living Index
    d. Exchange rate

22. A _____ or a flexible exchange rate is a type of exchange rate regime wherein a currency's value is allowed to fluctuate according to the foreign exchange market. A currency that uses a _____ is known as a floating currency. The opposite of a _____ is a fixed exchange rate.
    a. Floating exchange rate
    b. Trade Weighted US dollar Index
    c. Foreign exchange market
    d. Floating currency

23. In economics and finance, _____ is the change in total cost that arises when the quantity produced changes by one unit. It is the cost of producing one more unit of a good. Mathematically, the _____ function is expressed as the first derivative of the total cost (TC) function with respect to quantity (Q.)
    a. Quality costs
    b. Marginal cost
    c. Variable cost
    d. Khozraschyot

24. _____ is a common market structure where many competing producers sell products that are differentiated from one another (ie. the products are substitutes, but are not exactly alike.) Many markets are monopolistically competitive, common examples include the markets for restaurants, cereal, clothing, shoes and service industries in large cities.
    a. Mathematical economics
    b. Financial crisis
    c. Perfect competition
    d. Monopolistic competition

25. An _____ is a market form in which a market or industry is dominated by a small number of sellers (oligopolists.) Because there are few participants in this type of market, each oligopolist is aware of the actions of the others. The decisions of one firm influence, and are influenced by, the decisions of other firms.
    a. Oligopoly
    b. Oligopsony
    c. ACCRA Cost of Living Index
    d. ACEA agreement

26. In business and accounting, _____ are everything of value that is owned by a person or company. It is a claim on the property your income of a borrower. The balance sheet of a firm records the monetary value of the _____ owned by the firm.
    a. Amortization schedule
    b. ACEA agreement
    c. ACCRA Cost of Living Index
    d. Assets

27. In economics, economic equilibrium is simply a state of the world where economic forces are balanced and in the absence of external influences the (equilibrium) values of economic variables will not change. It is the point at which quantity demanded and quantity supplied are equal. _____, for example, refers to a condition where a market price is established through competition such that the amount of goods or services sought by buyers is equal to the amount of goods or services produced by sellers.

Chapter 6. Economies of Scale, Imperfect Competition, and International Trade

    a. Marketization
    b. Regulated market
    c. Product-Market Growth Matrix
    d. Market equilibrium

28. The _____ is the official currency of 16 of the 27 member states of the European Union (EU.) The states, known collectively as the Eurozone, are Austria, Belgium, Cyprus, Finland, France, Germany, Greece, Ireland, Italy, Luxembourg, Malta, the Netherlands, Portugal, Slovakia, Slovenia, and Spain. The currency is also used in a further five European countries, with and without formal agreements and is consequently used daily by some 327 million Europeans.
    a. Euro
    b. IRS Code 3401
    c. Import and Export Price Indices
    d. Equity capital market

29. In calculus, a function f defined on a subset of the real numbers with real values is called _____, if for all x and y such that x >≤ y one has f(x) >≤ f(y), so f preserves the order. In layman's terms, the sign of the slope is always positive (the curve tending upwards) or zero (i.e., non-decreasing, or asymptotic, or depicted as a horizontal, flat line) Likewise, a function is called monotonically decreasing (non-increasing) if, whenever x >≤ y, then f(x) >≥ f(y), so it reverses the order.
    a. 1921 recession
    b. 100-year flood
    c. Monotonic
    d. 130-30 fund

30. The _____ was a period of financial crisis that gripped much of Asia beginning in July 1997, and raised fears of a worldwide economic meltdown (financial contagion.)

The crisis started in Thailand with the financial collapse of the Thai baht caused by the decision of the Thai government to float the baht, cutting its peg to the USD, after exhaustive efforts to support it in the face of a severe financial overextension that was in part real estate driven. At the time, Thailand had acquired a burden of foreign debt that made the country effectively bankrupt even before the collapse of its currency.

    a. AD-IA Model
    b. ACEA agreement
    c. ACCRA Cost of Living Index
    d. Asian financial crisis

31. A _____ is a customs union with common policies on product regulation, and freedom of movement of the factors of production (capital and labour) and of enterprise. The goal is that the movement of capital, labour, goods, and services between the members is as easy as within them. This is the fourth stage of economic integration.
    a. Competitiveness
    b. Mutual recognition agreement
    c. Grey market
    d. Common Market

32. In economics, _____ is how a natione;s total economy is distributed among its population. ._____ has always been a central concern of economic theory and economic policy. Classical economists such as Adam Smith, Thomas Malthus and David Ricardo were mainly concerned with factor _____, that is, the distribution of income between the main factors of production, land, labour and capital.
    a. Equipment trust certificate
    b. Authorised capital
    c. Eco commerce
    d. Income distribution

33. The _____ is a trilateral trade bloc in North America created by the governments of the United States, Canada, and Mexico. The agreement creating the trade bloc came into force on January 1, 1994. It superseded the Canada-United States Free Trade Agreement between the U.S. and Canada.

Chapter 6. Economies of Scale, Imperfect Competition, and International Trade

a. Demand-side technologies
b. Federal Reserve Bank Notes
c. Case-Shiller Home Price Indices
d. North American Free Trade Agreement

34. The term _____ is applied broadly to a variety of situations in which some financial institutions or assets suddenly lose a large part of their value. In the 19th and early 20th centuries, many financial crises were associated with banking panics, and many recessions coincided with these panics. Other situations that are often called financial crises include stock market crashes and the bursting of other financial bubbles, currency crises, and sovereign defaults.
   a. Macroeconomics
   b. Co-operative economics
   c. Market failure
   d. Financial crisis

35. A variety of measures of _____ and output are used in economics to estimate total economic activity in a country or region, including gross domestic product (GDP), gross national product (GNP), and net _____

There are three main ways of calculating these numbers; the output approach, the income approach and the expenditure approach. In theory, the three must yield the same, because total expenditures on goods and services must equal the total income paid to the producers (Gnational income), and that must also equal the total value of the output of goods and services (GNP.)

   a. Volume index
   b. GNI per capita
   c. Gross world product
   d. National income

36. _____ exists when sales of identical goods or services are transacted at different prices from the same provider. In a theoretical market with perfect information, no transaction costs or prohibition on secondary exchange (or re-selling) to prevent arbitrage, _____ can only be a feature of monopoly and oligopoly markets, where market power can be exercised. Otherwise, the moment the seller tries to sell the same good at different prices, the buyer at the lower price can arbitrage by selling to the consumer buying at the higher price but with a tiny discount.
   a. Transfer pricing
   b. Loss leader
   c. Price discrimination
   d. Lerner Index

37. _____ is the economic policy of restraining trade between states, through methods such as tariffs on imported goods, restrictive quotas, and a variety of other restrictive government regulations designed to discourage imports, and prevent foreign take-over of local markets and companies. This policy is closely aligned with anti-globalization, and contrasts with free trade, where government barriers to trade are kept to a minimum. The term is mostly used in the context of economics, where _____ refers to policies or doctrines which 'protect' businesses and workers within a country by restricting or regulating trade with foreign nations.
   a. Google economy
   b. Knowledge economy
   c. Digital economy
   d. Protectionism

38. In economics, _____ are the resources employed to produce goods and services. They facilitate production but do not become part of the product (as with raw materials) or significantly transformed by the production process (as with fuel used to power machinery.) To 19th century economists, the _____ were land (natural resources, gifts from nature), labor (the ability to work), and capital goods (human-made tools and equipment.)
   a. Factors of production
   b. Long-run
   c. Hicks-neutral technical change
   d. Product Pipeline

Chapter 6. Economies of Scale, Imperfect Competition, and International Trade   39

39. A _____ is:

- Rewrite _____, in generative grammar and computer science
- Standardization, a formal and widely-accepted statement, fact, definition, or qualification
- Operation, a determinate _____ for performing a mathematical operation and obtaining a certain result (Mathematics, Logic)
    - Unary operation
    - Binary operation
- _____ of inference, a function from sets of formulae to formulae (Mathematics, Logic)
- _____ of thumb, principle with broad application that is not intended to be strictly accurate or reliable for every situation. Also often simply referred to as a _____
- Moral, an atomic element of a moral code for guiding choices in human behavior
- Heuristic, a quantized '_____' which shows a tendency or probability for successful function
- A regulation, as in sports
- A Production _____, as in computer science
- Procedural law, a _____ set governing the application of laws to cases
    - A law, which may informally be called a '_____'
    - A court ruling, a decision by a court
- In the U.S. Government, a regulation mandated by Congress, but written or expanded upon by the Executive Branch.
- Norm (sociology), an informal but widely accepted _____, concept, truth, definition, or qualification (social norms, legal norms, coding norms)
- Norm (philosophy), a kind of sentence or a reason to act, feel or believe
- 'Rulership' is the concept of governance by a government:
    - Military _____, governance by a military body
    - Monastic _____, a collection of precepts that guides the life of monks or nuns in a religious order where the superior holds the place of Christ
- Slide _____

- '_____,' a song by Ayumi Hamasaki
- '_____,' a song by rapper Nas
- '_____s,' an album by the band The Whitest Boy Alive
- _____s: Pyaar Ka Superhit Formula, a 2003 Bollywood film
- ruler, an instrument for measuring lengths
- _____, a component of an astrolabe, circumferator or similar instrument
- The _____s, a bestselling self-help book
- _____ Project (Run Up-to-date Linux Everywhere), a project that aims to use up-to-date Linux software on old PCs
- _____ engine, a software system that helps managing business _____s
- Ja _____, a hip hop artist
    - R.U.L.E., a 2005 greatest hits album by rapper Ja _____
- '_____s,' a KMFDM song

a. Technocracy
c. Procter ' Gamble
b. Demand
d. Rule

Chapter 6. Economies of Scale, Imperfect Competition, and International Trade

40. _____s are a type of administrative division, in some countries managed by a local government. They vary greatly in size, spanning entire regions or counties, several municipalities, or subdivisions of municipalities.

In Austria, a _____ or Bezirk is an administrative division normally encompassing several municipalities, roughly equivalent to the Landkreis in Germany.

a. 100-year flood
b. District
c. 1921 recession
d. 130-30 fund

41. The _____ is an economic reason for protectionism. The crux of the argument is that nascent industries often do not have the economies of scale that their older competitors from other countries may have, and thus need to be protected until they can attain similar economies of scale. It was first used by Alexander Hamilton in 1790 and later by Friedrich List, in 1841, to support protection for German manufacturing against British industry.

a. Infant industry argument
b. AD-IA Model
c. ACCRA Cost of Living Index
d. ACEA agreement

42. In economics, an _____ is any good or commodity, transported from one country to another country in a legitimate fashion, typically for use in trade. _____ goods or services are provided to foreign consumers by domestic producers. _____ is an important part of international trade.

a. Export
b. AD-IA Model
c. ACEA agreement
d. ACCRA Cost of Living Index

Chapter 7. International Factor Movements

1. _____ or worker mobility is the socioeconomic ease with which an individual or groups of individuals who are currently receiving remuneration in the form of wages can take advantage of various economic opportunities.

Worker mobility is best gauged by the lack of impediments to such mobility. Impediments to mobility are easily divided into two distinct classes with one being personal and the other being systemic.

   a. Labor mobility
   b. Genuine progress indicator
   c. Purchasing power
   d. Physical quality-of-life index

2. In economics, the _____ or marginal physical product is the extra output produced by one more unit of an input (for instance, the difference in output when a firm's labour is increased from five to six units.) Assuming that no other inputs to production change, the _____ of a given input (X) can be expressed as:

   _____ = ΔY/ΔX = (the change of Y)/(the change of X.)

   -
     - ○
       - Pending approval by Thomas Sowell***

In neoclassical economics, this is the mathematical derivative of the production function.... Note that the 'product' (Y) is typically defined ignoring external costs and benefits.

   a. Labor problem
   b. Productive capacity
   c. Factor prices
   d. Marginal product

3. In economics, the _____ also known as MPL or MPN is the change in output from hiring one additional unit of labor. It is the increase in output added by the last unit of labor. Assuming that no other inputs to production change, the marginal product of a given input (X) can be expressed as:

   MP = ΔY/ΔX = (the change of Y)/(the change of X.)

   a. Marginal product of labor
   b. Marginal product
   c. Production function
   d. Product Pipeline

4. In microeconomics, _____ is quite simply the conversion of inputs into outputs. It is an economic process that uses resources to create a good or service that is suitable for exchange. This can include manufacturing, storing, shipping, and packaging.

   a. Production
   b. MET
   c. Solved
   d. Red Guards

5. In economics, a _____ is a function that specifies the output of a firm, an industry, or an entire economy for all combinations of inputs. A meta-_____ compares the practice of the existing entities converting inputs X into output y to determine the most efficient practice _____ of the existing entities, whether the most efficient feasible practice production or the most efficient actual practice production. In either case, the maximum output of a technologically-determined production process is a mathematical function of input factors of production.

Chapter 7. International Factor Movements

a. Short-run
b. Post-Fordism
c. Production function
d. Constant elasticity of substitution

6. Economics:

  - _____, the desire to own something and the ability to pay for it
  - _____ curve, a graphic representation of a _____ schedule
  - _____ deposit, the money in checking accounts
  - _____ pull theory, the theory that inflation occurs when _____ for goods and services exceeds existing supplies
  - _____ schedule, a table that lists the quantity of a good a person will buy it each different price
  - _____ side economics, the school of economics at believes government spending and tax cuts open economy by raising _____

a. Variability
b. Production
c. McKesson ' Robbins scandal
d. Demand

7. In economics, _____ is when quantity demanded is more than quantity supplied. See Economic shortage.
a. AD-IA Model
b. Excess demand
c. ACCRA Cost of Living Index
d. ACEA agreement

8. A _____ is a place of residence or refuge and comfort. It is usually a place in which an individual or a family can rest and be able to store personal property. Most modern-day households contain sanitary facilities and a means of preparing food.
a. 1921 recession
b. 130-30 fund
c. 100-year flood
d. Home

9. The term _____s refers to wages that have been adjusted for inflation. This term is used in contrast to nominal wages or unadjusted wages.

The use of adjusted figures is in undertaking some form of economic analysis.

a. Real wage
b. Profit sharing
c. Federal Wage System
d. Living wage

10. In economics, the people in the _____ are the suppliers of labor. The _____ is all the nonmilitary people who are employed or unemployed. In 2005, the worldwide _____ was over 3 billion people.
a. Distributed workforce
b. Departmentalization
c. Grenelle agreements
d. Labor force

11. In economics, _____ is the transfer of income, wealth or property from some individuals to others.

One premise of _____ is that money should be distributed to benefit the poorer members of society, and that the rich have an obligation to assist the poor, thus creating a more financially egalitarian society. Another argument is that the rich exploit the poor or otherwise gain unfair benefits.

a. 130-30 fund
b. 100-year flood
c. Redistribution
d. 1921 recession

12. The _____ is a general equilibrium mathematical model of international trade, developed by Eli Heckscher and Bertil Ohlin at the Stockholm School of Economics. It builds on David Ricardo's theory of comparative advantage by predicting patterns of commerce and production based on the factor endowments of a trading region. The model essentially says that countries will export products that utilize their abundant and cheap factor(s) of production and import products that utilize the countries' scarce factor(s.)
    a. Heckscher-Ohlin model
    b. Free trade zone
    c. Jamaican Free Zones
    d. Linder hypothesis

13. The _____ is an international organization that oversees the global financial system by following the macroeconomic policies of its member countries, in particular those with an impact on exchange rates and the balance of payments. It is an organization formed to stabilize international exchange rates and facilitate development. It also offers financial and technical assistance to its members, making it an international lender of last resort.
    a. International Monetary Fund
    b. Office of Thrift Supervision
    c. ACEA agreement
    d. ACCRA Cost of Living Index

14. The _____ is the largest national economy in the world. Its gross domestic product (GDP) was estimated as $14.2 trillion in 2008. The U.S. economy maintains a high level of output per person (GDP per capita, $46,800 in 2008, ranked at around number ten in the world.)
    a. ACCRA Cost of Living Index
    b. ACEA agreement
    c. AD-IA Model
    d. Economy of the United States

15. In business and accounting, _____ are everything of value that is owned by a person or company. It is a claim on the property your income of a borrower. The balance sheet of a firm records the monetary value of the _____ owned by the firm.
    a. ACCRA Cost of Living Index
    b. ACEA agreement
    c. Amortization schedule
    d. Assets

16. _____ to the arrival of new individuals into a habitat or population. It is a biological concept and is important in population ecology, differentiated from emigration and migration.

    _____ is a modern phenomenon.

    a. ACEA agreement
    b. AD-IA Model
    c. Immigration
    d. ACCRA Cost of Living Index

17. _____ is a fee paid on borrowed assets. It is the price paid for the use of borrowed money, or, money earned by deposited funds. Assets that are sometimes lent with _____ include money, shares, consumer goods through hire purchase, major assets such as aircraft, and even entire factories in finance lease arrangements.
    a. Insolvency
    b. Internal debt
    c. Asset protection
    d. Interest

Chapter 7. International Factor Movements

18. An _____ is the price a borrower pays for the use of money they do not own, for instance a small company might borrow from a bank to kick start their business, and the return a lender receives for deferring the use of funds, by lending it to the borrower. _____s are normally expressed as a percentage rate over the period of one year.

_____s targets are also a vital tool of monetary policy and are used to control variables like investment, inflation, and unemployment.

   a. Enterprise value
   b. Arrow-Debreu model
   c. ACCRA Cost of Living Index
   d. Interest rate

19. The '_____' is approximately the nominal interest rate minus the inflation rate Since the inflation rate over the course of a loan is not known initially, volatility in inflation represents a risk to both the lender and the borrower.

In economics and finance, an individual who lends money for repayment at a later point in time expects to be compensated for the time value of money, or not having the use of that money while it is lent.

   a. Core inflation
   b. Cost-push inflation
   c. Reflation
   d. Real interest rate

20. In economics, _____ refers to the ability of a person or a country to produce a particular good at a lower marginal cost and opportunity cost than another person or country. It is the ability to produce a product most efficiently given all the other products that could be produced. It can be contrasted with absolute advantage which refers to the ability of a person or a country to produce a particular good at a lower absolute cost than another.
   a. Gravity model of trade
   b. Triffin dilemma
   c. Hot money
   d. Comparative advantage

21. _____ is that which is owed; usually referencing assets owed, but the term can also cover moral obligations and other interactions not requiring money. In the case of assets, _____ is a means of using future purchasing power in the present before a summation has been earned. Some companies and corporations use _____ as a part of their overall corporate finance strategy.
   a. Debenture
   b. Hard money loan
   c. Collateral Management
   d. Debt

22. In finance, _____ is investment originating from other countries. See Foreign direct investment.
   a. Horizontal merger
   b. Demand side economics
   c. Preclusive purchasing
   d. Foreign investment

23. A _____ is a duty imposed on goods when they are moved across a political boundary. They are usually associated with protectionism, the economic policy of restraining trade between nations. For political reasons, _____s are usually imposed on imported goods, although they may also be imposed on exported goods.
   a. 130-30 fund
   b. 100-year flood
   c. 1921 recession
   d. Tariff

24. _____ is the process of sharing of skills, knowledge, technologies, methods of manufacturing, samples of manufacturing and facilities among governments and other institutions to ensure that scientific and technological developments are accessible to a wider range of users who can then further develop and exploit the technology into new products, processes, applications, materials or services. It is closely related to (and may arguably be considered a subset of) Knowledge transfer. Related terms, used almost synonymously, include 'technology valorisation' and 'technology commercialisation'.
   a. Judgment summons
   b. Patent
   c. Law of increasing relative cost
   d. Technology transfer

25. _____ in its classic form is defined as a company from one country making a physical investment into building a factory in another country. It is the establishment of an enterprise by a foreigner. Its definition can be extended to include investments made to acquire lasting interest in enterprises operating outside of the economy of the investor.
   a. Federal Deposit Insurance Corporation
   b. Foreign direct investment
   c. Non-governmental organization
   d. Financial Stability Forum

26. The _____ consists of a number of economic theories which describe the nature of the firm, company including its existence, its behaviour, and its relationship with the market.

In simplified terms, the _____ aims to answer these questions:

1. Existence - why do firms emerge, why are not all transactions in the economy mediated over the market?
2. Boundaries - why the boundary between firms and the market is located exactly there? Which transactions are performed internally and which are negotiated on the market?
3. Organization - why are firms structured in such specific way? What is the interplay of formal and informal relationships?

Despite looking simple, these questions are not answered by the established economic theory, which usually views firms as given, and treats them as black boxes without any internal structure.

The First World War period saw a change of emphasis in economic theory away from industry-level analysis which mainly included analysing markets to analysis at the level of the firm, as it became increasingly clear that perfect competition was no longer an adequate model of how firms behaved. Economic theory till then had focussed on trying to understand markets alone and there had been little study on understanding why firms or organisations exist.

   a. Policy Ineffectiveness Proposition
   b. Technology gap
   c. Khazzoom-Brookes postulate
   d. Theory of the firm

27. _____s is the social science that studies the production, distribution, and consumption of goods and services. The term _____s comes from the Ancient Greek oá¼°κονομῖα from oá¼¶κος (oikos, 'house') + vÏŒμος (nomos, 'custom' or 'law'), hence 'rules of the house(hold)'. Current _____ models developed out of the broader field of political economy in the late 19th century, owing to a desire to use an empirical approach more akin to the physical sciences.
   a. Energy economics
   b. Economic
   c. Inflation
   d. Opportunity cost

Chapter 7. International Factor Movements

28. _____ is a term used to describe how different aspects between economies are integrated. The basics of this theory were written by the Hungarian Economist Béla Balassa in the 1960s. As _____ increases, the barriers of trade between markets diminishes.

   a. Import
   b. Economic integration
   c. Import license
   d. Inward investment

29. A _____ represents the combinations of goods and services that a consumer can purchase given current prices and his income. Consumer theory uses the concepts of a _____ and a preference map to analyze consumer choices. Both concepts have a ready graphical representation in the two-good case.

   a. Budget constraint
   b. Joint demand
   c. Quality bias
   d. Revealed preference

Chapter 8. The Instruments of Trade Policy

1. A _____ is a duty imposed on goods when they are moved across a political boundary. They are usually associated with protectionism, the economic policy of restraining trade between nations. For political reasons, _____s are usually imposed on imported goods, although they may also be imposed on exported goods.
   - a. 1921 recession
   - b. 100-year flood
   - c. 130-30 fund
   - d. Tariff

2. In economics, an _____ is any good (e.g. a commodity) or service brought into one country from another country in a legitimate fashion, typically for use in trade. It is a good that is brought in from another country for sale. _____ goods or services are provided to domestic consumers by foreign producers. An _____ in the receiving country is an export to the sending country.
   - a. Economic integration
   - b. Import quota
   - c. Incoterms
   - d. Import

3. An _____ is a type of protectionist trade restriction that sets a physical limit on the quantity of a good that can be imported into a country in a given period of time. Quotas, like other trade restrictions, are used to benefit the producers of a good in a domestic economy at the expense of all consumers of the good in that economy.

   Critics say quotas often lead to corruption (bribes to get a quota allocation), smuggling (circumventing a quota), and higher prices for consumers.
   - a. Economic integration
   - b. Import quota
   - c. Agreement on Agriculture
   - d. International Monetary Systems

4. _____ describes a set of laws relating to domestic agriculture and imports of foreign agricultural products. Governments usually implement agricultural policies with the goal of achieving a specific outcome in the domestic agricultural product markets. Outcomes can involve, for example, a guaranteed supply level, price stability, product quality, product selection, land use or employment.
   - a. Intercropping
   - b. ACEA agreement
   - c. ACCRA Cost of Living Index
   - d. Agricultural Policy

5. Economics:

   - _____, the desire to own something and the ability to pay for it
   - _____ curve, a graphic representation of a _____ schedule
   - _____ deposit, the money in checking accounts
   - _____ pull theory, the theory that inflation occurs when _____ for goods and services exceeds existing supplies
   - _____ schedule, a table that lists the quantity of a good a person will buy it each different price
   - _____ side economics, the school of economics at believes government spending and tax cuts open economy by raising _____

   - a. Production
   - b. Variability
   - c. McKesson ' Robbins scandal
   - d. Demand

6. In economics, an _____ is any good or commodity, transported from one country to another country in a legitimate fashion, typically for use in trade. _____ goods or services are provided to foreign consumers by domestic producers. _____ is an important part of international trade.
   a. AD-IA Model
   b. ACCRA Cost of Living Index
   c. ACEA agreement
   d. Export

7. _____ theory is a branch of theoretical economics. It seeks to explain the behavior of supply, demand and prices in a whole economy with several or many markets. It is often assumed that agents are price takers and in that setting two common notions of equilibrium exist: Walrasian (or competitive) equilibrium, and its generalization; a price equilibrium with transfers.
   a. Rational choice theory
   b. New Keynesian economics
   c. Human capital
   d. General equilibrium

8. A _____ is a type of economic equilibrium, where the clearance on the market of some specific goods is obtained independently from prices and quantities demanded and supplied in other markets. In other words, the prices of all substitutes and complements, as well as income levels of consumers are constant. Here the dynamic process is that prices adjust until supply equals demand.
   a. Horizontal market
   b. Market depth
   c. Market system
   d. Partial equilibrium

9. In finance, the _____s between two currencies specifies how much one currency is worth in terms of the other. It is the value of a foreign natione;s currency in terms of the home natione;s currency. For example an _____ of 102 Japanese yen to the United States dollar means that JPY 102 is worth the same as USD 1.
   a. Exchange rate
   b. ACCRA Cost of Living Index
   c. ACEA agreement
   d. Interbank market

10. In economic models, the _____ time frame assumes no fixed factors of production. Firms can enter or leave the marketplace, and the cost (and availability) of land, labor, raw materials, and capital goods can be assumed to vary. In contrast, in the short-run time frame, certain factors are assumed to be fixed, because there is not sufficient time for them to change.
    a. Price/performance ratio
    b. Diseconomies of scale
    c. Productivity world
    d. Long-run

11. _____ is an economic model based on price, utility and quantity in a market. It predicts that in a competitive market, price will function to equalize the quantity demanded by consumers, and the quantity supplied by producers, resulting in an economic equilibrium of price and quantity. The model incorporates other factors changing equilibrium as a shift of demand and/or supply.
    a. Joint demand
    b. Deferred gratification
    c. Supply and demand
    d. Rational addiction

12. In economics, economic equilibrium is simply a state of the world where economic forces are balanced and in the absence of external influences the (equilibrium) values of economic variables will not change. It is the point at which quantity demanded and quantity supplied are equal. _____, for example, refers to a condition where a market price is established through competition such that the amount of goods or services sought by buyers is equal to the amount of goods or services produced by sellers.

Chapter 8. The Instruments of Trade Policy

a. Market equilibrium
b. Marketization
c. Regulated market
d. Product-Market Growth Matrix

13. In economics, the _____ refers to the decision-making time frame of a firm in which at least one factor of production is fixed. Costs which are fixed in the _____ have no impact on a firms decisions. For example a firm can raise output by increasing the amount of labour through overtime.
   a. Product Pipeline
   b. Hicks-neutral technical change
   c. Productivity model
   d. Short-run

14. In economics, the _____ measures the payments that flow between any individual country and all other countries. It is used to summarize all international economic transactions for that country during a specific time period, usually a year. The _____ is determined by the country's exports and imports of goods, services, and financial capital, as well as financial transfers.
   a. Gross domestic product per barrel
   b. Skyscraper Index
   c. Gross world product
   d. Balance of payments

15. The _____ is where currency trading takes place. It is where banks and other official institutions facilitate the buying and selling of foreign currencies. FX transactions typically involve one party purchasing a quantity of one currency in exchange for paying a quantity of another.
   a. Currency swap
   b. Covered interest arbitrage
   c. Foreign exchange market
   d. Floating currency

16. In finance, the _____ is the global financial market for short-term borrowing and lending. It provides short-term liquidity funding for the global financial system. The _____ is where short-term obligations such as Treasury bills, commercial paper and bankers' acceptances are bought and sold.
   a. Consignment stock
   b. Deferred compensation
   c. T-Model
   d. Money market

17. A _____ is the transfer of wealth from one party (such as a person or company) to another. A _____ is usually made in exchange for the provision of goods, services or both, or to fulfill a legal obligation.

The simplest and oldest form of _____ is barter, the exchange of one good or service for another.

   a. Going concern
   b. Soft count
   c. Social gravity
   d. Payment

18. In economics, the _____ is a measure of the total effect of the entire tariff structure on the value added per unit of output in each industry, when both intermediate and final goods are imported. This statistic is used by economists to measure the real amount of protection afforded to a particular industry by import duties, tariffs or other trade restrictions.

Consider a simple case, there is a tradable good (shoes) that uses one tradable input to produce (leather.)

   a. Export function
   b. Aras Free Zone
   c. IATT
   d. Effective rate of protection

19. _____ is a broad label that refers to any individuals or households that use goods and services generated within the economy. The concept of a _____ is used in different contexts, so that the usage and significance of the term may vary.

Typically when business people and economists talk of _____s they are talking about person as _____, an aggregated commodity item with little individuality other than that expressed in the buy/not-buy decision.

a. 1921 recession
b. 130-30 fund
c. 100-year flood
d. Consumer

20. The term surplus is used in economics for several related quantities. The _____ is the amount that consumers benefit by being able to purchase a product for a price that is less than they would be willing to pay. The producer surplus is the amount that producers benefit by selling at a market price mechanism that is higher than they would be willing to sell for.

a. Microeconomic reform
b. Consumer surplus
c. Necessity good
d. Marginal rate of technical substitution

21. _____ is a term that refers both to:

- a formal discipline used to help appraise, or assess, the case for a project or proposal, which itself is a process known as project appraisal; and
- an informal approach to making decisions of any kind.

Under both definitions the process involves, whether explicitly or implicitly, weighing the total expected costs against the total expected benefits of one or more actions in order to choose the best or most profitable option. The formal process is often referred to as either CBA (_____) or BCost-benefit analysis

A hallmark of CBA is that all benefits and all costs are expressed in money terms, and are adjusted for the time value of money, so that all flows of benefits and flows of project costs over time (which tend to occur at different points in time) are expressed on a common basis in terms of their e;present value.e; Closely related, but slightly different, formal techniques include Cost-effectiveness analysis, Economic impact analysis, Fiscal impact analysis and Social Return on Investment(SROI) analysis. The latter builds upon the logic of _____, but differs in that it is explicitly designed to inform the practical decision-making of enterprise managers and investors focused on optimising their social and environmental impacts.

a. Cost-benefit analysis
b. Decision theory
c. 100-year flood
d. 130-30 fund

22. The term surplus is used in economics for several related quantities. The consumer surplus is the amount that consumers benefit by being able to purchase a product for a price that is less than they would be willing to pay. The _____ is the amount that producers benefit by selling at a market price mechanism that is higher than they would be willing to sell for.

a. Producer surplus
b. Returns to scale
c. Schedule delay
d. Long term

Chapter 8. The Instruments of Trade Policy

23. In international economics and international trade, _____ or _____ is the relative prices of a country's export to import. '_____' are sometimes used as a proxy for the relative social welfare of a country, but this heuristic is technically questionable and should be used with extreme caution. An improvement in a nation's _____ is good for that country in the sense that it has to pay less for the products it import.
    a. Commercial invoice
    b. Terms of trade
    c. Kennedy Round
    d. Common market

24. _____ is a common concept in economics, and gives rise to derived concepts such as consumer debt. Generally _____ is defined by opposition to production. But the precise definition can vary because different schools of economists define production quite differently.
    a. Cash or share options
    b. Foreclosure data providers
    c. Federal Reserve Bank Notes
    d. Consumption

25. _____ is a government policy to encourage export of goods and discourage sale of goods on the domestic market through low-cost loans or tax relief for exporters, or government financed international advertising or R'D. An _____ reduces the price paid by foreign importers, which means domestic consumers pay more than foreign consumers. The WTO prohibits most subsidies directly linked to the volume of exports.
    a. Illicit financial flows
    b. Export subsidy
    c. Economic repression
    d. Economic activity rate

26. In microeconomics, _____ is quite simply the conversion of inputs into outputs. It is an economic process that uses resources to create a good or service that is suitable for exchange. This can include manufacturing, storing, shipping, and packaging.
    a. Red Guards
    b. Solved
    c. Production
    d. MET

27. Economic _____ is defined as an excess distribution to any factor in a production process above that which is required to induce the factor into the process or any excess above that which is necessary to keep the factor in its current use..

    Classical Factor _____ is primarily concerned with the fee paid for the use of fixed (e.g. natural) resources. The classical definition is expressed as any excess payment above that required to induce or provide for production.

    a. 100-year flood
    b. Rent
    c. 1921 recession
    d. 130-30 fund

28. The _____ is a general equilibrium mathematical model of international trade, developed by Eli Heckscher and Bertil Ohlin at the Stockholm School of Economics. It builds on David Ricardo's theory of comparative advantage by predicting patterns of commerce and production based on the factor endowments of a trading region. The model essentially says that countries will export products that utilize their abundant and cheap factor(s) of production and import products that utilize the countries' scarce factor(s.)
    a. Heckscher-Ohlin model
    b. Jamaican Free Zones
    c. Free trade zone
    d. Linder hypothesis

Chapter 8. The Instruments of Trade Policy

29. _____ is the acquisition of goods and/or services at the best possible total cost of ownership, in the right quantity and quality, at the right time, in the right place and from the right source for the direct benefit or use of corporations or individuals, generally via a contract. Simple _____ may involve nothing more than repeat purchasing. Complex _____ could involve finding long term partners - or even 'co-destiny' suppliers that might fundamentally commit one organization to another.
   - a. Sole proprietorship
   - b. Golden umbrella
   - c. Procurement
   - d. Pre-emerging markets

30. A _____ refers to any type debt instrument, such as a loan, bond, mortgage that does not have a fixed rate of interest over the life of the instrument. Such debt typically uses an index or other base rate for establishing the interest rate for each relevant period. One of the most common rates to use as the basis for applying interest rates is the London Inter-bank Offered Rate, or LIBOR
   - a. Money market
   - b. Moneylender
   - c. Disposal tax effect
   - d. Floating interest rate

31. _____ is a type of trade policy that allows traders to act and transact without interference from government. Thus, the policy permits trading partners mutual gains from trade, with goods and services produced according to the theory of comparative advantage.

    Under a _____ policy, prices are a reflection of true supply and demand, and are the sole determinant of resource allocation.
   - a. 1921 recession
   - b. 130-30 fund
   - c. 100-year flood
   - d. Free trade

32. In economics, a _____ exists when a specific individual or enterprise has sufficient control over a particular product or service to determine significantly the terms on which other individuals shall have access to it. Monopolies are thus characterized by a lack of economic competition for the good or service that they provide and a lack of viable substitute goods. The verb 'monopolize' refers to the process by which a firm gains persistently greater market share than what is expected under perfect competition.
   - a. 130-30 fund
   - b. 1921 recession
   - c. 100-year flood
   - d. Monopoly

Chapter 9. The Political Economy of Trade Policy

1. _____ originally was the term for studying production, buying and selling, and their relations with law, custom, and government. _____ originated in moral philosophy. It developed in the 18th century as the study of the economies of states -- polities, hence _____.
   a. Dirigisme
   b. Productive and unproductive labour
   c. Political economy
   d. Geoeconomics

2. In economics, an _____ is any good (e.g. a commodity) or service brought into one country from another country in a legitimate fashion, typically for use in trade. It is a good that is brought in from another country for sale. _____ goods or services are provided to domestic consumers by foreign producers. An _____ in the receiving country is an export to the sending country.
   a. Import quota
   b. Incoterms
   c. Import
   d. Economic integration

3. An _____ is a type of protectionist trade restriction that sets a physical limit on the quantity of a good that can be imported into a country in a given period of time. Quotas, like other trade restrictions, are used to benefit the producers of a good in a domestic economy at the expense of all consumers of the good in that economy.

   Critics say quotas often lead to corruption (bribes to get a quota allocation), smuggling (circumventing a quota), and higher prices for consumers.

   a. International Monetary Systems
   b. Import quota
   c. Agreement on Agriculture
   d. Economic integration

4. _____ is a type of trade policy that allows traders to act and transact without interference from government. Thus, the policy permits trading partners mutual gains from trade, with goods and services produced according to the theory of comparative advantage.

   Under a _____ policy, prices are a reflection of true supply and demand, and are the sole determinant of resource allocation.

   a. 100-year flood
   b. Free trade
   c. 1921 recession
   d. 130-30 fund

5. _____s is the social science that studies the production, distribution, and consumption of goods and services. The term _____s comes from the Ancient Greek oá¼°κονομῖα from oá¼¶κος (oikos, 'house') + vΐŒμος (nomos, 'custom' or 'law'), hence 'rules of the house(hold)'. Current _____ models developed out of the broader field of political economy in the late 19th century, owing to a desire to use an empirical approach more akin to the physical sciences.
   a. Opportunity cost
   b. Economic
   c. Energy economics
   d. Inflation

6. _____, in microeconomics, are the cost advantages that a business obtains due to expansion. They are factors that cause a producere;s average cost per unit to fall as scale is increased. _____ is a long run concept and refers to reductions in unit cost as the size of a facility, or scale, increases.
   a. Economic production quantity
   b. Economies of scale
   c. Underinvestment employment relationship
   d. Isoquant

7. In economics, _____ refers to the ability of a person or a country to produce a particular good at a lower marginal cost and opportunity cost than another person or country. It is the ability to produce a product most efficiently given all the other products that could be produced. It can be contrasted with absolute advantage which refers to the ability of a person or a country to produce a particular good at a lower absolute cost than another.
   a. Hot money
   b. Comparative advantage
   c. Triffin dilemma
   d. Gravity model of trade

8. _____ is money accepted for exchange of goods in an economy. The prevalence of one money over another arises, usually, when a government designates through decrees that the government shall accept only particular notes and coins in payment for taxes. Typically, money of _____ consists of stamped coins and minted paper bills.
   a. Security thread
   b. Totnes pound
   c. Local currency
   d. Currency

9. A _____ is a duty imposed on goods when they are moved across a political boundary. They are usually associated with protectionism, the economic policy of restraining trade between nations. For political reasons, _____s are usually imposed on imported goods, although they may also be imposed on exported goods.
   a. 130-30 fund
   b. 100-year flood
   c. 1921 recession
   d. Tariff

10. In international economics and international trade, _____ or _____ is the relative prices of a country's export to import. '_____' are sometimes used as a proxy for the relative social welfare of a country, but this heuristic is technically questionable and should be used with extreme caution. An improvement in a nation's _____ is good for that country in the sense that it has to pay less for the products it import.
    a. Kennedy Round
    b. Common market
    c. Commercial invoice
    d. Terms of trade

11. In economics, a _____ exists when the production or use of goods and services by the market is not efficient. That is, there exists another outcome where all involved can be made better off. _____s can be viewed as scenarios where individuals' pursuit of pure self-interest leads to results that are not efficient - that can be improved upon from the societal point-of-view.
    a. Financial economics
    b. General equilibrium
    c. Market failure
    d. Fixed exchange rate

12. The _____ concerns what happens when one or more optimality conditions cannot be satisfied in an economic model. Canadian economist Richard Lipsey and Australian-American economist Kelvin Lancaster showed in a 1956 paper that if one optimality condition in an economic model cannot be satisfied, it is possible that the next-best solution involves changing other variables away from the ones that are usually assumed to be optimal.

This means that in an economy with some unavoidable market failure in one sector, there can actually be a decrease in efficiency due to a move toward greater market perfection in another sector.

   a. Theory of the second best
   b. Technology gap
   c. Developmentalism
   d. Diamond model

Chapter 9. The Political Economy of Trade Policy

13. In economics, _____ is how a natione;s total economy is distributed among its population. ._____ has always been a central concern of economic theory and economic policy. Classical economists such as Adam Smith, Thomas Malthus and David Ricardo were mainly concerned with factor _____, that is, the distribution of income between the main factors of production, land, labour and capital.
    a. Authorised capital
    b. Income distribution
    c. Eco commerce
    d. Equipment trust certificate

14. In probability theory and statistics, a _____ is described as the number separating the higher half of a sample, a population from the lower half. The _____ of a finite list of numbers can be found by arranging all the observations from lowest value to highest value and picking the middle one. If there is an even number of observations, the _____ is not unique, so one often takes the mean of the two middle values.
    a. Median
    b. Labour vouchers
    c. First player wins
    d. Fiscal stimulus plans

15. A _____ is a group of people who share or are motivated by at least one common issue or interest, or work together on a specific project(s) to achieve a common objective. _____s are also characterised by attempts to share and exercise political and social power and to make decisions on a consensus-driven and egalitarian basis. _____s differ from cooperatives in that they are not necessarily focused upon an economic benefit or saving (but can be that as well.)
    a. 1921 recession
    b. 130-30 fund
    c. 100-year flood
    d. Collective

16. The _____ or gross domestic income (GDI), a basic measure of an economy's economic performance, is the market value of all final goods and services produced within the borders of a nation in a year. _____ can be defined in three ways, all of which are conceptually identical. First, it is equal to the total expenditures for all final goods and services produced within the country in a stipulated period of time (usually a 365-day year.)
    a. Countercyclical
    b. Monopolistic competition
    c. Market structure
    d. Gross domestic product

17. The _____ is a trilateral trade bloc in North America created by the governments of the United States, Canada, and Mexico. The agreement creating the trade bloc came into force on January 1, 1994. It superseded the Canada-United States Free Trade Agreement between the U.S. and Canada.
    a. Federal Reserve Bank Notes
    b. Demand-side technologies
    c. Case-Shiller Home Price Indices
    d. North American Free Trade Agreement

18. _____ describes a set of laws relating to domestic agriculture and imports of foreign agricultural products. Governments usually implement agricultural policies with the goal of achieving a specific outcome in the domestic agricultural product markets. Outcomes can involve, for example, a guaranteed supply level, price stability, product quality, product selection, land use or employment.
    a. ACCRA Cost of Living Index
    b. Intercropping
    c. ACEA agreement
    d. Agricultural Policy

56 *Chapter 9. The Political Economy of Trade Policy*

19. Economics:

   - _____, the desire to own something and the ability to pay for it
   - _____ curve, a graphic representation of a _____ schedule
   - _____ deposit, the money in checking accounts
   - _____ pull theory, the theory that inflation occurs when _____ for goods and services exceeds existing supplies
   - _____ schedule, a table that lists the quantity of a good a person will buy it each different price
   - _____ side economics, the school of economics at believes government spending and tax cuts open economy by raising _____

   a. Production
   b. Demand
   c. McKesson ' Robbins scandal
   d. Variability

20. _____ is the income of individuals or nations after adjusting for inflation. It is calculated by subtracting inflation from the nominal income. Real variables, such as _____, real GDP, and real interest rate are variables that are measured in physical units, while nominal variables such as nominal income, nominal GDP, and nominal interest rate are measured in monetary units.

   a. Windfall gain
   b. Net national income
   c. Real income
   d. Family income

21. The General Agreement on Tariffs and Trade was the outcome of the failure of negotiating governments to create the International Trade Organization (ITO). _____ was formed in 1947 and lasted until 1994, when it was replaced by the World Trade Organization. The Bretton Woods Conference had introduced the idea for an organization to regulate trade as part of a larger plan for economic recovery after World War II.

   a. GATT
   b. General Agreement on Tariffs and Trade
   c. General Agreement on Trade in Services
   d. Dutch-Scandinavian Economic Pact

22. The _____ is an important selective, mainly private, international organization designed by its founders to supervise and liberalize international trade. The organization officially commenced on 1 January 1995, under the Marrakesh Agreement, succeeding the 1947 General Agreement on Tariffs and Trade (GATT.)

   The _____ deals with regulation of trade between participating countries; it provides a framework for negotiating and formalising trade agreements, and a dispute resolution process aimed at enforcing participants' adherence to _____ agreements which are signed by representatives of member governments and ratified by their parliaments.

   a. Backus-Kehoe-Kydland consumption correlation puzzle
   b. 2009 G-20 London summit protests
   c. Bio-energy village
   d. World Trade Organization

23. The _____ was an act signed into law on June 17, 1930, that raised U.S. tariffs on over 20,000 imported goods to record levels. In the United States 1,028 economists signed a petition against this legislation, and after it was passed, many countries retaliated with their own increased tariffs on U.S. goods, and American exports and imports were reduced by more than half.

Chapter 9. The Political Economy of Trade Policy

Although rated capacity had increased tremendously, actual output, income, and expenditure had not.

a. Judgment summons
b. Loss of use
c. Patent Law Treaty
d. Smoot-Hawley Tariff Act

24. _____ is exchange of capital, goods, and services across international borders or territories. In most countries, it represents a significant share of gross domestic product (GDP.) While _____ has been present throughout much of history, its economic, social, and political importance has been on the rise in recent centuries.

a. Intra-industry trade
b. International Trade
c. Incoterms
d. Import license

25. _____s are payments made by a corporation to its shareholders. It is the portion of corporate profits paid out to stockholders. When a corporation earns a profit or surplus, that money can be put to two uses: it can either be re-invested in the business (called retained earnings), or it can be paid to the shareholders as a _____.

a. Dividend cover
b. Dividend yield
c. Dividend
d. Dividend puzzle

26. The _____ was the outcome of the failure of negotiating governments to create the International Trade Organization (ITO.) GATT was formed in 1947 and lasted until 1994, when it was replaced by the World Trade Organization. The Bretton Woods Conference had introduced the idea for an organization to regulate trade as part of a larger plan for economic recovery after World War II.

a. GATT
b. Dutch-Scandinavian Economic Pact
c. General Agreement on Trade in Services
d. General Agreement on Tariffs and Trade

27. The _____ is an international organization that oversees the global financial system by following the macroeconomic policies of its member countries, in particular those with an impact on exchange rates and the balance of payments. It is an organization formed to stabilize international exchange rates and facilitate development. It also offers financial and technical assistance to its members, making it an international lender of last resort.

a. ACCRA Cost of Living Index
b. International Monetary Fund
c. Office of Thrift Supervision
d. ACEA agreement

28. The _____ commenced in September 1986 and continued until April 1994. The round, based on the General Agreement on Tariffs and Trade (GATT) ministerial meeting in Geneva (1982), was launched in Punta del Este in Uruguay (hence the name), followed by negotiations in Montreal, Geneva, Brussels, Washington, D.C., and Tokyo, with the 20 agreements finally being signed in Marrakech - the Marrakesh Agreement. The Round transformed the GATT into the World Trade Organization.

a. ACEA agreement
b. AD-IA Model
c. Uruguay Round
d. ACCRA Cost of Living Index

29. The _____ is an international financial institution that provides financial and technical assistance to developing countries for development programs (e.g. bridges, roads, schools, etc.) with the stated goal of reducing poverty.

The _____ differs from the _____ Group, in that the _____ comprises only two institutions:

- International Bank for Reconstruction and Development (IBRD)
- International Development Association (IDA)

Whereas the latter incorporates these two in addition to three more:

- International Finance Corporation (IFC)
- Multilateral Investment Guarantee Agency (MIGA)
- International Centre for Settlement of Investment Disputes (ICSID)

John Maynard Keynes (right) represented the UK at the conference, and Harry Dexter White represented the US.

The _____ is one of two major financial institutions created as a result of the Bretton Woods Conference in 1944. The International Monetary Fund, a related but separate institution, is the second.

   a. Flow to Equity-Approach
   b. Financial costs of the 2003 Iraq War
   c. Bank-State-Branch
   d. World Bank

30. The _____ was the sixth session of General Agreement on Tariffs and Trade (GATT) trade negotiations held in 1964-1967 in Geneva, Switzerland. Congressional passage of the US Trade Expansion Act in 1962 authorized the White House to conduct mutual tariff negotiations ultimately leading to the _____. The _____ had four major goals: to slash tariffs by half with a minimum of exceptions, to break down farm trade restrictions, to strip away nontariff regulations, and to aid developing nations.

   a. Special Drawing Rights
   b. Jamaican Free Zones
   c. Heckscher-Ohlin model
   d. Kennedy Round

31. The _____ is a treaty of the World Trade Organization (WTO) that entered into force in January 1995 as a result of the Uruguay Round negotiations. The treaty was created to extend the multilateral trading system to service sector, in the same way the General Agreement on Tariffs and Trade (GATT) provides such a system for merchandise trade.

All members of the WTO are signatories to the GATS.

   a. General Agreement on Tariffs and Trade
   b. Dutch-Scandinavian Economic Pact
   c. GATT
   d. General Agreement on Trade in Services

32. _____ is the acquisition of goods and/or services at the best possible total cost of ownership, in the right quantity and quality, at the right time, in the right place and from the right source for the direct benefit or use of corporations or individuals, generally via a contract. Simple _____ may involve nothing more than repeat purchasing. Complex _____ could involve finding long term partners - or even 'co-destiny' suppliers that might fundamentally commit one organization to another.

Chapter 9. The Political Economy of Trade Policy

a. Golden umbrella
c. Pre-emerging markets
b. Sole proprietorship
d. Procurement

33. The _____ movement is movement of movements which are critical of the globalization of capitalism. Participants base their criticisms on a number of related ideas. What is shared is that participants stand in opposition to the unregulated political power of large, multi-national corporations and to the powers exercised through trade agreements.

a. Overcapitalisation
c. Anti-consumerism
b. Anti-globalization
d. Asset price inflation

34. _____ is a term that refers both to:

- a formal discipline used to help appraise, or assess, the case for a project or proposal, which itself is a process known as project appraisal; and
- an informal approach to making decisions of any kind.

Under both definitions the process involves, whether explicitly or implicitly, weighing the total expected costs against the total expected benefits of one or more actions in order to choose the best or most profitable option. The formal process is often referred to as either CBA (_____) or BCost-benefit analysis

A hallmark of CBA is that all benefits and all costs are expressed in money terms, and are adjusted for the time value of money, so that all flows of benefits and flows of project costs over time (which tend to occur at different points in time) are expressed on a common basis in terms of their e;present value.e; Closely related, but slightly different, formal techniques include Cost-effectiveness analysis, Economic impact analysis, Fiscal impact analysis and Social Return on Investment(SROI) analysis. The latter builds upon the logic of _____, but differs in that it is explicitly designed to inform the practical decision-making of enterprise managers and investors focused on optimising their social and environmental impacts.

a. 130-30 fund
c. Decision theory
b. 100-year flood
d. Cost-benefit analysis

35. _____ are legal property rights over creations of the mind, both artistic and commercial, and the corresponding fields of law. Under _____ law, owners are granted certain exclusive rights to a variety of intangible assets, such as musical, literary, and artistic works; ideas, discoveries and inventions; and words, phrases, symbols, and designs. Common types of _____ include copyrights, trademarks, patents, industrial design rights and trade secrets.

a. Intellectual property
c. Independent contractor
b. Ease of Doing Business Index
d. Expedited Funds Availability Act

36. In general _____ refers to any non-human asset made by humans and then used in production. Often, it refers to economic capital in some ambiguous combination of infrastructural capital and natural capital. As these are combined in process-specific and firm-specific ways that neoclassical macroeconomics does not differentiate at its level of analysis, it is common to refer only to physical vs. human capital and seek so-called 'balanced growth' that develops both in tandem

Such analyses, however, fails to make distinctions considered critical by many modern economists.

Chapter 9. The Political Economy of Trade Policy

a. Physical capital
c. Net domestic product
b. Linkage principle
d. Factor cost

37. _____ is the practice within the banking industry of authorizing electronic transactions done with a debit card or credit card and holding this balance as unavailable either until the merchant clears the transaction _____s can fall off the account anywhere from 1-5 days after the transaction date depending on the bank's policy; in the case of credit cards, holds may last as long as 30 days, depending on the issuing bank.

Signature-based credit and debit card transactions are a two-step process, consisting of an authorization and a settlement.

When a merchant swipes a customer's credit card, the credit card terminal connects to the merchant's acquirer which verifies that the customer's account is valid and that sufficient funds are available to cover the transaction's cost.

a. Interbank network
c. Issuing bank
b. Authorization hold
d. Electronic funds transfer

38. A _____ is a free trade area with a common external tariff. The participant countries set up common external trade policy, but in some cases they use different import quotas. Common competition policy is also helpful to avoid competition deficiency.

a. Customs union
c. Grey market
b. Bilateral Investment Treaty
d. Common market

39. _____ is a designated group of countries that have agreed to eliminate tariffs, quotas and preferences on most (if not all) goods and services traded between them. It can be considered the second stage of economic integration. Countries choose this kind of economic integration form if their economical structures are complementary.

a. 100-year flood
c. MERCOSUR
b. 130-30 fund
d. Free trade area

40. The _____, alternately called the Group of African, Caribbean and Pacific countries are the countries that are signatories of the Lomé Convention with the European Commission (48 African, 16 Caribbean and 15 Pacific countries.)

The first Lomé Convention was signed in Lomé, Togo, in 1975. It arose out of Europe's wish to guarantee itself regular supplies of raw materials, and to maintain its privileged position in its overseas markets.

a. Intra-industry trade
c. Export function
b. Economic and monetary union
d. ACP States

41. The _____ are two of the treaties of the European Union signed on March 25, 1957. Both treaties were signed by The Six: Belgium, France, Italy, Luxembourg, the Netherlands and West Germany.

The first established the European Economic Community and the second established the European Atomic Energy Community (EAEC or Euratom.)

Chapter 9. The Political Economy of Trade Policy

a. Maastricht Treaty
b. Treaty of Amsterdam
c. 100-year flood
d. Treaties of Rome

42. _____ is a Regional Trade Agreement among Argentina, Brazil, Paraguay and Uruguay founded in 1991 by the Treaty of Asunci>ón, which was later amended and updated by the 1994 Treaty of Ouro Preto. Its purpose is to promote free trade and the fluid movement of goods, people, and currency.

_____ origins trace back to 1985 when Presidents Ra>úl Alfons>ín of Argentina and Jos>é Sarney of Brazil signed the Argentina-Brazil Integration and Economics Cooperation Program or PICE .

a. 100-year flood
b. 130-30 fund
c. Free trade area
d. Mercosur

43. _____ is the price of a commodity such as a good or service in terms of another; ie, the ratio of two prices. A _____ may be expressed in terms of a ratio between any two prices or the ratio between the price of one particular good and a weighted average of all other goods available in the market. A _____ is an opportunity cost.

a. False economy
b. Food cooperative
c. False shortage
d. Relative price

44. _____ in economics and business is the result of an exchange and from that trade we assign a numerical monetary value to a good, service or asset. If Alice trades Bob 4 apples for an orange, the _____ of an orange is 4 apples. Inversely, the _____ of an apple is 1/4 oranges.

a. Price war
b. Premium pricing
c. Price book
d. Price

Chapter 10. Trade Policy in Developing Countries

1. _____ is that which is owed; usually referencing assets owed, but the term can also cover moral obligations and other interactions not requiring money. In the case of assets, _____ is a means of using future purchasing power in the present before a summation has been earned. Some companies and corporations use _____ as a part of their overall corporate finance strategy.
   a. Debenture
   b. Collateral Management
   c. Hard money loan
   d. Debt

2. _____ ndustrialization in North America, is the process of social and economic change whereby a human group is transformed from a pre-industrial society into an industrial one. _____ t is a part of a wider modernisation process, where social change and economic development are closely related with technological innovation, particularly with the development of large-scale energy and metallurgy production. _____ t is the extensive organisation of an economy for the purpose of manufacturing.
   a. AD-IA Model
   b. ACEA agreement
   c. Industrialization
   d. ACCRA Cost of Living Index

3. The _____ is an economic reason for protectionism. The crux of the argument is that nascent industries often do not have the economies of scale that their older competitors from other countries may have, and thus need to be protected until they can attain similar economies of scale. It was first used by Alexander Hamilton in 1790 and later by Friedrich List, in 1841, to support protection for German manufacturing against British industry.
   a. ACCRA Cost of Living Index
   b. ACEA agreement
   c. Infant industry argument
   d. AD-IA Model

4. An _____ company is one which produces goods mainly for exports, rather than for the domestic market. The term is commonly used to describe factories in developing countries producing goods for developed countries.

   Such companies are heavily dependent on the exchange rate, usually wanting their domestic currency to be weak, as this allows them to sell their products cheaply abroad.

   a. Inferior good
   b. Information good
   c. Independent goods
   d. Export-oriented

5. The _____ was a period of financial crisis that gripped much of Asia beginning in July 1997, and raised fears of a worldwide economic meltdown (financial contagion.)

   The crisis started in Thailand with the financial collapse of the Thai baht caused by the decision of the Thai government to float the baht, cutting its peg to the USD, after exhaustive efforts to support it in the face of a severe financial overextension that was in part real estate driven. At the time, Thailand had acquired a burden of foreign debt that made the country effectively bankrupt even before the collapse of its currency.

   a. Asian financial crisis
   b. ACEA agreement
   c. AD-IA Model
   d. ACCRA Cost of Living Index

6. The term _____ is applied broadly to a variety of situations in which some financial institutions or assets suddenly lose a large part of their value. In the 19th and early 20th centuries, many financial crises were associated with banking panics, and many recessions coincided with these panics. Other situations that are often called financial crises include stock market crashes and the bursting of other financial bubbles, currency crises, and sovereign defaults.

Chapter 10. Trade Policy in Developing Countries

    a. Macroeconomics
    b. Market failure
    c. Financial crisis
    d. Co-operative economics

7. In economics, a _____ exists when the production or use of goods and services by the market is not efficient. That is, there exists another outcome where all involved can be made better off. _____s can be viewed as scenarios where individuals' pursuit of pure self-interest leads to results that are not efficient - that can be improved upon from the societal point-of-view.
    a. Market failure
    b. Fixed exchange rate
    c. General equilibrium
    d. Financial economics

8. The _____ is the market for securities, where companies and governments can raise longterm funds. It is a market in which money is lent for periods longer than a year. The _____ includes the stock market and the bond market.
    a. Multi-family office
    b. Financial instrument
    c. Performance attribution
    d. Capital market

9. In economics, an _____ is any good (e.g. a commodity) or service brought into one country from another country in a legitimate fashion, typically for use in trade. It is a good that is brought in from another country for sale. _____ goods or services are provided to domestic consumers by foreign producers. An _____ in the receiving country is an export to the sending country.
    a. Economic integration
    b. Import quota
    c. Incoterms
    d. Import

10. _____ industrialization is a trade and economic policy based on the premise that a country should attempt to reduce its foreign dependency through the local production of industrialized products. Adopted in many Latin American countries from the 1930s until the late 1980s, and in some Asian and African countries from the 1950s on, Import substitutionl was theoretically organized in the works of Raúl Prebisch, Hans Singer, Celso Furtado and other structural economic thinkers, and gained prominence with the creation of the United Nations Economic Commission for Latin America and the Caribbean . Insofar as its suggestion of state-induced industrialization through governmental spending, it is largely influenced by Keynesian thinking, as well as the infant industry arguments adopted by some highly industrialized countries, such as the United States, until the 1940s.
    a. AD-IA Model
    b. ACCRA Cost of Living Index
    c. ACEA agreement
    d. Import substitution

11. _____ is exchange of capital, goods, and services across international borders or territories. In most countries, it represents a significant share of gross domestic product (GDP.) While _____ has been present throughout much of history, its economic, social, and political importance has been on the rise in recent centuries.
    a. Intra-industry trade
    b. International trade
    c. Import license
    d. Incoterms

Chapter 10. Trade Policy in Developing Countries

12. In mathematics, an _____ is a statement about the relative size or order of two objects, or about whether they are the same or not

- The notation a < b means that a is less than b.
- The notation a > b means that a is greater than b.
- The notation a ≠ b means that a is not equal to b, but does not say that one is greater than the other or even that they can be compared in size.

In each statement above, a is not equal to b. These relations are known as strict inequalities. The notation a < b may also be read as 'a is strictly less than b'.

a. AD-IA Model
b. ACCRA Cost of Living Index
c. ACEA agreement
d. Inequality

13. In economics, an _____ is any good or commodity, transported from one country to another country in a legitimate fashion, typically for use in trade. _____ goods or services are provided to foreign consumers by domestic producers. _____ is an important part of international trade.

a. AD-IA Model
b. ACEA agreement
c. ACCRA Cost of Living Index
d. Export

14. _____ sometimes called export substitution industrialization (ESI) or export led industrialization (ELI) is a trade and economic policy aiming to speed-up the industrialization process of a country through exporting goods for which the nation has a comparative advantage. Export-led growth implies opening domestic markets to foreign competition in exchange for market access in other countries. Reduced tariff barriers, floating exchange rate (devaluation of national currency is often employed to facilitate exports), and government support for exporting sectors are all an example of policies adopted to promote EOI, and ultimately economic development.

a. Aras Free Zone
b. Export Yellow Pages
c. Export-oriented industrialization
d. Agreement on Agriculture

15. Economics:

- _____,the desire to own something and the ability to pay for it
- _____ curve,a graphic representation of a _____ schedule
- _____ deposit, the money in checking accounts
- _____ pull theory,the theory that inflation occurs when _____ for goods and services exceeds existing supplies
- _____ schedule,a table that lists the quantity of a good a person will buy it each different price
- _____ side economics,the school of economics at believes government spending and tax cuts open economy by raising _____

a. Variability
b. Production
c. McKesson ' Robbins scandal
d. Demand

Chapter 10. Trade Policy in Developing Countries

16. _____s is the social science that studies the production, distribution, and consumption of goods and services. The term _____s comes from the Ancient Greek oá¼°κονομῖα from oá¼¶κος (oikos, 'house') + vÏŒμος (nomos, 'custom' or 'law'), hence 'rules of the house(hold)'. Current _____ models developed out of the broader field of political economy in the late 19th century, owing to a desire to use an empirical approach more akin to the physical sciences.
   a. Opportunity cost
   b. Inflation
   c. Energy economics
   d. Economic

17. _____ is a type of trade policy that allows traders to act and transact without interference from government. Thus, the policy permits trading partners mutual gains from trade, with goods and services produced according to the theory of comparative advantage.

Under a _____ policy, prices are a reflection of true supply and demand, and are the sole determinant of resource allocation.

   a. 100-year flood
   b. 1921 recession
   c. 130-30 fund
   d. Free trade

18. In calculus, a function f defined on a subset of the real numbers with real values is called _____, if for all x and y such that x >≤ y one has f(x) >≤ f(y), so f preserves the order. In layman's terms, the sign of the slope is always positive (the curve tending upwards) or zero (i.e., non-decreasing, or asymptotic, or depicted as a horizontal, flat line) Likewise, a function is called monotonically decreasing (non-increasing) if, whenever x >≤ y, then f(x) >≥ f(y), so it reverses the order.
   a. Monotonic
   b. 130-30 fund
   c. 100-year flood
   d. 1921 recession

Chapter 11. Controversies in Trade Policy

1. In economics, an _____ is any good (e.g. a commodity) or service brought into one country from another country in a legitimate fashion, typically for use in trade. It is a good that is brought in from another country for sale. _____ goods or services are provided to domestic consumers by foreign producers. An _____ in the receiving country is an export to the sending country.
   a. Import quota
   b. Incoterms
   c. Economic integration
   d. Import

2. An _____ is a type of protectionist trade restriction that sets a physical limit on the quantity of a good that can be imported into a country in a given period of time. Quotas, like other trade restrictions, are used to benefit the producers of a good in a domestic economy at the expense of all consumers of the good in that economy.

   Critics say quotas often lead to corruption (bribes to get a quota allocation), smuggling (circumventing a quota), and higher prices for consumers.

   a. Economic integration
   b. Agreement on Agriculture
   c. Import quota
   d. International Monetary Systems

3. The phrase _____, according to the Organization for Economic Co-operation and Development, refers to 'creative work undertaken on a systematic basis in order to increase the stock of knowledge, including knowledge of man, culture and society, and the use of this stock of knowledge to devise new applications [sic]'

   New product design and development is more than often a crucial factor in the survival of a company. In an industry that is fast changing, firms must continually revise their design and range of products. This is necessary due to continuous technology change and development as well as other competitors and the changing preference of customers.

   a. 100-year flood
   b. 130-30 fund
   c. 1921 recession
   d. Research and development

4. In economic theory, _____ is the competitive situation in any market where the conditions necessary for perfect competition are not satisfied. It is a market structure that does not meet the conditions of perfect competition.

   Forms of _____ include:

   - Monopoly, in which there is only one seller of a good.
   - Oligopoly, in which there is a small number of sellers.
   - Monopolistic competition, in which there are many sellers producing highly differentiated goods.
   - Monopsony, in which there is only one buyer of a good.
   - Oligopsony, in which there is a small number of buyers.

   There may also be _____ in markets due to buyers or sellers lacking information about prices and the goods being traded.

   There may also be _____ due to a time lag in a market.

Chapter 11. Controversies in Trade Policy

a. AD-IA Model
c. Imperfect competition
b. ACEA agreement
d. ACCRA Cost of Living Index

5. The _____ is a trilateral trade bloc in North America created by the governments of the United States, Canada, and Mexico. The agreement creating the trade bloc came into force on January 1, 1994. It superseded the Canada-United States Free Trade Agreement between the U.S. and Canada.

a. Federal Reserve Bank Notes
c. North American Free Trade Agreement
b. Case-Shiller Home Price Indices
d. Demand-side technologies

6. _____ is a concept with somewhat disparate meanings in several fields. It also has a common meaning which has a loose connection with some of those more definite meanings.

Casually, it is typically used to denote a lack of order, or purpose, or cause.

a. 1921 recession
c. 100-year flood
b. Randomness
d. 130-30 fund

7. The _____ movement is movement of movements which are critical of the globalization of capitalism. Participants base their criticisms on a number of related ideas. What is shared is that participants stand in opposition to the unregulated political power of large, multi-national corporations and to the powers exercised through trade agreements.

a. Asset price inflation
c. Anti-globalization
b. Overcapitalisation
d. Anti-consumerism

8. _____ is a type of trade policy that allows traders to act and transact without interference from government. Thus, the policy permits trading partners mutual gains from trade, with goods and services produced according to the theory of comparative advantage.

Under a _____ policy, prices are a reflection of true supply and demand, and are the sole determinant of resource allocation.

a. Free trade
c. 100-year flood
b. 1921 recession
d. 130-30 fund

9. _____ in its literal sense is the process of transformation of local or regional phenomena into global ones. It can be described as a process by which the people of the world are unified into a single society and function together.

This process is a combination of economic, technological, sociocultural and political forces.

a. Helsinki Process on Globalisation and Democracy
c. Globally Integrated Enterprise
b. Global Cosmopolitanism
d. Globalization

10. _____ is exchange of capital, goods, and services across international borders or territories. In most countries, it represents a significant share of gross domestic product (GDP.) While _____ has been present throughout much of history, its economic, social, and political importance has been on the rise in recent centuries.

Chapter 11. Controversies in Trade Policy

a. Incoterms
b. Import license
c. Intra-industry trade
d. International trade

11. The _____ commenced in September 1986 and continued until April 1994. The round, based on the General Agreement on Tariffs and Trade (GATT) ministerial meeting in Geneva (1982), was launched in Punta del Este in Uruguay (hence the name), followed by negotiations in Montreal, Geneva, Brussels, Washington, D.C., and Tokyo, with the 20 agreements finally being signed in Marrakech - the Marrakesh Agreement. The Round transformed the GATT into the World Trade Organization.

    a. AD-IA Model
    b. ACCRA Cost of Living Index
    c. ACEA agreement
    d. Uruguay Round

12. The _____ is an important selective, mainly private, international organization designed by its founders to supervise and liberalize international trade. The organization officially commenced on 1 January 1995, under the Marrakesh Agreement, succeeding the 1947 General Agreement on Tariffs and Trade (GATT.)

The _____ deals with regulation of trade between participating countries; it provides a framework for negotiating and formalising trade agreements, and a dispute resolution process aimed at enforcing participants' adherence to _____ agreements which are signed by representatives of member governments and ratified by their parliaments.

    a. 2009 G-20 London summit protests
    b. Bio-energy village
    c. Backus-Kehoe-Kydland consumption correlation puzzle
    d. World Trade Organization

13. _____ is that which is owed; usually referencing assets owed, but the term can also cover moral obligations and other interactions not requiring money. In the case of assets, _____ is a means of using future purchasing power in the present before a summation has been earned. Some companies and corporations use _____ as a part of their overall corporate finance strategy.

    a. Hard money loan
    b. Collateral Management
    c. Debenture
    d. Debt

14. Economics:

- _____, the desire to own something and the ability to pay for it
- _____ curve, a graphic representation of a _____ schedule
- _____ deposit, the money in checking accounts
- _____ pull theory, the theory that inflation occurs when _____ for goods and services exceeds existing supplies
- _____ schedule, a table that lists the quantity of a good a person will buy it each different price
- _____ side economics, the school of economics at believes government spending and tax cuts open economy by raising _____

a. Variability
b. Production
c. McKesson ' Robbins scandal
d. Demand

Chapter 11. Controversies in Trade Policy

15. In economics, _____ is when quantity demanded is more than quantity supplied. See Economic shortage.
    a. Excess demand
    b. AD-IA Model
    c. ACCRA Cost of Living Index
    d. ACEA agreement

16. The _____ of monetary management established the rules for commercial and financial relations among the world's major industrial states in the mid 20th Century. The _____ was the first example of a fully negotiated monetary order intended to govern monetary relations among independent nation-states.

Preparing to rebuild the international economic system as World War II was still raging, 730 delegates from all 44 Allied nations gathered at the Mount Washington Hotel in Bretton Woods, New Hampshire, United States, for the United Nations Monetary and Financial Conference.

   a. 130-30 fund
   b. 1921 recession
   c. 100-year flood
   d. Bretton Woods System

17. The _____ is an international financial institution that provides financial and technical assistance to developing countries for development programs (e.g. bridges, roads, schools, etc.) with the stated goal of reducing poverty.

The _____ differs from the _____ Group, in that the _____ comprises only two institutions:

- International Bank for Reconstruction and Development (IBRD)
- International Development Association (IDA)

Whereas the latter incorporates these two in addition to three more:

- International Finance Corporation (IFC)
- Multilateral Investment Guarantee Agency (MIGA)
- International Centre for Settlement of Investment Disputes (ICSID)

John Maynard Keynes (right) represented the UK at the conference, and Harry Dexter White represented the US.

The _____ is one of two major financial institutions created as a result of the Bretton Woods Conference in 1944. The International Monetary Fund, a related but separate institution, is the second.

   a. Bank-State-Branch
   b. Financial costs of the 2003 Iraq War
   c. Flow to Equity-Approach
   d. World Bank

18. The term _____s refers to wages that have been adjusted for inflation. This term is used in contrast to nominal wages or unadjusted wages.

The use of adjusted figures is in undertaking some form of economic analysis.

a. Federal Wage System
b. Profit sharing
c. Real wage
d. Living wage

19. The _____ was a period of financial crisis that gripped much of Asia beginning in July 1997, and raised fears of a worldwide economic meltdown (financial contagion.)

The crisis started in Thailand with the financial collapse of the Thai baht caused by the decision of the Thai government to float the baht, cutting its peg to the USD, after exhaustive efforts to support it in the face of a severe financial overextension that was in part real estate driven. At the time, Thailand had acquired a burden of foreign debt that made the country effectively bankrupt even before the collapse of its currency.

a. AD-IA Model
b. ACEA agreement
c. ACCRA Cost of Living Index
d. Asian financial crisis

20. A _____ describes one of a number of pieces of legislation relating to the reduction of smog and air pollution in general. The use by governments to enforce clean air standards has contributed to an improvement in human health and longer life spans. Critics argue it has also sapped corporate profits and contributed to outsourcing, while defenders counter that improved environmental air quality has generated more jobs than it has eliminated.

a. 130-30 fund
b. 100-year flood
c. Smog
d. Clean Air Act

21. The term _____ is applied broadly to a variety of situations in which some financial institutions or assets suddenly lose a large part of their value. In the 19th and early 20th centuries, many financial crises were associated with banking panics, and many recessions coincided with these panics. Other situations that are often called financial crises include stock market crashes and the bursting of other financial bubbles, currency crises, and sovereign defaults.

a. Co-operative economics
b. Financial crisis
c. Macroeconomics
d. Market failure

Chapter 12. National Income Accounting and the Balance of Payments

1. _____ is a branch of economics that deals with the performance, structure, and behavior of a national or regional economy as a whole. Along with microeconomics, _____ is one of the two most general fields in economics. It is the study of the behavior and decision-making of entire economies.
   a. Tobit model
   b. Nominal value
   c. New Trade Theory
   d. Macroeconomics

2. A variety of measures of _____ and output are used in economics to estimate total economic activity in a country or region, including gross domestic product (GDP), gross national product (GNP), and net _____

   There are three main ways of calculating these numbers; the output approach, the income approach and the expenditure approach. In theory, the three must yield the same, because total expenditures on goods and services must equal the total income paid to the producers (Gnational income), and that must also equal the total value of the output of goods and services (GNP.)

   a. Gross world product
   b. Volume index
   c. GNI per capita
   d. National income

3. In economics, the _____ measures the payments that flow between any individual country and all other countries. It is used to summarize all international economic transactions for that country during a specific time period, usually a year. The _____ is determined by the country's exports and imports of goods, services, and financial capital, as well as financial transfers.
   a. Balance of payments
   b. Skyscraper Index
   c. Gross domestic product per barrel
   d. Gross world product

4. _____ in economics and business is the result of an exchange and from that trade we assign a numerical monetary value to a good, service or asset. If Alice trades Bob 4 apples for an orange, the _____ of an orange is 4 apples. Inversely, the _____ of an apple is 1/4 oranges.
   a. Premium pricing
   b. Price book
   c. Price war
   d. Price

5. A _____ is a hypothetical measure of overall prices for some set of goods and services, in a given region during a given interval, normalized relative to some base set. Typically, a _____ is approximated with a price index.

   The classical dichotomy is the assumption that there is a relatively clean distinction between overall increases or decreases in prices and underlying, e;reale; economic variables.

   a. Discouraged worker
   b. Discretionary spending
   c. Price elasticity of supply
   d. Price level

6. In economics, _____ is the total demand for final goods and services in the economy (Y) at a given time and price level. It is the amount of goods and services in the economy that will be purchased at all possible price levels. This is the demand for the gross domestic product of a country when inventory levels are static.
   a. Aggregation problem
   b. Aggregate expenditure
   c. Aggregate demand
   d. Aggregate supply

7. Economics:

- _____, the desire to own something and the ability to pay for it
- _____ curve, a graphic representation of a _____ schedule
- _____ deposit, the money in checking accounts
- _____ pull theory, the theory that inflation occurs when _____ for goods and services exceeds existing supplies
- _____ schedule, a table that lists the quantity of a good a person will buy it each different price
- _____ side economics, the school of economics at believes government spending and tax cuts open economy by raising _____

a. Production
b. Variability
c. McKesson ' Robbins scandal
d. Demand

8. _____ is exchange of capital, goods, and services across international borders or territories. In most countries, it represents a significant share of gross domestic product (GDP.) While _____ has been present throughout much of history, its economic, social, and political importance has been on the rise in recent centuries.

a. Incoterms
b. International trade
c. Intra-industry trade
d. Import license

9. A _____ is the transfer of wealth from one party (such as a person or company) to another. A _____ is usually made in exchange for the provision of goods, services or both, or to fulfill a legal obligation.

The simplest and oldest form of _____ is barter, the exchange of one good or service for another.

a. Going concern
b. Payment
c. Social gravity
d. Soft count

10. A variety of measures of national income and output are used in economics to estimate total economic activity in a country or region, including gross domestic product (GDP), _____ , and net national income (NNI.)

There are three main ways of calculating these numbers; the output approach, the income approach and the expenditure approach. In theory, the three must yield the same, because total expenditures on goods and services must equal the total income paid to the producers (GNI), and that must also equal the total value of the output of goods and services (_____.)

a. Household final consumption expenditure
b. Gross world product
c. Purchasing power parity
d. Gross national product

11. The _____ is a trilateral trade bloc in North America created by the governments of the United States, Canada, and Mexico. The agreement creating the trade bloc came into force on January 1, 1994. It superseded the Canada-United States Free Trade Agreement between the U.S. and Canada.

a. Demand-side technologies
b. Federal Reserve Bank Notes
c. Case-Shiller Home Price Indices
d. North American Free Trade Agreement

Chapter 12. National Income Accounting and the Balance of Payments

12. _____ is a term used in accounting, economics and finance to spread the cost of an asset over the span of several years.

In simple words we can say that _____ is the reduction in the value of an asset due to usage, passage of time, wear and tear, technological outdating or obsolescence, depletion, inadequacy, rot, rust, decay or other such factors.

In accounting, _____ is a term used to describe any method of attributing the historical or purchase cost of an asset across its useful life, roughly corresponding to normal wear and tear.

   a. Salvage value
   b. Historical cost
   c. Net income per employee
   d. Depreciation

13. The _____ or gross domestic income (GDI), a basic measure of an economy's economic performance, is the market value of all final goods and services produced within the borders of a nation in a year. _____ can be defined in three ways, all of which are conceptually identical. First, it is equal to the total expenditures for all final goods and services produced within the country in a stipulated period of time (usually a 365-day year.)
   a. Countercyclical
   b. Market structure
   c. Monopolistic competition
   d. Gross domestic product

14. _____ is the total market value of all final goods and services produced by citizens of an economy during a given period of time (gross national product or GNP) minus depreciation. The _____ can be similarly applied at a country's domestic output level. The net domestic product (NDP) is the equivalent application of _____ within macroeconomics, and NDP is equal to gross domestic product (GDP) minus depreciation: NDP = GDP - depreciation.
   a. Net national product
   b. Compensation of employees
   c. Current account
   d. Gross private domestic investment

15. To _____ is to impose a financial charge or other levy upon a taxpayer by a state or the functional equivalent of a state.

_____es are also imposed by many subnational entities. _____es consist of direct _____ or indirect _____, and may be paid in money or as its labour equivalent (often but not always unpaid.)

   a. Tax
   b. 100-year flood
   c. 1921 recession
   d. 130-30 fund

16. To tax is to impose a financial charge or other levy upon a taxpayer by a state or the functional equivalent of a state.

_____ are also imposed by many subnational entities. _____ consist of direct tax or indirect tax, and may be paid in money or as its labour equivalent (often but not always unpaid.)

   a. 1921 recession
   b. Taxes
   c. 100-year flood
   d. 130-30 fund

Chapter 12. National Income Accounting and the Balance of Payments

17. _____ is a broad label that refers to any individuals or households that use goods and services generated within the economy. The concept of a _____ is used in different contexts, so that the usage and significance of the term may vary.

Typically when business people and economists talk of _____s they are talking about person as _____, an aggregated commodity item with little individuality other than that expressed in the buy/not-buy decision.

- a. 100-year flood
- b. 1921 recession
- c. 130-30 fund
- d. Consumer

18. The term surplus is used in economics for several related quantities. The _____ is the amount that consumers benefit by being able to purchase a product for a price that is less than they would be willing to pay. The producer surplus is the amount that producers benefit by selling at a market price mechanism that is higher than they would be willing to sell for.
- a. Necessity good
- b. Consumer surplus
- c. Microeconomic reform
- d. Marginal rate of technical substitution

19. _____ is a common concept in economics, and gives rise to derived concepts such as consumer debt. Generally _____ is defined by opposition to production. But the precise definition can vary because different schools of economists define production quite differently.
- a. Federal Reserve Bank Notes
- b. Cash or share options
- c. Foreclosure data providers
- d. Consumption

20. _____ or amortisation is the process of increasing an amount over a period of time. The word comes from Middle English amortisen to kill, alienate in mortmain, from Anglo-French amorteser, alteration of amortir, from Vulgar Latin admortire to kill, from Latin ad- + mort-, mors death. Particular instances of the term include:

- _____, the allocation of a lump sum amount to different time periods, particularly for loans and other forms of finance, including related interest or other finance charges.
    - _____ schedule, a table detailing each periodic payment on a loan (typically a mortgage), as generated by an _____ calculator.
    - Negative _____, an _____ schedule where the loan amount actually increases through not paying the full interest
- Amortized analysis, analyzing the execution cost of algorithms over a sequence of operations.
- _____ of capital expenditures of certain assets under accounting rules, particularly intangible assets, in a manner analogous to depreciation.
- _____ (tax law)

_____ is also used in the context of zoning regulations and describes the time in which a property owner has to relocate when the property's use constitutes a preexisting nonconforming use under zoning regulations.

- a. Economic miracle
- b. Oslo Agreements
- c. Augmentation
- d. Amortization

21. In finance, _____ is investment originating from other countries. See Foreign direct investment.

Chapter 12. National Income Accounting and the Balance of Payments

a. Foreign investment
c. Demand side economics
b. Preclusive purchasing
d. Horizontal merger

22. _____ is a fee paid on borrowed assets. It is the price paid for the use of borrowed money, or, money earned by deposited funds. Assets that are sometimes lent with _____ include money, shares, consumer goods through hire purchase, major assets such as aircraft, and even entire factories in finance lease arrangements.
    a. Insolvency
    c. Asset protection
    b. Internal debt
    d. Interest

23. An _____ is an economy in which people, including businesses, can trade in goods and services with other people and businesses in the international community at large. This contrasts with a closed economy in which international trade cannot take place.

The act of selling goods or services to a foreign country is called exporting.

    a. Information economy
    c. Attention work
    b. Open economy
    d. Indicative planning

24. _____ refers to a business or organization attempting to acquire goods or services to accomplish the goals of the enterprise. Though there are several organizations that attempt to set standards in the _____ process, processes can vary greatly between organizations. Typically the word '_____' is not used interchangeably with the word 'procurement', since procurement typically includes Expediting, Supplier Quality, and Traffic and Logistics (T'L) in addition to _____.
    a. 100-year flood
    c. Purchasing
    b. Free port
    d. 130-30 fund

25. In economics, the _____ is one of the two primary components of the balance of payments, the other being the capital account. It is the sum of the balance of trade (exports minus imports of goods and services), net factor income (such as interest and dividends) and net transfer payments (such as foreign aid.)

$$\text{Current account} = \text{Balance of trade} \\ + \text{Net factor income from abroad} \\ + \text{Net unilateral transfers from abroad}$$

The _____ balance is one of two major metrics of the nature of a country's foreign trade (the other being the net capital outflow.)

    a. Compensation of employees
    c. National Income and Product Accounts
    b. Gross private domestic investment
    d. Current account

26. An autarky is an economy that is self-sufficient and does not take part in international trade, or severely limits trade with the outside world. Likewise the term refers to an ecosystem not affected by influences from the outside, which relies entirely on its own resources. In the economic meaning, it is also referred to as a _____.
    a. Digital economy
    c. Network Economy
    b. Transition economy
    d. Closed economy

Chapter 12. National Income Accounting and the Balance of Payments

27. A _____ is a legal document that is often passed by the legislature, and approved by the chief executive-or president. For example, only certain types of revenue may be imposed and collected. Property tax is frequently the basis for municipal and county revenues, while sales tax and/or income tax are the basis for state revenues, and income tax and corporate tax are the basis for national revenues.
   - a. Government budget
   - b. Structural deficit
   - c. Lump-sum tax
   - d. Right-financing

28. A _____ occurs when an entity spends more money than it takes in. The opposite of a _____ is a budget surplus. Debt is essentially an accumulated flow of deficits.
   - a. Public Financial Management
   - b. Funding body
   - c. Lump-sum tax
   - d. Budget deficit

29. The _____ is an economic and political union of 27 member states, located primarily in Europe. It was established by the Treaty of Maastricht on 1 November 1993, upon the foundations of the pre-existing European Economic Community. With a population of almost 500 million, the _____ generates an estimated 30% share (US$18.4 trillion in 2008) of the nominal gross world product.
   - a. European Court of Justice
   - b. European Union
   - c. ACEA agreement
   - d. ACCRA Cost of Living Index

30. _____, is an economic theory that suggests consumers internalise the government's budget constraint and thus the timing of any tax change does not affect their change in spending. Consequently, _____ suggests that it does not matter whether a government finances its spending with debt or a tax increase, the effect on total level of demand in an economy will be the same. It was proposed, and then rejected, by the 19th-century economist David Ricardo.
   - a. Social discount rate
   - b. Quasi-market
   - c. Municipalization
   - d. Ricardian equivalence

31. The _____ hypothesis is a concept from macroeconomics that contends that there is a strong link between a national economy's current account balance and its government budget balance. As an example, it is hypothesized that a large budget deficit leads to a large current account deficit. The theory goes as follows:

$Y = C + I + G + NX$

where Y represents National Income or GDP, C is consumption, I is investment, G is government spending and NX stands for net exports.

   - a. 100-year flood
   - b. Power of the purse
   - c. Public-private partnership
   - d. Twin deficits

32. In finance, the _____s between two currencies specifies how much one currency is worth in terms of the other. It is the value of a foreign natione;s currency in terms of the home natione;s currency. For example an _____ of 102 Japanese yen to the United States dollar means that JPY 102 is worth the same as USD 1.
   - a. ACEA agreement
   - b. Interbank market
   - c. Exchange rate
   - d. ACCRA Cost of Living Index

33. In financial accounting, the _____ is one of the accounts in shareholders' equity. Sole proprietorships have a single _____ in the owner's equity. Partnerships maintain a _____ for each of the partners.

Chapter 12. National Income Accounting and the Balance of Payments

a. Compensation of employees
b. Net national product
c. Current account
d. Capital account

34. _____ is an economic term describing capital flowing out of (or leaving) a particular economy. Outflowing capital can be caused by any number of economic or political reasons but can often originate from instability in either sphere.

Regardless of cause, capital outflowing is generally perceived as always undesirable and many countries create laws to restrict the movement of capital out of the nations' borders (called capital controls.)

a. Whitemail
b. Hedonic treadmill
c. Minsky moment
d. Capital outflow

35. The _____ of monetary management established the rules for commercial and financial relations among the world's major industrial states in the mid 20th Century. The _____ was the first example of a fully negotiated monetary order intended to govern monetary relations among independent nation-states.

Preparing to rebuild the international economic system as World War II was still raging, 730 delegates from all 44 Allied nations gathered at the Mount Washington Hotel in Bretton Woods, New Hampshire, United States, for the United Nations Monetary and Financial Conference.

a. 130-30 fund
b. 1921 recession
c. 100-year flood
d. Bretton Woods system

36. The _____ is the central banking system of the United States. Created in 1913 by the enactment of the Federal Reserve Act (signed by Woodrow Wilson), it is a quasi-public and quasi-private (government entity with private components) banking system that comprises (1) the presidentially appointed Board of Governors of the _____ in Washington, D.C.; (2) the Federal Open Market Committee; (3) twelve regional Federal Reserve Banks located in major cities throughout the nation acting as fiscal agents for the U.S. Treasury, each with its own nine-member board of directors; (4) numerous other private U.S. member banks, which subscribe to required amounts of non-transferable stock in their regional Federal Reserve Banks; and (5) various advisory councils. Since February 2006, Ben Bernanke has served as the Chairman of the Board of Governors of the _____.

a. Term auction facility
b. Federal Reserve System
c. Monetary Policy Report to the Congress
d. Federal Reserve System Open Market Account

37. In business and accounting, _____ are everything of value that is owned by a person or company. It is a claim on the property your income of a borrower. The balance sheet of a firm records the monetary value of the _____ owned by the firm.

a. ACEA agreement
b. Assets
c. ACCRA Cost of Living Index
d. Amortization schedule

38. In microeconomics, _____ is quite simply the conversion of inputs into outputs. It is an economic process that uses resources to create a good or service that is suitable for exchange. This can include manufacturing, storing, shipping, and packaging.

a. Red Guards
b. MET
c. Solved
d. Production

Chapter 12. National Income Accounting and the Balance of Payments

39. _____ is the practice within the banking industry of authorizing electronic transactions done with a debit card or credit card and holding this balance as unavailable either until the merchant clears the transaction _____s can fall off the account anywhere from 1-5 days after the transaction date depending on the bank's policy; in the case of credit cards, holds may last as long as 30 days, depending on the issuing bank.

Signature-based credit and debit card transactions are a two-step process, consisting of an authorization and a settlement.

When a merchant swipes a customer's credit card, the credit card terminal connects to the merchant's acquirer which verifies that the customer's account is valid and that sufficient funds are available to cover the transaction's cost.

    a. Interbank network
    b. Authorization hold
    c. Electronic funds transfer
    d. Issuing bank

40. _____s is the social science that studies the production, distribution, and consumption of goods and services. The term _____s comes from the Ancient Greek oá¼°κονομῖα from oá¼¶κος (oikos, 'house') + vÏŒμος (nomos, 'custom' or 'law'), hence 'rules of the house(hold)'. Current _____ models developed out of the broader field of political economy in the late 19th century, owing to a desire to use an empirical approach more akin to the physical sciences.
    a. Inflation
    b. Economic
    c. Energy economics
    d. Opportunity cost

41. _____ is the price at which an asset would trade in a competitive Walrasian auction setting. _____ is often used interchangeably with open _____, fair value or fair _____, although these terms have distinct definitions in different standards, and may differ in some circumstances.

International Valuation Standards defines _____ as 'the estimated amount for which a property should exchange on the date of valuation between a willing buyer and a willing seller in an arm's-length transaction after proper marketing wherein the parties had each acted knowledgeably, prudently, and without compulsion.'

_____ is a concept distinct from market price, which is 'the price at which one can transact', while _____ is 'the true underlying value' according to theoretical standards.

    a. Personal financial management
    b. Secured loan
    c. Market value
    d. Netting

42. The accounting equation relates assets, _____, and owner's equity:

    Assets = _____ + Owner's Equity

The accounting equation is the mathematical structure of the balance sheet.

The Australian Accounting Research Foundation defines _____ as: 'future sacrifice of economic benefits that the entity is presently obliged to make to other entities as a result of past transactions and other past events.'

Chapter 12. National Income Accounting and the Balance of Payments

Probably the most accepted accounting definition of liability is the one used by the International Accounting Standards Board (IASB.) The following is a quotation from IFRS Framework:

A liability is a present obligation of the enterprise arising from past events, the settlement of which is expected to result in an outflow from the enterprise of resources embodying economic benefits

-

Regulations as to the recognition of _____ are different all over the world, but are roughly similar to those of the IASB.

a. Liabilities
b. Community property
c. Competition law theory
d. Coase theorem

43. _____ is the a method of technical and economic research of the systems for purpose to optimize a parity between system's consumer functions or properties and expenses to achieve those functions or properties.

This methodology for continuous perfection of production, industrial technologies, organizational structures was developed by Juryj Sobolev in 1948 at the 'Perm telephone factory'

- 1948 Juryj Sobolev - the first success in application of a method analysis at the 'Perm telephone factory' .
- 1949 - the first application for the invention as result of use of the new method.

Today in economically developed countries practically each enterprise or the company use methodology of the kind of functional-cost analysis as a practice of the quality management, most full satisfying to principles of standards of series ISO 9000.

- Interest of consumer not in products itself, but the advantage which it will receive from its usage.
- The consumer aspires to reduce his expenses
- Functions needed by consumer can be executed in the various ways, and, hence, with various efficiency and expenses. Among possible alternatives of realization of functions exist such in which the parity of quality and the price is the optimal for the consumer.

The goal of _____ is achievement of the highest consumer satisfaction of production at simultaneous decrease in all kinds of industrial expenses Classical _____ has three English synonyms - Value Engineering, Value Management, Value Analysis.

a. Staple financing
b. Monopoly wage
c. Function cost analysis
d. Willingness to pay

44. Preparing to rebuild the international economic system as World War II was still raging, 730 delegates from all 44 Allied nations gathered at the Mount Washington Hotel in Bretton Woods, New Hampshire, United States, for the United Nations Monetary and Financial Conference. The delegates deliberated upon and signed the _____ during the first three weeks of July 1944.

Setting up a system of rules, institutions, and procedures to regulate the international monetary system, the planners at Bretton Woods established the International Monetary Fund (IMF) and the International Bank for Reconstruction and Development (IBRD), which today is part of the World Bank Group.

- a. Dromography
- b. Land reform
- c. Heavy-Chemical Industry Drive
- d. Bretton Woods Agreements

45. A _____, sometimes called a pegged exchange rate, is a type of exchange rate regime wherein a currency's value is matched to the value of another single currency or to a basket of other currencies such as gold.

A _____ is usually used to stabilize the value of a currency, vis-a-vis the currency it is pegged to. This facilitates trade and investments between the two countries, and is especially useful for small economies where external trade forms a large part of their GDP.

- a. Fixed exchange rate
- b. Monetary economics
- c. Leading indicators
- d. Law of supply

46. A _____ or a flexible exchange rate is a type of exchange rate regime wherein a currency's value is allowed to fluctuate according to the foreign exchange market. A currency that uses a _____ is known as a floating currency. The opposite of a _____ is a fixed exchange rate.

- a. Trade Weighted US dollar Index
- b. Foreign exchange market
- c. Floating exchange rate
- d. Floating currency

47. The _____ is a monetary system in which a region's common medium of exchange are paper notes that are normally freely convertible into pre-set, fixed quantities of gold. The _____ is not currently used by any government, having been replaced completely by fiat currency. Gold certificates were used as paper currency in the United States from 1882 to 1933, these certificates were freely convertible into gold coins.

In the 1790s Britain suffered a massive shortage of silver coinage and ceased to mint larger silver coins.

- a. 1921 recession
- b. 100-year flood
- c. 130-30 fund
- d. Gold standard

48. _____ is that which is owed; usually referencing assets owed, but the term can also cover moral obligations and other interactions not requiring money. In the case of assets, _____ is a means of using future purchasing power in the present before a summation has been earned. Some companies and corporations use _____ as a part of their overall corporate finance strategy.

- a. Collateral Management
- b. Debenture
- c. Hard money loan
- d. Debt

49. _____ is that part of the total debt in a country that is owed to creditors outside the country. The debtors can be the government, corporations or private households. The debt includes money owed to private commercial banks, other governments, or international financial institutions such as the IMF and World Bank.

a. Internal debt
b. International debt collection
c. Asset protection
d. External debt

Chapter 13. Exchange Rates and the Foreign Exchange Market: An Asset Approach

1. In business and accounting, _____ are everything of value that is owned by a person or company. It is a claim on the property your income of a borrower. The balance sheet of a firm records the monetary value of the _____ owned by the firm.
   a. ACEA agreement
   b. Amortization schedule
   c. ACCRA Cost of Living Index
   d. Assets

2. Preparing to rebuild the international economic system as World War II was still raging, 730 delegates from all 44 Allied nations gathered at the Mount Washington Hotel in Bretton Woods, New Hampshire, United States, for the United Nations Monetary and Financial Conference. The delegates deliberated upon and signed the _____ during the first three weeks of July 1944.

   Setting up a system of rules, institutions, and procedures to regulate the international monetary system, the planners at Bretton Woods established the International Monetary Fund (IMF) and the International Bank for Reconstruction and Development (IBRD), which today is part of the World Bank Group.

   a. Dromography
   b. Land reform
   c. Heavy-Chemical Industry Drive
   d. Bretton Woods Agreements

3. A _____, sometimes called a pegged exchange rate, is a type of exchange rate regime wherein a currency's value is matched to the value of another single currency or to a basket of other currencies such as gold.

   A _____ is usually used to stabilize the value of a currency, vis-a-vis the currency it is pegged to. This facilitates trade and investments between the two countries, and is especially useful for small economies where external trade forms a large part of their GDP.

   a. Law of supply
   b. Fixed exchange rate
   c. Leading indicators
   d. Monetary economics

4. A _____ or a flexible exchange rate is a type of exchange rate regime wherein a currency's value is allowed to fluctuate according to the foreign exchange market. A currency that uses a _____ is known as a floating currency. The opposite of a _____ is a fixed exchange rate.
   a. Trade Weighted US dollar Index
   b. Foreign exchange market
   c. Floating exchange rate
   d. Floating currency

5. The _____ is where currency trading takes place. It is where banks and other official institutions facilitate the buying and selling of foreign currencies. FX transactions typically involve one party purchasing a quantity of one currency in exchange for paying a quantity of another.
   a. Foreign exchange market
   b. Floating currency
   c. Covered interest arbitrage
   d. Currency swap

6. The _____ is a monetary system in which a region's common medium of exchange are paper notes that are normally freely convertible into pre-set, fixed quantities of gold. The _____ is not currently used by any government, having been replaced completely by fiat currency. Gold certificates were used as paper currency in the United States from 1882 to 1933, these certificates were freely convertible into gold coins.

   In the 1790s Britain suffered a massive shortage of silver coinage and ceased to mint larger silver coins.

Chapter 13. Exchange Rates and the Foreign Exchange Market: An Asset Approach

a. 100-year flood
b. Gold standard
c. 130-30 fund
d. 1921 recession

7. In finance, the _____s between two currencies specifies how much one currency is worth in terms of the other. It is the value of a foreign natione;s currency in terms of the home natione;s currency. For example an _____ of 102 Japanese yen to the United States dollar means that JPY 102 is worth the same as USD 1.
   a. ACCRA Cost of Living Index
   b. Interbank market
   c. ACEA agreement
   d. Exchange rate

8. _____ is the price of a commodity such as a good or service in terms of another; ie, the ratio of two prices. A _____ may be expressed in terms of a ratio between any two prices or the ratio between the price of one particular good and a weighted average of all other goods available in the market. A _____ is an opportunity cost.
   a. Food cooperative
   b. False economy
   c. Relative price
   d. False shortage

9. Economics:
   - _____,the desire to own something and the ability to pay for it
   - _____ curve,a graphic representation of a _____ schedule
   - _____ deposit, the money in checking accounts
   - _____ pull theory,the theory that inflation occurs when _____ for goods and services exceeds existing supplies
   - _____ schedule,a table that lists the quantity of a good a person will buy it each different price
   - _____ side economics,the school of economics at believes government spending and tax cuts open economy by raising _____

   a. Variability
   b. Production
   c. McKesson ' Robbins scandal
   d. Demand

10. _____ is exchange of capital, goods, and services across international borders or territories. In most countries, it represents a significant share of gross domestic product (GDP.) While _____ has been present throughout much of history , its economic, social, and political importance has been on the rise in recent centuries.
    a. Import license
    b. Incoterms
    c. Intra-industry trade
    d. International trade

11. _____ in economics and business is the result of an exchange and from that trade we assign a numerical monetary value to a good, service or asset. If Alice trades Bob 4 apples for an orange, the _____ of an orange is 4 apples. Inversely, the _____ of an apple is 1/4 oranges.
    a. Price
    b. Price book
    c. Premium pricing
    d. Price war

12. _____ is a term used in accounting, economics and finance to spread the cost of an asset over the span of several years.

Chapter 13. Exchange Rates and the Foreign Exchange Market: An Asset Approach

In simple words we can say that _____ is the reduction in the value of an asset due to usage, passage of time, wear and tear, technological outdating or obsolescence, depletion, inadequacy, rot, rust, decay or other such factors.

In accounting, _____ is a term used to describe any method of attributing the historical or purchase cost of an asset across its useful life, roughly corresponding to normal wear and tear.

a. Net income per employee
b. Historical cost
c. Salvage value
d. Depreciation

13. _____ is money accepted for exchange of goods in an economy. The prevalence of one money over another arises, usually, when a government designates through decrees that the government shall accept only particular notes and coins in payment for taxes. Typically, money of _____ consists of stamped coins and minted paper bills.

a. Security thread
b. Currency
c. Local currency
d. Totnes pound

14. The _____ is the official currency of 16 of the 27 member states of the European Union (EU.) The states, known collectively as the Eurozone, are Austria, Belgium, Cyprus, Finland, France, Germany, Greece, Ireland, Italy, Luxembourg, Malta, the Netherlands, Portugal, Slovakia, Slovenia, and Spain. The currency is also used in a further five European countries, with and without formal agreements and is consequently used daily by some 327 million Europeans.

a. Equity capital market
b. IRS Code 3401
c. Euro
d. Import and Export Price Indices

15. _____ is a term used in accounting relating to the increase in value of an asset. In this sense it is the reverse of depreciation, which measures the fall in value of assets over their normal life-time.

_____ is a rise of a currency in a floating exchange rate.

a. AD-IA Model
b. ACCRA Cost of Living Index
c. ACEA agreement
d. Appreciation

16.

A _____ is a type of financial intermediary and a type of bank. Commercial banking is also known as business banking. It is a bank that provides checking accounts, savings accounts, and money market accounts and that accepts time deposits.

a. Bought deal
b. Lombard banking
c. Daylight overdraft
d. Commercial bank

17. The _____ of monetary management established the rules for commercial and financial relations among the world's major industrial states in the mid 20th Century. The _____ was the first example of a fully negotiated monetary order intended to govern monetary relations among independent nation-states.

Chapter 13. Exchange Rates and the Foreign Exchange Market: An Asset Approach

Preparing to rebuild the international economic system as World War II was still raging, 730 delegates from all 44 Allied nations gathered at the Mount Washington Hotel in Bretton Woods, New Hampshire, United States, for the United Nations Monetary and Financial Conference.

a. 1921 recession
b. 100-year flood
c. Bretton Woods system
d. 130-30 fund

18. The _____ consists of a number of economic theories which describe the nature of the firm, company including its existence, its behaviour, and its relationship with the market.

In simplified terms, the _____ aims to answer these questions:

1. Existence - why do firms emerge, why are not all transactions in the economy mediated over the market?
2. Boundaries - why the boundary between firms and the market is located exactly there? Which transactions are performed internally and which are negotiated on the market?
3. Organization - why are firms structured in such specific way? What is the interplay of formal and informal relationships?

Despite looking simple, these questions are not answered by the established economic theory, which usually views firms as given, and treats them as black boxes without any internal structure.

The First World War period saw a change of emphasis in economic theory away from industry-level analysis which mainly included analysing markets to analysis at the level of the firm, as it became increasingly clear that perfect competition was no longer an adequate model of how firms behaved. Economic theory till then had focussed on trying to understand markets alone and there had been little study on understanding why firms or organisations exist.

a. Khazzoom-Brookes postulate
b. Theory of the firm
c. Technology gap
d. Policy Ineffectiveness Proposition

19. A _____ association is a financial institution that specializes in accepting savings deposits and making mortgage and other loans. The S'L or thrift term is mainly used in the United States; similar institutions in the United Kingdom, Ireland and some Commonwealth countries include building societies and trustee savings banks.

They are often mutually held, meaning that the depositors and borrowers are members with voting rights, and have the ability to direct the financial and managerial goals of the organization, similar to the policyholders of a mutual insurance company.

a. Participating policy
b. Collective investment scheme
c. Fonds commun de placement
d. Savings and loan

86 Chapter 13. Exchange Rates and the Foreign Exchange Market: An Asset Approach

20. _____ has several particular meanings:

- in mathematics
    - _____ function
    - Euler _____
    - _____
    - _____ subgroup
    - method of _____s (partial differential equations)
- in physics and engineering
    - any _____ curve that shows the relationship between certain input- and output parameters, e.g.
    - an I-V or current-voltage _____ is the current in a circuit as a function of the applied voltage
    - Receiver-Operator _____
- in fiction
    - in Dungeons ' Dragons, _____ is another name for ability score

a. Russian financial crisis
b. Characteristic
c. Technocracy
d. Demand

21. In economics and finance, _____ is the practice of taking advantage of a price differential between two or more markets: striking a combination of matching deals that capitalize upon the imbalance, the profit being the difference between the market prices. When used by academics, an _____ is a transaction that involves no negative cash flow at any probabilistic or temporal state and a positive cash flow in at least one state; in simple terms, a risk-free profit. A person who engages in _____ is called an arbitrageur--such as a bank or brokerage firm.

a. Arbitrage
b. Electronic trading
c. Options Price Reporting Authority
d. Alternext

22. The term _____ refers to government debt, expenditures and revenues, or to finance (particularly financial revenue) in general.

- _____ deficit is the budget deficit of federal or local government
- _____ policy is the discretionary spending of governments. Contrasts with monetary policy.
- _____ year and _____ quarter are reporting periods for firms and other agencies.

a. Procter ' Gamble
b. Bucket shop
c. Fiscal
d. Drawdown

23. In economics, _____ is the use of government spending and revenue collection to influence the economy.

_____ can be contrasted with the other main type of economic policy, monetary policy, which attempts to stabilize the economy by controlling interest rates and the supply of money. The two main instruments of _____ are government spending and taxation.

Chapter 13. Exchange Rates and the Foreign Exchange Market: An Asset Approach

a. Sustainable investment rule
b. Fiscalism
c. 100-year flood
d. Fiscal policy

24. The _____ or gross domestic income (GDI), a basic measure of an economy's economic performance, is the market value of all final goods and services produced within the borders of a nation in a year. _____ can be defined in three ways, all of which are conceptually identical. First, it is equal to the total expenditures for all final goods and services produced within the country in a stipulated period of time (usually a 365-day year.)

a. Market structure
b. Monopolistic competition
c. Countercyclical
d. Gross domestic product

25. _____ is the a method of technical and economic research of the systems for purpose to optimize a parity between system's consumer functions or properties and expenses to achieve those functions or properties.

This methodology for continuous perfection of production, industrial technologies, organizational structures was developed by Juryj Sobolev in 1948 at the 'Perm telephone factory'

- 1948 Juryj Sobolev - the first success in application of a method analysis at the 'Perm telephone factory' .
- 1949 - the first application for the invention as result of use of the new method.

Today in economically developed countries practically each enterprise or the company use methodology of the kind of functional-cost analysis as a practice of the quality management, most full satisfying to principles of standards of series ISO 9000.

- Interest of consumer not in products itself, but the advantage which it will receive from its usage.
- The consumer aspires to reduce his expenses
- Functions needed by consumer can be executed in the various ways, and, hence, with various efficiency and expenses. Among possible alternatives of realization of functions exist such in which the parity of quality and the price is the optimal for the consumer.

The goal of _____ is achievement of the highest consumer satisfaction of production at simultaneous decrease in all kinds of industrial expenses Classical _____ has three English synonyms - Value Engineering, Value Management, Value Analysis.

a. Staple financing
b. Monopoly wage
c. Willingness to pay
d. Function cost analysis

26. The _____ is the future yield on a bond. It is calculated using the yield curve.

For example, the yield on a three-month Treasury bill six months from now is a _____ .

a. Single-index model
b. Forward rate
c. Capital asset
d. Settlement date

Chapter 13. Exchange Rates and the Foreign Exchange Market: An Asset Approach

27. _____ is a common concept in economics, and gives rise to derived concepts such as consumer debt. Generally _____ is defined by opposition to production. But the precise definition can vary because different schools of economists define production quite differently.
   a. Consumption
   b. Cash or share options
   c. Federal Reserve Bank Notes
   d. Foreclosure data providers

28. A _____ is a financial contract between two parties, the buyer and the seller of this type of option. It is the option to buy shares of stock at a specified time in the future. Often it is simply labeled a 'call'. The buyer of the option has the right, but not the obligation to buy an agreed quantity of a particular commodity or financial instrument (the underlying instrument) from the seller of the option at a certain time (the expiration date) for a certain price (the strike price.)
   a. Synthetic underlying position
   b. Call option
   c. Moneyness
   d. Put option

29. In finance, a _____ is a derivative financial instrument where the owner has the right but not the obligation to exchange money denominated in one currency into another currency at a pre-agreed exchange rate on a specified date.

The FX options market is the deepest, largest and most liquid market for options of any kind in the world. Most of the FX option volume is traded OTC and is lightly regulated, but a fraction is traded on exchanges like the International Securities Exchange, Philadelphia Stock Exchange, or the Chicago Mercantile Exchange for options on futures contracts.

   a. Floating exchange rate
   b. Foreign exchange reserves
   c. Spot market
   d. Foreign exchange option

30. In finance, a _____ is a standardized contract, to buy or sell a specified commodity of standardized quality at a certain date in the future, at a market determined price (the futures price.)

The price is determined by the instantaneous equilibrium between the forces of supply and demand among competing buy and sell orders on the exchange at the time of the purchase or sale of the contract.

In many cases, the items may be such non-traditional 'commodities' as foreign currencies, commercial or government paper [e.g., bonds], or 'baskets' of corporate equity ['stock indices'] or other financial instruments.

   a. Futures contract
   b. Power reverse dual currency note
   c. Dual currency deposit
   d. Local volatility

31. A _____ is a financial contract between two parties, the seller (writer) and the buyer of the option. The buyer acquires a short position offering the right, but not obligation, to sell the underlying instrument at an agreed-upon price (the strike price.) If the buyer exercises the right granted by the option, the seller has the obligation to purchase the underlying at the strike price.
   a. Bull spread
   b. Synthetic underlying position
   c. Bear spread
   d. Put option

Chapter 13. Exchange Rates and the Foreign Exchange Market: An Asset Approach

32. In finance, _____ rate of profit or sometimes just return, is the ratio of money gained or lost on an investment relative to the amount of money invested. The amount of money gained or lost may be referred to as interest, profit/loss, gain/loss, or net income/loss. The money invested may be referred to as the asset, capital, principal, or the cost basis of the investment.
    a. Cost accrual ratio
    b. Sortino ratio
    c. Current ratio
    d. Rate of return

33. _____ is a fee paid on borrowed assets. It is the price paid for the use of borrowed money, or, money earned by deposited funds. Assets that are sometimes lent with _____ include money, shares, consumer goods through hire purchase, major assets such as aircraft, and even entire factories in finance lease arrangements.
    a. Asset protection
    b. Interest
    c. Insolvency
    d. Internal debt

34. An _____ is the price a borrower pays for the use of money they do not own, for instance a small company might borrow from a bank to kick start their business, and the return a lender receives for deferring the use of funds, by lending it to the borrower. _____s are normally expressed as a percentage rate over the period of one year.

    _____s targets are also a vital tool of monetary policy and are used to control variables like investment, inflation, and unemployment.

    a. Enterprise value
    b. Arrow-Debreu model
    c. Interest rate
    d. ACCRA Cost of Living Index

35. Market _____ is a business, economics or investment term that refers to an asset's ability to be easily converted through an act of buying or selling without causing a significant movement in the price and with minimum loss of value. Money, or cash on hand, is the most liquid asset. An act of exchange of a less liquid asset with a more liquid asset is called liquidation.
    a. Liquidity
    b. 130-30 fund
    c. 1921 recession
    d. 100-year flood

36. A variety of measures of _____ and output are used in economics to estimate total economic activity in a country or region, including gross domestic product (GDP), gross national product (GNP), and net _____

    There are three main ways of calculating these numbers; the output approach, the income approach and the expenditure approach. In theory, the three must yield the same, because total expenditures on goods and services must equal the total income paid to the producers (Gnational income), and that must also equal the total value of the output of goods and services (GNP.)

    a. GNI per capita
    b. Volume index
    c. Gross world product
    d. National income

37. _____ is a form of risk that arises from the change in price of one currency against another. Whenever investors or companies have assets or business operations across national borders, they face _____ if their positions are not hedged.

- Transaction risk is the risk that exchange rates will change unfavourably over time. It can be hedged against using forward currency contracts;
- Translation risk is an accounting risk, proportional to the amount of assets held in foreign currencies. Changes in the exchange rate over time will render a report inaccurate, and so assets are usually balanced by borrowings in that currency.

The exchange risk associated with a foreign denominated instrument is a key element in foreign investment. This risk flows from differential monetary policy and growth in real productivity, which results in differential inflation rates.

a. Transaction risk
b. Risk neutral
c. Currency risk
d. Taleb distribution

38. _____ is a business, economics or investment term that refers to an asset's ability to be easily converted through an act of buying or selling without causing a significant movement in the price and with minimum loss of value. Money, or cash on hand, is the most liquid asset. An act of exchange of a less liquid asset with a more liquid asset is called liquidation.

a. Paper trading
b. Principal trade
c. Market maker
d. Market Liquidity

39. In economics, economic equilibrium is simply a state of the world where economic forces are balanced and in the absence of external influences the (equilibrium) values of economic variables will not change. It is the point at which quantity demanded and quantity supplied are equal. _____, for example, refers to a condition where a market price is established through competition such that the amount of goods or services sought by buyers is equal to the amount of goods or services produced by sellers.

a. Product-Market Growth Matrix
b. Marketization
c. Regulated market
d. Market equilibrium

40. In economics, the concept of the _____ refers to the decision-making time frame of a firm in which at least one factor of production is fixed. Costs which are fixed in the _____ have no impact on a firms decisions. For example a firm can raise output by increasing the amount of labour through overtime.

a. Product Pipeline
b. Hicks-neutral technical change
c. Short-run
d. Productivity model

41. In economics, the _____ measures the payments that flow between any individual country and all other countries. It is used to summarize all international economic transactions for that country during a specific time period, usually a year. The _____ is determined by the country's exports and imports of goods, services, and financial capital, as well as financial transfers.

a. Gross domestic product per barrel
b. Skyscraper Index
c. Gross world product
d. Balance of payments

42. A _____ is the transfer of wealth from one party (such as a person or company) to another. A _____ is usually made in exchange for the provision of goods, services or both, or to fulfill a legal obligation.

Chapter 13. Exchange Rates and the Foreign Exchange Market: An Asset Approach

The simplest and oldest form of _____ is barter, the exchange of one good or service for another.

a. Social gravity
c. Soft count
b. Payment
d. Going concern

43. The _____ is the weighted-average most likely outcome in gambling, probability theory, economics or finance.

What Does _____ Mean? The average of a probability distribution of possible returns, calculated by using the following formula:

E(R)= Sum: probability (in scenario i) * the return (in scenario i)

How do you calculate the average of a probability distribution? As denoted by the above formula, simply take the probability of each possible return outcome and multiply it by the return outcome itself. For example, if you knew a given investment had a 50% chance of earning a 10% return, a 25% chance of earning 20% and a 25% chance of earning -10%, the _____ would be equal to 7.5%:

= (0.5) (0.1) + (0.25) (0.2) + (0.25) (-0.1) = 0.075 = 7.5%

Although this is what you expect the return to be, there is no guarantee that it will be the actual return.

a. ACCRA Cost of Living Index
c. AD-IA Model
b. Expected return
d. ACEA agreement

44. In microeconomics, _____ is quite simply the conversion of inputs into outputs. It is an economic process that uses resources to create a good or service that is suitable for exchange. This can include manufacturing, storing, shipping, and packaging.

a. MET
c. Red Guards
b. Production
d. Solved

Chapter 14. Money, Interest Rates, and Exchange Rates

1. Preparing to rebuild the international economic system as World War II was still raging, 730 delegates from all 44 Allied nations gathered at the Mount Washington Hotel in Bretton Woods, New Hampshire, United States, for the United Nations Monetary and Financial Conference. The delegates deliberated upon and signed the _____ during the first three weeks of July 1944.

Setting up a system of rules, institutions, and procedures to regulate the international monetary system, the planners at Bretton Woods established the International Monetary Fund (IMF) and the International Bank for Reconstruction and Development (IBRD), which today is part of the World Bank Group.

    a. Dromography
    c. Land reform
    b. Bretton Woods Agreements
    d. Heavy-Chemical Industry Drive

2. A _____, sometimes called a pegged exchange rate, is a type of exchange rate regime wherein a currency's value is matched to the value of another single currency or to a basket of other currencies such as gold.

A _____ is usually used to stabilize the value of a currency, vis-a-vis the currency it is pegged to. This facilitates trade and investments between the two countries, and is especially useful for small economies where external trade forms a large part of their GDP.

    a. Leading indicators
    c. Monetary economics
    b. Fixed exchange rate
    d. Law of supply

3. A _____ or a flexible exchange rate is a type of exchange rate regime wherein a currency's value is allowed to fluctuate according to the foreign exchange market. A currency that uses a _____ is known as a floating currency. The opposite of a _____ is a fixed exchange rate.

    a. Floating currency
    c. Trade Weighted US dollar Index
    b. Foreign exchange market
    d. Floating exchange rate

4. The _____ is a monetary system in which a region's common medium of exchange are paper notes that are normally freely convertible into pre-set, fixed quantities of gold. The _____ is not currently used by any government, having been replaced completely by fiat currency. Gold certificates were used as paper currency in the United States from 1882 to 1933, these certificates were freely convertable into gold coins.

In the 1790s Britain suffered a massive shortage of silver coinage and ceased to mint larger silver coins.

    a. 1921 recession
    c. 100-year flood
    b. Gold standard
    d. 130-30 fund

5. In economics, _____ is the total amount of money available in an economy at a particular point in time. There are several ways to define 'money', but standard measures usually include currency in circulation and demand deposits.

_____ data are recorded and published, usually by the government or the central bank of the country.

    a. Velocity of money
    c. Veil of money
    b. Money supply
    d. Neutrality of money

Chapter 14. Money, Interest Rates, and Exchange Rates

6. In business and accounting, _____ are everything of value that is owned by a person or company. It is a claim on the property your income of a borrower. The balance sheet of a firm records the monetary value of the _____ owned by the firm.
   a. Amortization schedule
   b. ACEA agreement
   c. Assets
   d. ACCRA Cost of Living Index

7. In economics, the _____ measures the payments that flow between any individual country and all other countries. It is used to summarize all international economic transactions for that country during a specific time period, usually a year. The _____ is determined by the country's exports and imports of goods, services, and financial capital, as well as financial transfers.
   a. Gross world product
   b. Balance of payments
   c. Gross domestic product per barrel
   d. Skyscraper Index

8. Economics:

   - _____, the desire to own something and the ability to pay for it
   - _____ curve, a graphic representation of a _____ schedule
   - _____ deposit, the money in checking accounts
   - _____ pull theory, the theory that inflation occurs when _____ for goods and services exceeds existing supplies
   - _____ schedule, a table that lists the quantity of a good a person will buy it each different price
   - _____ side economics, the school of economics at believes government spending and tax cuts open economy by raising _____

   a. McKesson ' Robbins scandal
   b. Variability
   c. Production
   d. Demand

9. In finance, the _____s between two currencies specifies how much one currency is worth in terms of the other. It is the value of a foreign natione;s currency in terms of the home natione;s currency. For example an _____ of 102 Japanese yen to the United States dollar means that JPY 102 is worth the same as USD 1.
   a. Interbank market
   b. ACEA agreement
   c. Exchange rate
   d. ACCRA Cost of Living Index

10. A _____ is the transfer of wealth from one party (such as a person or company) to another. A _____ is usually made in exchange for the provision of goods, services or both, or to fulfill a legal obligation.

    The simplest and oldest form of _____ is barter, the exchange of one good or service for another.
    a. Soft count
    b. Payment
    c. Going concern
    d. Social gravity

11. _____ is a misspelled phrase from Latin 'pro capite' phrase meaning per head with pro meaning 'per' or 'for each' and capite meaning 'head.' Both words together equate to the phrase 'for each head.'

It is usually used in the field of statistics to indicate the average per person for any given concern, such as income, crime rate, etc.

It is also used in wills to indicate that each of the named beneficiaries should receive, by devise or bequest, equal shares of the estate. This is in contrast to a per stirpes division, in which each branch of the inheriting family inherits an equal share of the estate.

    a. Per capita
    c. False positive rate
    b. Population statistics
    d. Sargan test

12. _____ in economics and business is the result of an exchange and from that trade we assign a numerical monetary value to a good, service or asset. If Alice trades Bob 4 apples for an orange, the _____ of an orange is 4 apples. Inversely, the _____ of an apple is 1/4 oranges.
    a. Price
    c. Premium pricing
    b. Price war
    d. Price book

13. _____ is an economic model based on price, utility and quantity in a market. It predicts that in a competitive market, price will function to equalize the quantity demanded by consumers, and the quantity supplied by producers, resulting in an economic equilibrium of price and quantity. The model incorporates other factors changing equilibrium as a shift of demand and/or supply.
    a. Joint demand
    c. Deferred gratification
    b. Rational addiction
    d. Supply and demand

14. The term '_____' refers to the concept of collecting information and attempting to spot a pattern in the information. In some fields of study, the term '_____' has more formally-defined meanings.

In project management _____ is a mathematical technique that uses historical results to predict future outcome.

    a. Probit model
    c. Coefficient of determination
    b. Quantile regression
    d. Trend analysis

15. The term _____, 'the state or characteristic of being variable', _____ describes how spread out or closely clustered a set of data is. may be applied to many different subjects:

- Climate _____
- Genetic _____
- Heart rate _____
- Human _____
- Solar van
- Spatial _____
- Statistical _____
- _____

a. Characteristic
b. Total product
c. Demand
d. Variability

16. A _____ is an intermediary used in trade to avoid the inconveniences of a pure barter system.

By contrast, as William Stanley Jevons argued, in a barter system there must be a coincidence of wants before two people can trade - one must want exactly what the other has to offer, when and where it is offered, so that the exchange can occur. A _____ permits the value of goods to be assessed and rendered in terms of the intermediary, most often, a form of money widely accepted to buy any other good.

a. Consumer theory
b. Medium of exchange
c. Price revolution
d. Labour economics

17. A _____ is a standard monetary unit of measurement of the market value/cost of goods, services, or assets. It is one of three well-known functions of money. It lends meaning to profits, losses, liability, or assets.

a. ACCRA Cost of Living Index
b. AD-IA Model
c. Unit of account
d. ACEA agreement

18. In economics, _____ is the total demand for final goods and services in the economy (Y) at a given time and price level. It is the amount of goods and services in the economy that will be purchased at all possible price levels. This is the demand for the gross domestic product of a country when inventory levels are static.

a. Aggregation problem
b. Aggregate expenditure
c. Aggregate supply
d. Aggregate demand

19. In economic models, the _____ time frame assumes no fixed factors of production. Firms can enter or leave the marketplace, and the cost (and availability) of land, labor, raw materials, and capital goods can be assumed to vary. In contrast, in the short-run time frame, certain factors are assumed to be fixed, because there is not sufficient time for them to change.

a. Diseconomies of scale
b. Productivity world
c. Price/performance ratio
d. Long-run

20. To act as a _____, a commodity, a form of money stored, and retrieved - and be predictably useful when it is so retrieved.

This is distinct from the standard of deferred payment function which requires acceptability to parties one owes a debt to and a minimum of opportunity to cheat others.

a. Fiat money
b. Petrodollar
c. World currency
d. Store of value

21. _____ is the a method of technical and economic research of the systems for purpose to optimize a parity between system's consumer functions or properties and expenses to achieve those functions or properties.

This methodology for continuous perfection of production, industrial technologies, organizational structures was developed by Juryj Sobolev in 1948 at the 'Perm telephone factory'

- 1948 Juryj Sobolev - the first success in application of a method analysis at the 'Perm telephone factory' .
- 1949 - the first application for the invention as result of use of the new method.

Today in economically developed countries practically each enterprise or the company use methodology of the kind of functional-cost analysis as a practice of the quality management, most full satisfying to principles of standards of series ISO 9000.

- Interest of consumer not in products itself, but the advantage which it will receive from its usage.
- The consumer aspires to reduce his expenses
- Functions needed by consumer can be executed in the various ways, and, hence, with various efficiency and expenses. Among possible alternatives of realization of functions exist such in which the parity of quality and the price is the optimal for the consumer.

The goal of _____ is achievement of the highest consumer satisfaction of production at simultaneous decrease in all kinds of industrial expenses Classical _____ has three English synonyms - Value Engineering, Value Management, Value Analysis.

   a. Willingness to pay   b. Function cost analysis
   c. Staple financing   d. Monopoly wage

22. The _____ is the weighted-average most likely outcome in gambling, probability theory, economics or finance.

What Does _____ Mean? The average of a probability distribution of possible returns, calculated by using the following formula:

E(R)= Sum: probability (in scenario i) * the return (in scenario i)

How do you calculate the average of a probability distribution? As denoted by the above formula, simply take the probability of each possible return outcome and multiply it by the return outcome itself. For example, if you knew a given investment had a 50% chance of earning a 10% return, a 25% chance of earning 20% and a 25% chance of earning -10%, the _____ would be equal to 7.5%:

   = (0.5) (0.1) + (0.25) (0.2) + (0.25) (-0.1) = 0.075 = 7.5%

Although this is what you expect the return to be, there is no guarantee that it will be the actual return.

   a. ACEA agreement   b. AD-IA Model
   c. Expected return   d. ACCRA Cost of Living Index

Chapter 14. Money, Interest Rates, and Exchange Rates

23. Market _____ is a business, economics or investment term that refers to an asset's ability to be easily converted through an act of buying or selling without causing a significant movement in the price and with minimum loss of value. Money, or cash on hand, is the most liquid asset. An act of exchange of a less liquid asset with a more liquid asset is called liquidation.
    a. 1921 recession
    b. 100-year flood
    c. 130-30 fund
    d. Liquidity

24. The _____ is the desired holding of money balances in the form of cash or bank deposits.

Money is dominated as store of value by interest bearing assets. However, money is necessary to carry out transactions, or in other words, it provides liquidity.

    a. Conglomerate merger
    b. Borrowing base
    c. Market neutral
    d. Demand for Money

25. _____ is a fee paid on borrowed assets. It is the price paid for the use of borrowed money, or, money earned by deposited funds. Assets that are sometimes lent with _____ include money, shares, consumer goods through hire purchase, major assets such as aircraft, and even entire factories in finance lease arrangements.
    a. Insolvency
    b. Interest
    c. Internal debt
    d. Asset protection

26. An _____ is the price a borrower pays for the use of money they do not own, for instance a small company might borrow from a bank to kick start their business, and the return a lender receives for deferring the use of funds, by lending it to the borrower. _____s are normally expressed as a percentage rate over the period of one year.

_____s targets are also a vital tool of monetary policy and are used to control variables like investment, inflation, and unemployment.

    a. ACCRA Cost of Living Index
    b. Enterprise value
    c. Arrow-Debreu model
    d. Interest rate

27. In finance, _____ rate of profit or sometimes just return, is the ratio of money gained or lost on an investment relative to the amount of money invested. The amount of money gained or lost may be referred to as interest, profit/loss, gain/loss, or net income/loss. The money invested may be referred to as the asset, capital, principal, or the cost basis of the investment.
    a. Current ratio
    b. Sortino ratio
    c. Cost accrual ratio
    d. Rate of return

28. A _____ is a hypothetical measure of overall prices for some set of goods and services, in a given region during a given interval, normalized relative to some base set. Typically, a _____ is approximated with a price index.

The classical dichotomy is the assumption that there is a relatively clean distinction between overall increases or decreases in prices and underlying, e;reale; economic variables.

a. Price elasticity of supply
b. Price level
c. Discretionary spending
d. Discouraged worker

29. _____ is exchange of capital, goods, and services across international borders or territories. In most countries, it represents a significant share of gross domestic product (GDP.) While _____ has been present throughout much of history, its economic, social, and political importance has been on the rise in recent centuries.
   a. International trade
   b. Intra-industry trade
   c. Import license
   d. Incoterms

30. A variety of measures of national income and output are used in economics to estimate total economic activity in a country or region, including gross domestic product (GDP), _____ , and net national income (NNI.)

There are three main ways of calculating these numbers; the output approach, the income approach and the expenditure approach. In theory, the three must yield the same, because total expenditures on goods and services must equal the total income paid to the producers (GNI), and that must also equal the total value of the output of goods and services (_____.)

   a. Purchasing power parity
   b. Household final consumption expenditure
   c. Gross world product
   d. Gross national product

31. A variety of measures of _____ and output are used in economics to estimate total economic activity in a country or region, including gross domestic product (GDP), gross national product (GNP), and net _____

There are three main ways of calculating these numbers; the output approach, the income approach and the expenditure approach. In theory, the three must yield the same, because total expenditures on goods and services must equal the total income paid to the producers (Gnational income), and that must also equal the total value of the output of goods and services (GNP.)

   a. Gross world product
   b. GNI per capita
   c. Volume index
   d. National income

32. In economics, economic equilibrium is simply a state of the world where economic forces are balanced and in the absence of external influences the (equilibrium) values of economic variables will not change. It is the point at which quantity demanded and quantity supplied are equal. _____, for example, refers to a condition where a market price is established through competition such that the amount of goods or services sought by buyers is equal to the amount of goods or services produced by sellers.
   a. Regulated market
   b. Product-Market Growth Matrix
   c. Marketization
   d. Market equilibrium

33. In finance, the _____ is the global financial market for short-term borrowing and lending. It provides short-term liquidity funding for the global financial system. The _____ is where short-term obligations such as Treasury bills, commercial paper and bankers' acceptances are bought and sold.
   a. Deferred compensation
   b. Consignment stock
   c. T-Model
   d. Money market

Chapter 14. Money, Interest Rates, and Exchange Rates

34. In economics, the concept of the _____ refers to the decision-making time frame of a firm in which at least one factor of production is fixed. Costs which are fixed in the _____ have no impact on a firms decisions. For example a firm can raise output by increasing the amount of labour through overtime.

   a. Short-run
   b. Hicks-neutral technical change
   c. Product Pipeline
   d. Productivity model

35. A _____, reserve bank, or monetary authority is the entity responsible for the monetary policy of a country or of a group of member states. It is a bank that can lend money to other banks in times of need. Its primary responsibility is to maintain the stability of the national currency and money supply, but more active duties include controlling subsidized-loan interest rates, and acting as a lender of last resort to the banking sector during times of financial crisis (private banks often being integral to the national financial system.)

   a. 1921 recession
   b. 100-year flood
   c. Central Bank
   d. 130-30 fund

36. The _____ is composed of the European Central Bank (ECB) and the national central banks (NCBs) of all 27 European Union (EU) Member States.

Since not all the EU states have joined the Euro, the ESCB could not be used as the monetary authority of the eurozone. For this reason the Eurosystem (which excludes all the NCBs which have not adopted the Euro) became the institution in charge of those tasks which in principle had to be managed by the ESCB.

   a. AD-IA Model
   b. ACEA agreement
   c. ACCRA Cost of Living Index
   d. European System of Central Banks

37. _____, in economics, is the period of time required for economic agents to reallocate resources, and generally reestablish equilibrium.

The actual length of this period, usually numbered in years or decades, varies widely depending on circumstantial context. During the _____, all factors are variable.

   a. Producer surplus
   b. Long Term
   c. Temporary equilibrium method
   d. Government surplus

38. The term _____ refers to government debt, expenditures and revenues, or to finance (particularly financial revenue) in general.

   - _____ deficit is the budget deficit of federal or local government
   - _____ policy is the discretionary spending of governments. Contrasts with monetary policy.
   - _____ year and _____ quarter are reporting periods for firms and other agencies.

   a. Bucket shop
   b. Drawdown
   c. Procter ' Gamble
   d. Fiscal

39. In economics, _____ is the use of government spending and revenue collection to influence the economy.

Chapter 14. Money, Interest Rates, and Exchange Rates

_____ can be contrasted with the other main type of economic policy, monetary policy, which attempts to stabilize the economy by controlling interest rates and the supply of money. The two main instruments of _____ are government spending and taxation.

a. Sustainable investment rule
b. Fiscal policy
c. 100-year flood
d. Fiscalism

40. The _____ is a general equilibrium mathematical model of international trade, developed by Eli Heckscher and Bertil Ohlin at the Stockholm School of Economics. It builds on David Ricardo's theory of comparative advantage by predicting patterns of commerce and production based on the factor endowments of a trading region. The model essentially says that countries will export products that utilize their abundant and cheap factor(s) of production and import products that utilize the countries' scarce factor(s.)

a. Free trade zone
b. Linder hypothesis
c. Jamaican Free Zones
d. Heckscher-Ohlin model

41. A country's _____ is a financial statement setting out the value and composition of that country's external financial assets and liabilities.

The difference between a country's external financial assets and liabilities is the net _____

_____ = domestically owned foreign assets - foreign owned domestic assets

a. International finance
b. Overshooting model
c. Optimum currency area
d. International investment position

42. The _____ was a period of financial crisis that gripped much of Asia beginning in July 1997, and raised fears of a worldwide economic meltdown (financial contagion.)

The crisis started in Thailand with the financial collapse of the Thai baht caused by the decision of the Thai government to float the baht, cutting its peg to the USD, after exhaustive efforts to support it in the face of a severe financial overextension that was in part real estate driven. At the time, Thailand had acquired a burden of foreign debt that made the country effectively bankrupt even before the collapse of its currency.

a. Asian financial crisis
b. AD-IA Model
c. ACCRA Cost of Living Index
d. ACEA agreement

43. The term _____ is applied broadly to a variety of situations in which some financial institutions or assets suddenly lose a large part of their value. In the 19th and early 20th centuries, many financial crises were associated with banking panics, and many recessions coincided with these panics. Other situations that are often called financial crises include stock market crashes and the bursting of other financial bubbles, currency crises, and sovereign defaults.

a. Co-operative economics
b. Macroeconomics
c. Market failure
d. Financial crisis

Chapter 14. Money, Interest Rates, and Exchange Rates

44. _____ is money accepted for exchange of goods in an economy. The prevalence of one money over another arises, usually, when a government designates through decrees that the government shall accept only particular notes and coins in payment for taxes. Typically, money of _____ consists of stamped coins and minted paper bills.
    a. Currency
    b. Totnes pound
    c. Local currency
    d. Security thread

45. _____ is the loss of value of a country's currency with respect to one or more foreign reference currencies, typically in a floating exchange rate system. It is most often used for the unofficial increase of the exchange rate due to market forces, though sometimes it appears interchangeably with devaluation. Its opposite is called appreciation.
    a. Quote currency
    b. Hero Card
    c. Fed Shreds
    d. Currency depreciation

46. _____ is a term used in accounting, economics and finance to spread the cost of an asset over the span of several years.

    In simple words we can say that _____ is the reduction in the value of an asset due to usage, passage of time, wear and tear, technological outdating or obsolescence, depletion, inadequacy, rot, rust, decay or other such factors.

    In accounting, _____ is a term used to describe any method of attributing the historical or purchase cost of an asset across its useful life, roughly corresponding to normal wear and tear.

    a. Net income per employee
    b. Salvage value
    c. Historical cost
    d. Depreciation

47. In economics, _____ is a rise in the general level of prices of goods and services in an economy over a period of time. When the general price level rises, each unit of currency buys fewer goods and services; consequently, _____ is also a decline in the real value of money--a loss of purchasing power in the medium of exchange which is also the monetary unit of account in the economy. A chief measure of general price-level _____ is the general _____ rate, which is the percentage change in a general price index (normally the Consumer Price Index) over time.
    a. Energy economics
    b. Opportunity cost
    c. Economic
    d. Inflation

48. In economics, _____ is a sustained decrease in the general price level of goods and services. _____ occurs when the annual inflation rate falls below zero percent, resulting in an increase in the real value of money -- a negative inflation rate. This should not be confused with disinflation, a slow-down in the inflation rate (i.e. when the inflation decreases, but still remains positive.)
    a. Literacy rate
    b. Price revolution
    c. Deflation
    d. Tobit model

49. _____ is a decrease in the rate of inflation. This phase of the business cycle, in which retailers can no longer pass on higher prices to their customers, often occurs during a recession. In contrast, deflation occurs when prices are actually dropping.
    a. Mundell-Tobin effect
    b. Stealth inflation
    c. Reflation
    d. Disinflation

Chapter 14. Money, Interest Rates, and Exchange Rates

50. The _____ is the official currency of 16 of the 27 member states of the European Union (EU.) The states, known collectively as the Eurozone, are Austria, Belgium, Cyprus, Finland, France, Germany, Greece, Ireland, Italy, Luxembourg, Malta, the Netherlands, Portugal, Slovakia, Slovenia, and Spain. The currency is also used in a further five European countries, with and without formal agreements and is consequently used daily by some 327 million Europeans.
   a. Equity capital market
   b. IRS Code 3401
   c. Import and Export Price Indices
   d. Euro

51. _____ is the price of a commodity such as a good or service in terms of another; ie, the ratio of two prices. A _____ may be expressed in terms of a ratio between any two prices or the ratio between the price of one particular good and a weighted average of all other goods available in the market. A _____ is an opportunity cost.
   a. False shortage
   b. Food cooperative
   c. False economy
   d. Relative price

52. In economics, _____ is inflation that is very high or 'out of control', a condition in which prices increase rapidly as a currency loses its value. Definitions used by the media vary from a cumulative inflation rate over three years approaching 100% to 'inflation exceeding 50% a month.' In informal usage the term is often applied to much lower rates. As a rule of thumb, normal inflation is reported per year, but _____ is often reported for much shorter intervals, often per month.
   a. 100-year flood
   b. 130-30 fund
   c. 1921 recession
   d. Hyperinflation

53. In economics, economic output is divided into physical goods and intangible services. Consumption of _____ is assumed to produce utility. It is often used when referring to a _____ Tax.
   a. Manufactured goods
   b. Composite good
   c. Private good
   d. Goods and services

54. _____ are goods that have been processed by way of machinery. As such, they are the opposite of raw materials, but include intermediate goods as well as final goods.
   a. Superior goods
   b. Search good
   c. Pie method
   d. Manufactured goods

55. A _____ is something that is acted upon or used by or by human labor or industry, for use as a building material to create some product or structure. Often the term is used to denote material that came from nature and is in an unprocessed or minimally processed state. Iron ore, logs, and crude oil, would be examples.
   a. 100-year flood
   b. 1921 recession
   c. 130-30 fund
   d. Raw material

56. In economics, _____ refers to the ability of a person or a country to produce a particular good at a lower marginal cost and opportunity cost than another person or country. It is the ability to produce a product most efficiently given all the other products that could be produced. It can be contrasted with absolute advantage which refers to the ability of a person or a country to produce a particular good at a lower absolute cost than another.
   a. Comparative advantage
   b. Gravity model of trade
   c. Hot money
   d. Triffin dilemma

57. In economics, _____ is when quantity demanded is more than quantity supplied. See Economic shortage.

a. Excess demand
c. AD-IA Model
b. ACEA agreement
d. ACCRA Cost of Living Index

58. A _____ is an object whose consumption increases the utility of the consumer, for which the quantity demanded exceeds the quantity supplied at zero price. _____s are usually modeled as having diminishing marginal utility. The first individual purchase has high utility; the second has less.
   a. Pie method
   c. Composite good
   b. Good
   d. Merit good

Chapter 15. Price Levels and the Exchange Rate in the Long Run

1. _____ in economics and business is the result of an exchange and from that trade we assign a numerical monetary value to a good, service or asset. If Alice trades Bob 4 apples for an orange, the _____ of an orange is 4 apples. Inversely, the _____ of an apple is 1/4 oranges.
   - a. Price
   - b. Price book
   - c. Premium pricing
   - d. Price war

2. A _____ is a hypothetical measure of overall prices for some set of goods and services, in a given region during a given interval, normalized relative to some base set. Typically, a _____ is approximated with a price index.

   The classical dichotomy is the assumption that there is a relatively clean distinction between overall increases or decreases in prices and underlying, e;reale; economic variables.

   - a. Discretionary spending
   - b. Discouraged worker
   - c. Price level
   - d. Price elasticity of supply

3. _____ is the price of a commodity such as a good or service in terms of another; ie, the ratio of two prices. A _____ may be expressed in terms of a ratio between any two prices or the ratio between the price of one particular good and a weighted average of all other goods available in the market. A _____ is an opportunity cost.
   - a. Relative price
   - b. False shortage
   - c. False economy
   - d. Food cooperative

4. In business and accounting, _____ are everything of value that is owned by a person or company. It is a claim on the property your income of a borrower. The balance sheet of a firm records the monetary value of the _____ owned by the firm.
   - a. ACEA agreement
   - b. ACCRA Cost of Living Index
   - c. Amortization schedule
   - d. Assets

5. Economics:
   - _____, the desire to own something and the ability to pay for it
   - _____ curve, a graphic representation of a _____ schedule
   - _____ deposit, the money in checking accounts
   - _____ pull theory, the theory that inflation occurs when _____ for goods and services exceeds existing supplies
   - _____ schedule, a table that lists the quantity of a good a person will buy it each different price
   - _____ side economics, the school of economics at believes government spending and tax cuts open economy by raising _____

   - a. Production
   - b. McKesson ' Robbins scandal
   - c. Demand
   - d. Variability

6. In finance, the _____s between two currencies specifies how much one currency is worth in terms of the other. It is the value of a foreign natione;s currency in terms of the home natione;s currency. For example an _____ of 102 Japanese yen to the United States dollar means that JPY 102 is worth the same as USD 1.

Chapter 15. Price Levels and the Exchange Rate in the Long Run

a. ACEA agreement
b. ACCRA Cost of Living Index
c. Interbank market
d. Exchange rate

7. _____ is exchange of capital, goods, and services across international borders or territories. In most countries, it represents a significant share of gross domestic product (GDP.) While _____ has been present throughout much of history, its economic, social, and political importance has been on the rise in recent centuries.

a. Intra-industry trade
b. International trade
c. Import license
d. Incoterms

8. In economics, economic equilibrium is simply a state of the world where economic forces are balanced and in the absence of external influences the (equilibrium) values of economic variables will not change. It is the point at which quantity demanded and quantity supplied are equal. _____, for example, refers to a condition where a market price is established through competition such that the amount of goods or services sought by buyers is equal to the amount of goods or services produced by sellers.

a. Marketization
b. Market equilibrium
c. Product-Market Growth Matrix
d. Regulated market

9. The _____ is an economic law stated as: 'In an efficient market all identical goods must have only one price.' The _____ relates to the outcome of free trade and globalization. It is the theory that some day all areas of the world will make the same amount of money as every other part of the world for equal work/product quality.

The intuition for this law is that all sellers will flock to the highest prevailing price, and all buyers to the lowest current market price.

a. Precaria
b. Law of one price
c. Leave of absence
d. Loss of use

10. _____ refers to a business or organization attempting to acquire goods or services to accomplish the goals of the enterprise. Though there are several organizations that attempt to set standards in the _____ process, processes can vary greatly between organizations. Typically the word '_____' is not used interchangeably with the word 'procurement', since procurement typically includes Expediting, Supplier Quality, and Traffic and Logistics (T'L) in addition to _____.

a. 130-30 fund
b. Purchasing
c. Free port
d. 100-year flood

11. _____ is the number of goods/services that can be purchased with a unit of currency. For example, if you had taken one dollar to a store in the 1950s, you would have been able to buy a greater number of items than you would today, indicating that you would have had a greater _____ in the 1950s. Currency can be either a commodity money, like gold or silver, or fiat currency like US dollars.

a. Human Poverty Index
b. Genuine progress indicator
c. Compliance cost
d. Purchasing power

12. The _____ theory uses the long-term equilibrium exchange rate of two currencies to equalize their purchasing power. Developed by Gustav Cassel in 1920, it is based on the law of one price: the theory states that, in ideally efficient markets, identical goods should have only one price.

This purchasing power SEM rate equalizes the purchasing power of different currencies in their home countries for a given basket of goods.

   a. Measures of national income and output
   b. Bureau of Labor Statistics
   c. Gross national product
   d. Purchasing power parity

13. Preparing to rebuild the international economic system as World War II was still raging, 730 delegates from all 44 Allied nations gathered at the Mount Washington Hotel in Bretton Woods, New Hampshire, United States, for the United Nations Monetary and Financial Conference. The delegates deliberated upon and signed the _____ during the first three weeks of July 1944.

Setting up a system of rules, institutions, and procedures to regulate the international monetary system, the planners at Bretton Woods established the International Monetary Fund (IMF) and the International Bank for Reconstruction and Development (IBRD), which today is part of the World Bank Group.

   a. Bretton Woods Agreements
   b. Heavy-Chemical Industry Drive
   c. Dromography
   d. Land reform

14. The _____ is the official currency of 16 of the 27 member states of the European Union (EU.) The states, known collectively as the Eurozone, are Austria, Belgium, Cyprus, Finland, France, Germany, Greece, Ireland, Italy, Luxembourg, Malta, the Netherlands, Portugal, Slovakia, Slovenia, and Spain. The currency is also used in a further five European countries, with and without formal agreements and is consequently used daily by some 327 million Europeans.

   a. Euro
   b. Import and Export Price Indices
   c. IRS Code 3401
   d. Equity capital market

15. The term _____ refers to government debt, expenditures and revenues, or to finance (particularly financial revenue) in general.

- _____ deficit is the budget deficit of federal or local government
- _____ policy is the discretionary spending of governments. Contrasts with monetary policy.
- _____ year and _____ quarter are reporting periods for firms and other agencies.

   a. Procter ' Gamble
   b. Drawdown
   c. Bucket shop
   d. Fiscal

16. In economics, _____ is the use of government spending and revenue collection to influence the economy.

_____ can be contrasted with the other main type of economic policy, monetary policy, which attempts to stabilize the economy by controlling interest rates and the supply of money. The two main instruments of _____ are government spending and taxation.

Chapter 15. Price Levels and the Exchange Rate in the Long Run

a. 100-year flood
c. Sustainable investment rule
b. Fiscalism
d. Fiscal policy

17. A _____, sometimes called a pegged exchange rate, is a type of exchange rate regime wherein a currency's value is matched to the value of another single currency or to a basket of other currencies such as gold.

A _____ is usually used to stabilize the value of a currency, vis-a-vis the currency it is pegged to. This facilitates trade and investments between the two countries, and is especially useful for small economies where external trade forms a large part of their GDP.

a. Law of supply
c. Leading indicators
b. Monetary economics
d. Fixed exchange rate

18. A _____ or a flexible exchange rate is a type of exchange rate regime wherein a currency's value is allowed to fluctuate according to the foreign exchange market. A currency that uses a _____ is known as a floating currency. The opposite of a _____ is a fixed exchange rate.

a. Foreign exchange market
c. Floating exchange rate
b. Trade Weighted US dollar Index
d. Floating currency

19. The _____ is a monetary system in which a region's common medium of exchange are paper notes that are normally freely convertible into pre-set, fixed quantities of gold. The _____ is not currently used by any government, having been replaced completely by fiat currency. Gold certificates were used as paper currency in the United States from 1882 to 1933, these certificates were freely convertable into gold coins.

In the 1790s Britain suffered a massive shortage of silver coinage and ceased to mint larger silver coins.

a. 100-year flood
c. 130-30 fund
b. 1921 recession
d. Gold standard

20. In economic models, the _____ time frame assumes no fixed factors of production. Firms can enter or leave the marketplace, and the cost (and availability) of land, labor, raw materials, and capital goods can be assumed to vary. In contrast, in the short-run time frame, certain factors are assumed to be fixed, because there is not sufficient time for them to change.

a. Long-run
c. Diseconomies of scale
b. Price/performance ratio
d. Productivity world

21. _____ is a fee paid on borrowed assets. It is the price paid for the use of borrowed money, or, money earned by deposited funds . Assets that are sometimes lent with _____ include money, shares, consumer goods through hire purchase, major assets such as aircraft, and even entire factories in finance lease arrangements.

a. Asset protection
c. Internal debt
b. Insolvency
d. Interest

22. An _____ is the price a borrower pays for the use of money they do not own, for instance a small company might borrow from a bank to kick start their business, and the return a lender receives for deferring the use of funds, by lending it to the borrower. _____s are normally expressed as a percentage rate over the period of one year.

_____s targets are also a vital tool of monetary policy and are used to control variables like investment, inflation, and unemployment.

a. Arrow-Debreu model
b. ACCRA Cost of Living Index
c. Enterprise value
d. Interest rate

23. In economics, _____ is the total amount of money available in an economy at a particular point in time. There are several ways to define 'money', but standard measures usually include currency in circulation and demand deposits.

_____ data are recorded and published, usually by the government or the central bank of the country.

a. Neutrality of money
b. Veil of money
c. Money supply
d. Velocity of money

24. In economics, the _____ measures the payments that flow between any individual country and all other countries. It is used to summarize all international economic transactions for that country during a specific time period, usually a year. The _____ is determined by the country's exports and imports of goods, services, and financial capital, as well as financial transfers.

a. Skyscraper Index
b. Gross domestic product per barrel
c. Balance of payments
d. Gross world product

25. _____s is the social science that studies the production, distribution, and consumption of goods and services. The term _____s comes from the Ancient Greek οἰκονομία from οἶκος (oikos, 'house') + νόμος (nomos, 'custom' or 'law'), hence 'rules of the house(hold)'. Current _____ models developed out of the broader field of political economy in the late 19th century, owing to a desire to use an empirical approach more akin to the physical sciences.

a. Opportunity cost
b. Inflation
c. Energy economics
d. Economic

26. A _____ is the transfer of wealth from one party (such as a person or company) to another. A _____ is usually made in exchange for the provision of goods, services or both, or to fulfill a legal obligation.

The simplest and oldest form of _____ is barter, the exchange of one good or service for another.

a. Social gravity
b. Soft count
c. Going concern
d. Payment

27. In economics, _____ is a rise in the general level of prices of goods and services in an economy over a period of time. When the general price level rises, each unit of currency buys fewer goods and services; consequently, _____ is also a decline in the real value of money--a loss of purchasing power in the medium of exchange which is also the monetary unit of account in the economy. A chief measure of general price-level _____ is the general _____ rate, which is the percentage change in a general price index (normally the Consumer Price Index) over time.

a. Opportunity cost
b. Energy economics
c. Inflation
d. Economic

Chapter 15. Price Levels and the Exchange Rate in the Long Run

28. _____ is a term used in accounting, economics and finance to spread the cost of an asset over the span of several years.

In simple words we can say that _____ is the reduction in the value of an asset due to usage, passage of time, wear and tear, technological outdating or obsolescence, depletion, inadequacy, rot, rust, decay or other such factors.

In accounting, _____ is a term used to describe any method of attributing the historical or purchase cost of an asset across its useful life, roughly corresponding to normal wear and tear.

a. Salvage value
b. Depreciation
c. Net income per employee
d. Historical cost

29. _____ was a survey conducted by the U.S. Department of Justice to gauge the prevalence of alcohol and illegal drug use among prior arrestees. It was a reformulation of the prior Drug Use Forecasting (DUF) program, focused on five drugs in particular: cocaine, marijuana, methamphetamine, opiates, and PCP.

Participants were randomly selected from arrest records in major metropolitan areas; because no personally identifying information is taken from each record chosen, the resulting data can be correlated to arrest rates, but not to the total population of persons charged.

a. ACEA agreement
b. AD-IA Model
c. ACCRA Cost of Living Index
d. Arrestee Drug Abuse Monitoring

30. _____ is a common concept in economics, and gives rise to derived concepts such as consumer debt. Generally _____ is defined by opposition to production. But the precise definition can vary because different schools of economists define production quite differently.

a. Federal Reserve Bank Notes
b. Cash or share options
c. Foreclosure data providers
d. Consumption

31. _____ is one of the four Ps of the marketing mix. The other three aspects are product, promotion, and place. It is also a key variable in microeconomic price allocation theory.

a. Pricing
b. Point of total assumption
c. Guaranteed Maximum Price
d. Premium pricing

32. A _____ is a general term that describes any government policy or regulation that restricts international trade. The barriers can take many forms, including the following terms that include many restrictions in international trade within multiple countries that import and export any items of trade.

- Import duty
- Import licenses
- Export licenses
- Import quotas
- Tariffs
- Subsidies
- Non-tariff barriers to trade
- Voluntary Export Restraints
- Local Content Requirements
- Embargo

Most _____s work on the same principle: the imposition of some sort of cost on trade that raises the price of the traded products. If two or more nations repeatedly use _____s against each other, then a trade war results.

a. National Foreign Trade Council
c. Trade barrier
b. Global financial system
d. Certificate of origin

33. A _____ is an object whose consumption increases the utility of the consumer, for which the quantity demanded exceeds the quantity supplied at zero price. _____s are usually modeled as having diminishing marginal utility. The first individual purchase has high utility; the second has less.

a. Pie method
c. Good
b. Composite good
d. Merit good

34. _____ is the income of individuals or nations after adjusting for inflation. It is calculated by subtracting inflation from the nominal income. Real variables, such as _____, real GDP, and real interest rate are variables that are measured in physical units, while nominal variables such as nominal income, nominal GDP, and nominal interest rate are measured in monetary units.

a. Windfall gain
c. Net national income
b. Real income
d. Family income

35. In economics, _____ is the total demand for final goods and services in the economy (Y) at a given time and price level. It is the amount of goods and services in the economy that will be purchased at all possible price levels. This is the demand for the gross domestic product of a country when inventory levels are static.

a. Aggregate expenditure
c. Aggregate supply
b. Aggregation problem
d. Aggregate demand

36. _____ is a term used in accounting relating to the increase in value of an asset. In this sense it is the reverse of depreciation, which measures the fall in value of assets over their normal life-time.

_____ is a rise of a currency in a floating exchange rate.

Chapter 15. Price Levels and the Exchange Rate in the Long Run

a. AD-IA Model
b. ACCRA Cost of Living Index
c. ACEA agreement
d. Appreciation

37. In economics, _____ is the total supply of goods and services produced by a national economy during a specific time period. It is the total amount of goods and services in the economy available at all possible price levels.
   a. Aggregation problem
   b. Aggregate demand
   c. Aggregate expenditure
   d. Aggregate supply

38. In finance, the _____ is the global financial market for short-term borrowing and lending. It provides short-term liquidity funding for the global financial system. The _____ is where short-term obligations such as Treasury bills, commercial paper and bankers' acceptances are bought and sold.
   a. Consignment stock
   b. T-Model
   c. Deferred compensation
   d. Money market

39. Later Keynesians economists took up the notion and redefined it in terms that ignored the microeconomic time structure of production. On this later definition, _____ is the idea that a change in the stock of money affects only nominal variables in the economy such as prices, wages and exchange rates but no effect on real (inflation-adjusted) variables, like employment, real GDP, and real consumption. It is an important idea in classical economics and is related to the classical dichotomy.
   a. Veil of money
   b. Neutrality of money
   c. Monetary reform
   d. Chartalism

40. _____ is a type of trade policy that allows traders to act and transact without interference from government. Thus, the policy permits trading partners mutual gains from trade, with goods and services produced according to the theory of comparative advantage.

Under a _____ policy, prices are a reflection of true supply and demand, and are the sole determinant of resource allocation.

   a. 1921 recession
   b. 100-year flood
   c. 130-30 fund
   d. Free trade

41. In economics and particularly in international trade, an _____ shows the quantity of one type of product that an agent will export ('offer') for each quantity of another type of product that it imports. The _____ was first derived by English economists Edgeworth and Marshall to help explain international trade.

The _____ is derived from the country's PPF.

   a. ACEA agreement
   b. AD-IA Model
   c. ACCRA Cost of Living Index
   d. Offer curve

Chapter 16. Output and the Exchange Rate in the Short Run

1. The _____ is a trilateral trade bloc in North America created by the governments of the United States, Canada, and Mexico. The agreement creating the trade bloc came into force on January 1, 1994. It superseded the Canada-United States Free Trade Agreement between the U.S. and Canada.
   a. Demand-side technologies
   b. North American Free Trade Agreement
   c. Federal Reserve Bank Notes
   d. Case-Shiller Home Price Indices

2. In business and accounting, _____ are everything of value that is owned by a person or company. It is a claim on the property your income of a borrower. The balance sheet of a firm records the monetary value of the _____ owned by the firm.
   a. Amortization schedule
   b. Assets
   c. ACEA agreement
   d. ACCRA Cost of Living Index

3. In finance, the _____s between two currencies specifies how much one currency is worth in terms of the other. It is the value of a foreign natione;s currency in terms of the home natione;s currency. For example an _____ of 102 Japanese yen to the United States dollar means that JPY 102 is worth the same as USD 1.
   a. Interbank market
   b. Exchange rate
   c. ACEA agreement
   d. ACCRA Cost of Living Index

4. In economics, economic equilibrium is simply a state of the world where economic forces are balanced and in the absence of external influences the (equilibrium) values of economic variables will not change. It is the point at which quantity demanded and quantity supplied are equal. _____, for example, refers to a condition where a market price is established through competition such that the amount of goods or services sought by buyers is equal to the amount of goods or services produced by sellers.
   a. Marketization
   b. Regulated market
   c. Product-Market Growth Matrix
   d. Market equilibrium

5. _____ is an economic concept with commonplace familiarity. It is the price that a good or service is offered at, or will fetch, in the marketplace. It is of interest mainly in the study of microeconomics.
   a. Market anomaly
   b. Noisy market hypothesis
   c. Paper trading
   d. Market price

6. _____ in economics and business is the result of an exchange and from that trade we assign a numerical monetary value to a good, service or asset. If Alice trades Bob 4 apples for an orange, the _____ of an orange is 4 apples. Inversely, the _____ of an apple is 1/4 oranges.
   a. Premium pricing
   b. Price war
   c. Price book
   d. Price

7. In economics, _____ is the total demand for final goods and services in the economy (Y) at a given time and price level. It is the amount of goods and services in the economy that will be purchased at all possible price levels. This is the demand for the gross domestic product of a country when inventory levels are static.
   a. Aggregate supply
   b. Aggregation problem
   c. Aggregate demand
   d. Aggregate expenditure

8. _____ is a common concept in economics, and gives rise to derived concepts such as consumer debt. Generally _____ is defined by opposition to production. But the precise definition can vary because different schools of economists define production quite differently.

a. Foreclosure data providers
c. Federal Reserve Bank Notes
b. Cash or share options
d. Consumption

9. Economics:

- _____, the desire to own something and the ability to pay for it
- _____ curve, a graphic representation of a _____ schedule
- _____ deposit, the money in checking accounts
- _____ pull theory, the theory that inflation occurs when _____ for goods and services exceeds existing supplies
- _____ schedule, a table that lists the quantity of a good a person will buy it each different price
- _____ side economics, the school of economics at believes government spending and tax cuts open economy by raising _____

a. McKesson ' Robbins scandal
c. Production
b. Variability
d. Demand

10. In algebra, a _____ is a function depending on n that associates a scalar, det(A), to an n×n square matrix A. The fundamental geometric meaning of a _____ is a scale factor for measure when A is regarded as a linear transformation. _____s are important both in calculus, where they enter the substitution rule for several variables, and in multilinear algebra.

For a fixed nonnegative integer n, there is a unique _____ function for the n×n matrices over any commutative ring R. In particular, this function exists when R is the field of real or complex numbers.

a. 100-year flood
c. 1921 recession
b. 130-30 fund
d. Determinant

11. _____ is a fee paid on borrowed assets. It is the price paid for the use of borrowed money, or, money earned by deposited funds. Assets that are sometimes lent with _____ include money, shares, consumer goods through hire purchase, major assets such as aircraft, and even entire factories in finance lease arrangements.

a. Asset protection
c. Internal debt
b. Insolvency
d. Interest

12. An _____ is an economy in which people, including businesses, can trade in goods and services with other people and businesses in the international community at large. This contrasts with a closed economy in which international trade cannot take place.

The act of selling goods or services to a foreign country is called exporting.

a. Information economy
c. Open economy
b. Indicative planning
d. Attention work

Chapter 16. Output and the Exchange Rate in the Short Run

13. In economics, the _____ is one of the two primary components of the balance of payments, the other being the capital account. It is the sum of the balance of trade (exports minus imports of goods and services), net factor income (such as interest and dividends) and net transfer payments (such as foreign aid.)

$$\begin{aligned}\text{Current account} = &\ \text{Balance of trade} \\ &+ \text{Net factor income from abroad} \\ &+ \text{Net unilateral transfers from abroad}\end{aligned}$$

The _____ balance is one of two major metrics of the nature of a country's foreign trade (the other being the net capital outflow.)

   a. Current account
   b. Gross private domestic investment
   c. National Income and Product Accounts
   d. Compensation of employees

14. _____ is a broad label that refers to any individuals or households that use goods and services generated within the economy. The concept of a _____ is used in different contexts, so that the usage and significance of the term may vary.

Typically when business people and economists talk of _____s they are talking about person as _____, an aggregated commodity item with little individuality other than that expressed in the buy/not-buy decision.

   a. 130-30 fund
   b. 1921 recession
   c. 100-year flood
   d. Consumer

15. A _____ is a measure of the average price of consumer goods and services purchased by households. A _____ measures a price change for a constant market basket of goods and services from one period to the next within the same area (city, region, or nation.) It is a price index determined by measuring the price of a standard group of goods meant to represent the typical market basket of a typical urban consumer.

   a. Cost-of-living index
   b. Consumer price index
   c. Lipstick index
   d. CPI

16. A _____ is a normalized average (typically a weighted average) of prices for a given class of goods or services in a given region, during a given interval of time. It is a statistic designed to help to compare how these prices, taken as a whole, differ between time periods or geographical locations.

Price indices have several potential uses.

   a. Transactional Net Margin Method
   b. Two-part tariff
   c. Product sabotage
   d. Price index

17. A _____ product is a product designed for cheapness and short-term convenience rather than medium to long-term durability, with most products only intended for single use. The term is also sometimes used for products that may last several months (ex. _____ air filters) to distinguish from similar products that last indefinitely (ex.

a. 100-year flood
c. 1921 recession
b. Disposable
d. 130-30 fund

18. _____ is gross income minus income tax on that income.

Discretionary income is income after subtracting taxes and normal expenses (such as rent or mortgage, utilities, insurance, medical, transportation, property maintenance, child support, inflation, food and sundries, 'c.') to maintain a certain standard of living.

a. Disposable personal income
c. Disposable income
b. Taxation as theft
d. Stamp Act

19. _____ is the income of individuals or nations after adjusting for inflation. It is calculated by subtracting inflation from the nominal income. Real variables, such as _____, real GDP, and real interest rate are variables that are measured in physical units, while nominal variables such as nominal income, nominal GDP, and nominal interest rate are measured in monetary units.

a. Family income
c. Net national income
b. Windfall gain
d. Real income

20. In economic models, the _____ time frame assumes no fixed factors of production. Firms can enter or leave the marketplace, and the cost (and availability) of land, labor, raw materials, and capital goods can be assumed to vary. In contrast, in the short-run time frame, certain factors are assumed to be fixed, because there is not sufficient time for them to change.

a. Price/performance ratio
c. Productivity world
b. Diseconomies of scale
d. Long-run

21. In economics, the _____ is a single mathematical function used to express consumer spending. It was developed by John Maynard Keynes and detailed most famously in his book The General Theory of Employment, Interest, and Money. The function is used to calculate the amount of total consumption in an economy.

a. Liquidity preference
c. Consumption function
b. Procyclical
d. DAD-SAS model

22. A _____ is an object whose consumption increases the utility of the consumer, for which the quantity demanded exceeds the quantity supplied at zero price. _____s are usually modeled as having diminishing marginal utility. The first individual purchase has high utility; the second has less.

a. Merit good
c. Good
b. Pie method
d. Composite good

23. In economics, the concept of the _____ refers to the decision-making time frame of a firm in which at least one factor of production is fixed. Costs which are fixed in the _____ have no impact on a firms decisions. For example a firm can raise output by increasing the amount of labour through overtime.

a. Hicks-neutral technical change
c. Productivity model
b. Product Pipeline
d. Short-run

Chapter 16. Output and the Exchange Rate in the Short Run

24. The term _____ refers to government debt, expenditures and revenues, or to finance (particularly financial revenue) in general.

- _____ deficit is the budget deficit of federal or local government
- _____ policy is the discretionary spending of governments. Contrasts with monetary policy.
- _____ year and _____ quarter are reporting periods for firms and other agencies.

    a. Drawdown   b. Fiscal
    c. Procter ' Gamble   d. Bucket shop

25. In economics, _____ is the use of government spending and revenue collection to influence the economy.

_____ can be contrasted with the other main type of economic policy, monetary policy, which attempts to stabilize the economy by controlling interest rates and the supply of money. The two main instruments of _____ are government spending and taxation.

    a. Fiscalism   b. Sustainable investment rule
    c. 100-year flood   d. Fiscal policy

26. _____ is the process by which the government, central bank (ii) availability of money, and (iii) cost of money or rate of interest, in order to attain a set of objectives oriented towards the growth and stability of the economy. Monetary theory provides insight into how to craft optimal _____.

_____ is referred to as either being an expansionary policy where an expansionary policy increases the total supply of money in the economy, and a contractionary policy decreases the total money supply.

    a. 100-year flood   b. 1921 recession
    c. 130-30 fund   d. Monetary policy

27. In economics, _____ is a rise in the general level of prices of goods and services in an economy over a period of time. When the general price level rises, each unit of currency buys fewer goods and services; consequently, _____ is also a decline in the real value of money--a loss of purchasing power in the medium of exchange which is also the monetary unit of account in the economy. A chief measure of general price-level _____ is the general _____ rate, which is the percentage change in a general price index (normally the Consumer Price Index) over time.

    a. Inflation   b. Economic
    c. Opportunity cost   d. Energy economics

28. _____ was an American economist, statistician and public intellectual, and a recipient of the Nobel Memorial Prize in Economic Sciences. He is best known among scholars for his theoretical and empirical research, especially consumption analysis, monetary history and theory, and for his demonstration of the complexity of stabilization policy. A global public followed his restatement of a political philosophy that insisted on minimizing the role of government in favor of the private sector.

Chapter 16. Output and the Exchange Rate in the Short Run   117

a. Adolph Fischer
b. Adolf Hitler
c. Adam Smith
d. Milton Friedman

29. The _____ is a monetary system in which a region's common medium of exchange are paper notes that are normally freely convertible into pre-set, fixed quantities of gold. The _____ is not currently used by any government, having been replaced completely by fiat currency. Gold certificates were used as paper currency in the United States from 1882 to 1933, these certificates were freely convertable into gold coins.

In the 1790s Britain suffered a massive shortage of silver coinage and ceased to mint larger silver coins.

a. 130-30 fund
b. Gold standard
c. 1921 recession
d. 100-year flood

30. _____ is a term used to described a tendency or preference towards a particular perspective, ideology or result, especially when the tendency interferes with the ability to be impartial, unprejudiced, or objective. The term _____ed is used to describe an action, judgment, or other outcome influenced by a prejudged perspective. It is also used to refer to a person or body of people whose actions or judgments exhibit _____.
a. 100-year flood
b. 1921 recession
c. Bias
d. 130-30 fund

31. A _____ occurs when an entity spends more money than it takes in. The opposite of a _____ is a budget surplus. Debt is essentially an accumulated flow of deficits.
a. Lump-sum tax
b. Budget deficit
c. Funding body
d. Public Financial Management

32. A _____ is a legal document that is often passed by the legislature, and approved by the chief executive-or president. For example, only certain types of revenue may be imposed and collected. Property tax is frequently the basis for municipal and county revenues, while sales tax and/or income tax are the basis for state revenues, and income tax and corporate tax are the basis for national revenues.
a. Structural deficit
b. Right-financing
c. Government budget
d. Lump-sum tax

33. In economics, _____ is the total amount of money available in an economy at a particular point in time. There are several ways to define 'money', but standard measures usually include currency in circulation and demand deposits.

_____ data are recorded and published, usually by the government or the central bank of the country.

a. Velocity of money
b. Neutrality of money
c. Money supply
d. Veil of money

34. In economics, the _____ measures the payments that flow between any individual country and all other countries. It is used to summarize all international economic transactions for that country during a specific time period, usually a year. The _____ is determined by the country's exports and imports of goods, services, and financial capital, as well as financial transfers.

a. Balance of payments
b. Gross world product
c. Gross domestic product per barrel
d. Skyscraper Index

35. A _____ is the transfer of wealth from one party (such as a person or company) to another. A _____ is usually made in exchange for the provision of goods, services or both, or to fulfill a legal obligation.

The simplest and oldest form of _____ is barter, the exchange of one good or service for another.

a. Social gravity
b. Going concern
c. Soft count
d. Payment

36. A _____, sometimes called a pegged exchange rate, is a type of exchange rate regime wherein a currency's value is matched to the value of another single currency or to a basket of other currencies such as gold.

A _____ is usually used to stabilize the value of a currency, vis-a-vis the currency it is pegged to. This facilitates trade and investments between the two countries, and is especially useful for small economies where external trade forms a large part of their GDP.

a. Leading indicators
b. Law of supply
c. Monetary economics
d. Fixed exchange rate

37. _____ is a type of trade policy that allows traders to act and transact without interference from government. Thus, the policy permits trading partners mutual gains from trade, with goods and services produced according to the theory of comparative advantage.

Under a _____ policy, prices are a reflection of true supply and demand, and are the sole determinant of resource allocation.

a. 1921 recession
b. 130-30 fund
c. 100-year flood
d. Free trade

38. _____ is exchange of capital, goods, and services across international borders or territories. In most countries, it represents a significant share of gross domestic product (GDP.) While _____ has been present throughout much of history , its economic, social, and political importance has been on the rise in recent centuries.

a. Intra-industry trade
b. Incoterms
c. International trade
d. Import license

39. Preparing to rebuild the international economic system as World War II was still raging, 730 delegates from all 44 Allied nations gathered at the Mount Washington Hotel in Bretton Woods, New Hampshire, United States, for the United Nations Monetary and Financial Conference. The delegates deliberated upon and signed the _____ during the first three weeks of July 1944.

Setting up a system of rules, institutions, and procedures to regulate the international monetary system, the planners at Bretton Woods established the International Monetary Fund (IMF) and the International Bank for Reconstruction and Development (IBRD), which today is part of the World Bank Group.

Chapter 16. Output and the Exchange Rate in the Short Run

a. Heavy-Chemical Industry Drive
c. Land reform
b. Dromography
d. Bretton Woods Agreements

40. A _____ or a flexible exchange rate is a type of exchange rate regime wherein a currency's value is allowed to fluctuate according to the foreign exchange market. A currency that uses a _____ is known as a floating currency. The opposite of a _____ is a fixed exchange rate.
   a. Floating exchange rate
   c. Floating currency
   b. Foreign exchange market
   d. Trade Weighted US dollar Index

41. To _____ is to impose a financial charge or other levy upon a taxpayer by a state or the functional equivalent of a state.

_____es are also imposed by many subnational entities. _____es consist of direct _____ or indirect _____, and may be paid in money or as its labour equivalent (often but not always unpaid.)

   a. 100-year flood
   c. 1921 recession
   b. Tax
   d. 130-30 fund

42. A _____ is a reduction in taxes. Economic stimulus via _____s, along with interest rate intervention and deficit spending, are one of the central tenets of Keynesian economics.

The immediate effects of a _____ are, generally, a decrease in the real income of the government and an increase in the real income of those whose tax rate has been lowered.

   a. Popiwek
   c. Direct taxes
   b. Withholding tax
   d. Tax cut

Chapter 17. Fixed Exchange Rates and Foreign Exchange Intervention

1. _____ in its classic form is defined as a company from one country making a physical investment into building a factory in another country. It is the establishment of an enterprise by a foreigner. Its definition can be extended to include investments made to acquire lasting interest in enterprises operating outside of the economy of the investor.
   a. Federal Deposit Insurance Corporation
   b. Non-governmental organization
   c. Financial Stability Forum
   d. Foreign direct investment

2. In finance, the _____s between two currencies specifies how much one currency is worth in terms of the other. It is the value of a foreign natione;s currency in terms of the home natione;s currency. For example an _____ of 102 Japanese yen to the United States dollar means that JPY 102 is worth the same as USD 1.
   a. Interbank market
   b. ACEA agreement
   c. ACCRA Cost of Living Index
   d. Exchange rate

3. A _____ or a flexible exchange rate is a type of exchange rate regime wherein a currency's value is allowed to fluctuate according to the foreign exchange market. A currency that uses a _____ is known as a floating currency. The opposite of a _____ is a fixed exchange rate.
   a. Foreign exchange market
   b. Floating exchange rate
   c. Floating currency
   d. Trade Weighted US dollar Index

4. Preparing to rebuild the international economic system as World War II was still raging, 730 delegates from all 44 Allied nations gathered at the Mount Washington Hotel in Bretton Woods, New Hampshire, United States, for the United Nations Monetary and Financial Conference. The delegates deliberated upon and signed the _____ during the first three weeks of July 1944.

   Setting up a system of rules, institutions, and procedures to regulate the international monetary system, the planners at Bretton Woods established the International Monetary Fund (IMF) and the International Bank for Reconstruction and Development (IBRD), which today is part of the World Bank Group.

   a. Bretton Woods Agreements
   b. Land reform
   c. Dromography
   d. Heavy-Chemical Industry Drive

5. The term _____ is used to describe a nation's social or business activity in the process of rapid growth and industrialization. Currently, there are approximately 28 _____ in the world, with the economies of China and India considered to be two of the largest. According to The Economist many people find the term dated, but a new term has yet to gain much traction.
   a. Occupational welfare
   b. Asymmetric price transmission
   c. Affinity diagram
   d. Emerging markets

6. The European _____, was a system introduced by the European Community in March 1979, as part of the European Monetary System (EMS), to reduce exchange rate variability and achieve monetary stability in Europe, in preparation for Economic and Monetary Union and the introduction of a single currency, the euro, which took place on 1 January 1999. Subsequent exchange rate agreements made with countries wishing to join the Eurozone are known as _____ II.

   The _____ is based on the concept of fixed currency exchange rate margins, but with exchange rates variable within those margins.

a. Exchange Rate Mechanism
b. Euro Interbank Offered Rate
c. European Monetary Union
d. European Monetary System

7. A _____, sometimes called a pegged exchange rate, is a type of exchange rate regime wherein a currency's value is matched to the value of another single currency or to a basket of other currencies such as gold.

A _____ is usually used to stabilize the value of a currency, vis-a-vis the currency it is pegged to. This facilitates trade and investments between the two countries, and is especially useful for small economies where external trade forms a large part of their GDP.

a. Monetary economics
b. Leading indicators
c. Fixed exchange rate
d. Law of supply

8. The _____ is a monetary system in which a region's common medium of exchange are paper notes that are normally freely convertible into pre-set, fixed quantities of gold. The _____ is not currently used by any government, having been replaced completely by fiat currency. Gold certificates were used as paper currency in the United States from 1882 to 1933, these certificates were freely convertable into gold coins.

In the 1790s Britain suffered a massive shortage of silver coinage and ceased to mint larger silver coins.

a. 100-year flood
b. Gold standard
c. 1921 recession
d. 130-30 fund

9. The _____ is an international organization that oversees the global financial system by following the macroeconomic policies of its member countries, in particular those with an impact on exchange rates and the balance of payments. It is an organization formed to stabilize international exchange rates and facilitate development. It also offers financial and technical assistance to its members, making it an international lender of last resort.

a. Office of Thrift Supervision
b. International Monetary Fund
c. ACEA agreement
d. ACCRA Cost of Living Index

10. In business and accounting, _____ are everything of value that is owned by a person or company. It is a claim on the property your income of a borrower. The balance sheet of a firm records the monetary value of the _____ owned by the firm.

a. Amortization schedule
b. ACCRA Cost of Living Index
c. ACEA agreement
d. Assets

11. _____ is money accepted for exchange of goods in an economy. The prevalence of one money over another arises, usually, when a government designates through decrees that the government shall accept only particular notes and coins in payment for taxes. Typically, money of _____ consists of stamped coins and minted paper bills.

a. Currency
b. Local currency
c. Security thread
d. Totnes pound

12. _____ is that which is owed; usually referencing assets owed, but the term can also cover moral obligations and other interactions not requiring money. In the case of assets, _____ is a means of using future purchasing power in the present before a summation has been earned. Some companies and corporations use _____ as a part of their overall corporate finance strategy.

a. Collateral Management
b. Debt
c. Hard money loan
d. Debenture

13. In financial accounting, a _____ or statement of financial position is a summary of a person's or organization's balances. Assets, liabilities and ownership equity are listed as of a specific date, such as the end of its financial year. A _____ is often described as a snapshot of a company's financial condition.

   a. 100-year flood
   b. Balance sheet
   c. 130-30 fund
   d. 1921 recession

14. A _____, reserve bank, or monetary authority is the entity responsible for the monetary policy of a country or of a group of member states. It is a bank that can lend money to other banks in times of need. Its primary responsibility is to maintain the stability of the national currency and money supply, but more active duties include controlling subsidized-loan interest rates, and acting as a lender of last resort to the banking sector during times of financial crisis (private banks often being integral to the national financial system.)

   a. 130-30 fund
   b. 100-year flood
   c. 1921 recession
   d. Central bank

15. In economics, _____ is the total amount of money available in an economy at a particular point in time. There are several ways to define 'money', but standard measures usually include currency in circulation and demand deposits.

   _____ data are recorded and published, usually by the government or the central bank of the country.

   a. Velocity of money
   b. Veil of money
   c. Neutrality of money
   d. Money supply

16. In economics, the _____ measures the payments that flow between any individual country and all other countries. It is used to summarize all international economic transactions for that country during a specific time period, usually a year. The _____ is determined by the country's exports and imports of goods, services, and financial capital, as well as financial transfers.

   a. Gross domestic product per barrel
   b. Skyscraper Index
   c. Gross world product
   d. Balance of payments

17. _____, in economics, occurs when assets and/or money rapidly flow out of a country, due to an economic event that disturbs investors and causes them to lower their valuation of the assets in that country, or otherwise to lose confidence in its economic strength. This leads to a disappearance of wealth and is usually accompanied by a sharp drop in the exchange rate of the affected country (depreciation in a variable exchange rate regime, or a forced devaluation in a fixed exchange rate regime.)

This fall is particularly damaging when the capital belongs to the people of the affected country, because not only are the citizens now burdened by the loss of faith in the economy and devaluation of their currency, but probably also their assets have lost much of their nominal value.

   a. Capital formation
   b. Firm-specific infrastructure
   c. Liquid capital
   d. Capital flight

Chapter 17. Fixed Exchange Rates and Foreign Exchange Intervention

18. _____ is a fee paid on borrowed assets. It is the price paid for the use of borrowed money, or, money earned by deposited funds. Assets that are sometimes lent with _____ include money, shares, consumer goods through hire purchase, major assets such as aircraft, and even entire factories in finance lease arrangements.

    a. Interest   b. Insolvency
    c. Asset protection   d. Internal debt

19. An _____ is the price a borrower pays for the use of money they do not own, for instance a small company might borrow from a bank to kick start their business, and the return a lender receives for deferring the use of funds, by lending it to the borrower. _____s are normally expressed as a percentage rate over the period of one year.

_____s targets are also a vital tool of monetary policy and are used to control variables like investment, inflation, and unemployment.

    a. Enterprise value   b. Interest rate
    c. ACCRA Cost of Living Index   d. Arrow-Debreu model

20. A _____ is the transfer of wealth from one party (such as a person or company) to another. A _____ is usually made in exchange for the provision of goods, services or both, or to fulfill a legal obligation.

The simplest and oldest form of _____ is barter, the exchange of one good or service for another.

    a. Going concern   b. Soft count
    c. Social gravity   d. Payment

21. The accounting equation relates assets, _____, and owner's equity:

    Assets = _____ + Owner's Equity

The accounting equation is the mathematical structure of the balance sheet.

The Australian Accounting Research Foundation defines _____ as: 'future sacrifice of economic benefits that the entity is presently obliged to make to other entities as a result of past transactions and other past events.'

Probably the most accepted accounting definition of liability is the one used by the International Accounting Standards Board (IASB.) The following is a quotation from IFRS Framework:

A liability is a present obligation of the enterprise arising from past events, the settlement of which is expected to result in an outflow from the enterprise of resources embodying economic benefits

-

Regulations as to the recognition of _____ are different all over the world, but are roughly similar to those of the IASB.

a. Liabilities
b. Competition law theory
c. Coase theorem
d. Community property

22. In finance, the _____ is the global financial market for short-term borrowing and lending. It provides short-term liquidity funding for the global financial system. The _____ is where short-term obligations such as Treasury bills, commercial paper and bankers' acceptances are bought and sold.
   a. Deferred compensation
   b. Consignment stock
   c. T-Model
   d. Money market

23. The most common mechanism used to measure this increase in the money supply is typically called the _____. It calculates the maximum amount of money that an initial deposit can be expanded to with a given reserve ratio - such a factor is called a multiplier.

The _____, m, is the inverse of the reserve requirement, R:

$$m = \frac{1}{R}$$

This formula stems from the fact that the sum of the 'amount loaned out' column above can be expressed mathematically as a geometric series with a common ratio of 1 − R.

   a. Flow to Equity-Approach
   b. Money multiplier
   c. Kibbutz volunteers
   d. Fixed-income arbitrage

24. In economics, economic equilibrium is simply a state of the world where economic forces are balanced and in the absence of external influences the (equilibrium) values of economic variables will not change. It is the point at which quantity demanded and quantity supplied are equal. _____, for example, refers to a condition where a market price is established through competition such that the amount of goods or services sought by buyers is equal to the amount of goods or services produced by sellers.
   a. Regulated market
   b. Marketization
   c. Product-Market Growth Matrix
   d. Market equilibrium

25. The _____ of monetary management established the rules for commercial and financial relations among the world's major industrial states in the mid 20th Century. The _____ was the first example of a fully negotiated monetary order intended to govern monetary relations among independent nation-states.

Preparing to rebuild the international economic system as World War II was still raging, 730 delegates from all 44 Allied nations gathered at the Mount Washington Hotel in Bretton Woods, New Hampshire, United States, for the United Nations Monetary and Financial Conference.

   a. 1921 recession
   b. 100-year flood
   c. 130-30 fund
   d. Bretton Woods system

26. The _____ is where currency trading takes place. It is where banks and other official institutions facilitate the buying and selling of foreign currencies. FX transactions typically involve one party purchasing a quantity of one currency in exchange for paying a quantity of another.

Chapter 17. Fixed Exchange Rates and Foreign Exchange Intervention

a. Currency swap
c. Covered interest arbitrage
b. Foreign exchange market
d. Floating currency

27. _____ is the process by which the government, central bank (ii) availability of money, and (iii) cost of money or rate of interest, in order to attain a set of objectives oriented towards the growth and stability of the economy. Monetary theory provides insight into how to craft optimal _____.

_____ is referred to as either being an expansionary policy where an expansionary policy increases the total supply of money in the economy, and a contractionary policy decreases the total money supply.

a. 100-year flood
c. 130-30 fund
b. 1921 recession
d. Monetary policy

28. A _____ is a monetary authority which is required to maintain a fixed exchange rate with a foreign currency. This policy objective requires the conventional objectives of a central bank to be subordinated to the exchange rate target.

The main qualities of an orthodox _____ are:

- A _____'s foreign currency reserves must be sufficient to ensure that all holders of its notes and coins (and all banks creditor of a Reserve Account at the _____) can convert them into the reserve currency (usually 110-115% of the monetary base M0.)
- A _____ maintains absolute, unlimited convertibility between its notes and coins and the currency against which they are pegged (the anchor currency), at a fixed rate of exchange, with no restrictions on current-account or capital-account transactions.
- A _____ only earns profit from interests on foreign reserves (less the expense of note-issuing), and does not engage in forward-exchange transactions. These foreign reserves exist (1) because local notes have been issued in exchange, or (2) because commercial banks must by regulation deposit a minimum reserve at the _____. (1) generates a seignorage revenue. (2) is the revenue on minimum reserves (revenue of investment activities less cost of minimum reserves remuneration)
- A _____ has no discretionary powers to effect monetary policy and does not lend to the government. Governments cannot print money, and can only tax or borrow to meet their spending commitments.
- A _____ does not act as a lender of last resort to commercial banks, and does not regulate reserve requirements.
- A _____ does not attempt to manipulate interest rates by establishing a discount rate like a central bank. The peg with the foreign currency tends to keep interest rates and inflation very closely aligned to those in the country against whose currency the peg is fixed.

The _____ in question will no longer issue fiat money but instead will only issue one unit of local currency for each unit (or decided amount) of foreign currency it has in its vault (often a hard currency such as the U.S. dollar or the euro.) The surplus on the balance of payments of that country is reflected by higher deposits local banks hold at the central bank as well as (initially) higher deposits of the (net) exporting firms at their local banks.

a. Petrodollar
c. Currency competition
b. Reserve currency
d. Currency board

Chapter 17. Fixed Exchange Rates and Foreign Exchange Intervention

29. The term _____ refers to government debt, expenditures and revenues, or to finance (particularly financial revenue) in general.

   - _____ deficit is the budget deficit of federal or local government
   - _____ policy is the discretionary spending of governments. Contrasts with monetary policy.
   - _____ year and _____ quarter are reporting periods for firms and other agencies.

   a. Drawdown
   b. Bucket shop
   c. Procter ' Gamble
   d. Fiscal

30. In economics, _____ is the use of government spending and revenue collection to influence the economy.

   _____ can be contrasted with the other main type of economic policy, monetary policy, which attempts to stabilize the economy by controlling interest rates and the supply of money. The two main instruments of _____ are government spending and taxation.

   a. 100-year flood
   b. Fiscal policy
   c. Sustainable investment rule
   d. Fiscalism

31. The _____ is the official currency of 16 of the 27 member states of the European Union (EU.) The states, known collectively as the Eurozone, are Austria, Belgium, Cyprus, Finland, France, Germany, Greece, Ireland, Italy, Luxembourg, Malta, the Netherlands, Portugal, Slovakia, Slovenia, and Spain. The currency is also used in a further five European countries, with and without formal agreements and is consequently used daily by some 327 million Europeans.

   a. Euro
   b. Equity capital market
   c. Import and Export Price Indices
   d. IRS Code 3401

32. _____ is a reduction in the value of a currency with respect to other monetary units. In common modern usage, it specifically implies an official lowering of the value of a country's currency within a fixed exchange rate system, by which the monetary authority formally sets a new fixed rate with respect to a foreign reference currency. In contrast, (currency) depreciation is used for the unofficial decrease in the exchange rate in a floating exchange rate system.

   a. Petrodollar recycling
   b. Devaluation
   c. Reserve currency
   d. Texas redbacks

33. _____ means a rise of a price of goods or products. This term is specially used as _____ of a currency, where it means a rise of currency to the relation with a foreign currency in a fixed exchange rate. In floating exchange rate correct term would be appreciation.

   a. Revaluation
   b. Death spiral financing
   c. Legal monopoly
   d. Deglobalization

Chapter 17. Fixed Exchange Rates and Foreign Exchange Intervention

34. In finance, _____ is a financial action that does not promise safety of the initial investment along with the return on the principal sum. _____ typically involves the lending of money or the purchase of assets, equity or debt but in a manner that has not been given thorough analysis or is deemed to have low margin of safety or a significant risk of the loss of the principal investment. The term, '_____,' which is formally defined as above in Graham and Dodd's 1934 text, Security Analysis, contrasts with the term 'investment,' which is a financial operation that, upon thorough analysis, promises safety of principal and a satisfactory return.
   a. Speculation
   b. Hybrid market
   c. Global Financial Centres Index
   d. Municipal Bond Arbitrage

35. A _____, which is also called a balance-of-payments crisis, occurs when the value of a currency changes quickly, undermining its ability to serve as a medium of exchange or a store of value. It is a type of financial crisis and is often associated with a real economic crisis. Currency crises can be especially destructive to small open economies or bigger, but not sufficiently stable ones.
   a. 130-30 fund
   b. 100-year flood
   c. Speculative attack
   d. Currency crisis

36. A currency crisis, which is also called a balance-of-payments crisis, occurs when the value of a currency changes quickly, undermining its ability to serve as a medium of exchange or a store of value. It is a type of financial crisis and is often associated with a real economic crisis. _____ can be especially destructive to small open economies or bigger, but not sufficiently stable ones.
   a. Currency crises
   b. 1921 recession
   c. 130-30 fund
   d. 100-year flood

37. In economics, the concept of the _____ refers to the decision-making time frame of a firm in which at least one factor of production is fixed. Costs which are fixed in the _____ have no impact on a firms decisions. For example a firm can raise output by increasing the amount of labour through overtime.
   a. Short-run
   b. Product Pipeline
   c. Hicks-neutral technical change
   d. Productivity model

38. A _____ is the minimum difference a person requires to be willing to take an uncertain bet, between the expected value of the bet and the certain value that he is indifferent to.

The certainty equivalent is the guaranteed payoff at which a person is 'indifferent' between accepting the guaranteed payoff and a higher but uncertain payoff. (It is the amount of the higher payout minus the _____.)

   a. Workers compensation
   b. Ruin theory
   c. Risk premium
   d. Linear model

39. A _____ secures the proper functioning of money by regulating economic agents, transaction types, and money supply.

_____s are traditionally formed by the policy decisions of individual governments and administrated as a domestic economic issue.

The current trend, however, is to use international trade and investment to alter the policy and legislation of individual governments.

- a. Monetary system
- b. Financial rand
- c. Netting
- d. Consumer basket

40. A _____ is a currency which is held in significant quantities by many governments and institutions as part of their foreign exchange reserves. It also tends to be the international pricing currency for products traded on a global market, such as oil, gold, etc.

This permits the issuing country to purchase the commodities at a marginally cheaper rate than other nations, which must exchange their currency with each purchase and pay a transaction cost.

- a. Currency board
- b. World currency
- c. Texas redbacks
- d. Reserve currency

41. An _____ is an economy in which people, including businesses, can trade in goods and services with other people and businesses in the international community at large. This contrasts with a closed economy in which international trade cannot take place.

The act of selling goods or services to a foreign country is called exporting.

- a. Information economy
- b. Indicative planning
- c. Attention work
- d. Open economy

42. In economics, _____ is a rise in the general level of prices of goods and services in an economy over a period of time. When the general price level rises, each unit of currency buys fewer goods and services; consequently, _____ is also a decline in the real value of money--a loss of purchasing power in the medium of exchange which is also the monetary unit of account in the economy. A chief measure of general price-level _____ is the general _____ rate, which is the percentage change in a general price index (normally the Consumer Price Index) over time.

- a. Economic
- b. Inflation
- c. Opportunity cost
- d. Energy economics

43. _____, 1st Baron Keynes was a renowned economist from Britain whose many ideas on economic and political theories as well as on many governments' monetary policies influenced America. He advocated a government that played an active role in the lives of people regarding business, economy, etc. In this role, the government would use fiscal measures to reduce the consequences of recessions, economic depressions and booms.

- a. Adam Smith
- b. Adolf Hitler
- c. Adolph Fischer
- d. John Maynard Keynes

44. In finance, a _____ is a debt security, in which the authorized issuer owes the holders a debt and, depending on the terms of the _____, is obliged to pay interest (the coupon) and/or to repay the principal at a later date, termed maturity. A _____ is a formal contract to repay borrowed money with interest at fixed intervals.

Thus a _____ is like a loan: the issuer is the borrower (debtor), the holder is the lender (creditor), and the coupon is the interest.

a. Zero-coupon
b. Callable
c. Prize Bond
d. Bond

45. Economics:

- _____, the desire to own something and the ability to pay for it
- _____ curve, a graphic representation of a _____ schedule
- _____ deposit, the money in checking accounts
- _____ pull theory, the theory that inflation occurs when _____ for goods and services exceeds existing supplies
- _____ schedule, a table that lists the quantity of a good a person will buy it each different price
- _____ side economics, the school of economics at believes government spending and tax cuts open economy by raising _____

a. Demand
b. Production
c. Variability
d. McKesson ' Robbins scandal

46. In economic models, the _____ time frame assumes no fixed factors of production. Firms can enter or leave the marketplace, and the cost (and availability) of land, labor, raw materials, and capital goods can be assumed to vary. In contrast, in the short-run time frame, certain factors are assumed to be fixed, because there is not sufficient time for them to change.

a. Productivity world
b. Diseconomies of scale
c. Price/performance ratio
d. Long-run

Chapter 18. The International Monetary System, 1870-1973

1. A _____ secures the proper functioning of money by regulating economic agents, transaction types, and money supply.

_____s are traditionally formed by the policy decisions of individual governments and administrated as a domestic economic issue.

The current trend, however, is to use international trade and investment to alter the policy and legislation of individual governments.

   a. Consumer basket
   b. Netting
   c. Financial rand
   d. Monetary system

2. The _____ of monetary management established the rules for commercial and financial relations among the world's major industrial states in the mid 20th Century. The _____ was the first example of a fully negotiated monetary order intended to govern monetary relations among independent nation-states.

Preparing to rebuild the international economic system as World War II was still raging, 730 delegates from all 44 Allied nations gathered at the Mount Washington Hotel in Bretton Woods, New Hampshire, United States, for the United Nations Monetary and Financial Conference.

   a. 130-30 fund
   b. 1921 recession
   c. 100-year flood
   d. Bretton Woods system

3. _____ was an American economist, statistician and public intellectual, and a recipient of the Nobel Memorial Prize in Economic Sciences. He is best known among scholars for his theoretical and empirical research, especially consumption analysis, monetary history and theory, and for his demonstration of the complexity of stabilization policy. A global public followed his restatement of a political philosophy that insisted on minimizing the role of government in favor of the private sector.
   a. Adam Smith
   b. Milton Friedman
   c. Adolph Fischer
   d. Adolf Hitler

4. _____ in economics is a state in which a country maintains full employment and price level stability. It is a function of a country's total output,

$$II = C(Yf - T) + I + G + CA(E \times P^*/P, Yf-T; Yf^* - T^*)$$

_____ = Consumption [determined by disposable income] + Investment + Government Spending + Current Account (determined by the real exchange rate, disposable income of home country and disposable income of the foreign country.)

External balance signifies a condition in which the country's current account, its exports minus imports, is neither too far in surplus nor in deficit.

   a. Internal balance
   b. Autonomous consumption
   c. Uneconomic growth
   d. Energy intensity

Chapter 18. The International Monetary System, 1870-1973

5. _____ in economics and business is the result of an exchange and from that trade we assign a numerical monetary value to a good, service or asset. If Alice trades Bob 4 apples for an orange, the _____ of an orange is 4 apples. Inversely, the _____ of an apple is 1/4 oranges.

   a. Price war
   b. Price
   c. Premium pricing
   d. Price book

6. A _____ is a hypothetical measure of overall prices for some set of goods and services, in a given region during a given interval, normalized relative to some base set. Typically, a _____ is approximated with a price index.

   The classical dichotomy is the assumption that there is a relatively clean distinction between overall increases or decreases in prices and underlying, e;reale; economic variables.

   a. Discouraged worker
   b. Price elasticity of supply
   c. Discretionary spending
   d. Price level

7. In economics, _____ is the total demand for final goods and services in the economy (Y) at a given time and price level. It is the amount of goods and services in the economy that will be purchased at all possible price levels. This is the demand for the gross domestic product of a country when inventory levels are static.

   a. Aggregation problem
   b. Aggregate supply
   c. Aggregate expenditure
   d. Aggregate demand

8. Economics:

   - _____,the desire to own something and the ability to pay for it
   - _____ curve,a graphic representation of a _____ schedule
   - _____ deposit, the money in checking accounts
   - _____ pull theory,the theory that inflation occurs when _____ for goods and services exceeds existing supplies
   - _____ schedule,a table that lists the quantity of a good a person will buy it each different price
   - _____ side economics,the school of economics at believes government spending and tax cuts open economy by raising _____

   a. Variability
   b. Production
   c. Demand
   d. McKesson ' Robbins scandal

9. In macroeconomics, _____ is a condition of the national economy, where all or nearly all persons willing and able to work at the prevailing wages and working conditions are able to do so. It is defined either as 0% unemployment, literally, no unemployment (the rate of unemployment is the fraction of the work force unable to find work), as by James Tobin, or as the level of employment rates when there is no cyclical unemployment. It is defined by the majority of mainstream economists as being an acceptable level of natural unemployment above 0%, the discrepancy from 0% being due to non-cyclical types of unemployment.

   a. Demand shock
   b. Harrod-Johnson diagram
   c. Marginal propensity to consume
   d. Full employment

10. The _____ is a monetary system in which a region's common medium of exchange are paper notes that are normally freely convertible into pre-set, fixed quantities of gold. The _____ is not currently used by any government, having been replaced completely by fiat currency. Gold certificates were used as paper currency in the United States from 1882 to 1933, these certificates were freely convertable into gold coins.

In the 1790s Britain suffered a massive shortage of silver coinage and ceased to mint larger silver coins.

- a. 100-year flood
- b. Gold standard
- c. 1921 recession
- d. 130-30 fund

11. _____ is a fee paid on borrowed assets. It is the price paid for the use of borrowed money , or, money earned by deposited funds . Assets that are sometimes lent with _____ include money, shares, consumer goods through hire purchase, major assets such as aircraft, and even entire factories in finance lease arrangements.
- a. Asset protection
- b. Internal debt
- c. Insolvency
- d. Interest

12. An _____ is an economy in which people, including businesses, can trade in goods and services with other people and businesses in the international community at large. This contrasts with a closed economy in which international trade cannot take place.

The act of selling goods or services to a foreign country is called exporting.

- a. Information economy
- b. Indicative planning
- c. Attention work
- d. Open economy

13. In economics, the _____ is one of the two primary components of the balance of payments, the other being the capital account. It is the sum of the balance of trade (exports minus imports of goods and services), net factor income (such as interest and dividends) and net transfer payments (such as foreign aid.)

$$\text{Current account} = \text{Balance of trade} \\ + \text{Net factor income from abroad} \\ + \text{Net unilateral transfers from abroad}$$

The _____ balance is one of two major metrics of the nature of a country's foreign trade (the other being the net capital outflow.)

- a. Current account
- b. Gross private domestic investment
- c. National Income and Product Accounts
- d. Compensation of employees

14. In economics, _____ is a sustained decrease in the general price level of goods and services. _____ occurs when the annual inflation rate falls below zero percent, resulting in an increase in the real value of money -- a negative inflation rate. This should not be confused with disinflation, a slow-down in the inflation rate (i.e. when the inflation decreases, but still remains positive.)

a. Tobit model
b. Literacy rate
c. Price revolution
d. Deflation

15. In algebra, a _____ is a function depending on n that associates a scalar, det(A), to an n×n square matrix A. The fundamental geometric meaning of a _____ is a scale factor for measure when A is regarded as a linear transformation. _____s are important both in calculus, where they enter the substitution rule for several variables, and in multilinear algebra.

For a fixed nonnegative integer n, there is a unique _____ function for the n×n matrices over any commutative ring R. In particular, this function exists when R is the field of real or complex numbers.

a. 1921 recession
b. Determinant
c. 100-year flood
d. 130-30 fund

16. In finance, the _____s between two currencies specifies how much one currency is worth in terms of the other. It is the value of a foreign natione;s currency in terms of the home natione;s currency. For example an _____ of 102 Japanese yen to the United States dollar means that JPY 102 is worth the same as USD 1.
a. Interbank market
b. ACEA agreement
c. ACCRA Cost of Living Index
d. Exchange rate

17. A _____ or a flexible exchange rate is a type of exchange rate regime wherein a currency's value is allowed to fluctuate according to the foreign exchange market. A currency that uses a _____ is known as a floating currency. The opposite of a _____ is a fixed exchange rate.
a. Foreign exchange market
b. Trade Weighted US dollar Index
c. Floating exchange rate
d. Floating currency

18. In economics, the _____ measures the payments that flow between any individual country and all other countries. It is used to summarize all international economic transactions for that country during a specific time period, usually a year. The _____ is determined by the country's exports and imports of goods, services, and financial capital, as well as financial transfers.
a. Gross world product
b. Gross domestic product per barrel
c. Skyscraper Index
d. Balance of payments

19. _____ is that part of the total debt in a country that is owed to creditors outside the country. The debtors can be the government, corporations or private households. The debt includes money owed to private commercial banks, other governments, or international financial institutions such as the IMF and World Bank.
a. International debt collection
b. Internal debt
c. Asset protection
d. External debt

20. In economics, economic equilibrium is simply a state of the world where economic forces are balanced and in the absence of external influences the (equilibrium) values of economic variables will not change. It is the point at which quantity demanded and quantity supplied are equal. _____, for example, refers to a condition where a market price is established through competition such that the amount of goods or services sought by buyers is equal to the amount of goods or services produced by sellers.

Chapter 18. The International Monetary System, 1870-1973

a. Marketization
c. Product-Market Growth Matrix
b. Regulated market
d. Market equilibrium

21. In economics, the concept of the _____ refers to the decision-making time frame of a firm in which at least one factor of production is fixed. Costs which are fixed in the _____ have no impact on a firms decisions. For example a firm can raise output by increasing the amount of labour through overtime.
   a. Short-run
   c. Product Pipeline
   b. Hicks-neutral technical change
   d. Productivity model

22. _____ is that which is owed; usually referencing assets owed, but the term can also cover moral obligations and other interactions not requiring money. In the case of assets, _____ is a means of using future purchasing power in the present before a summation has been earned. Some companies and corporations use _____ as a part of their overall corporate finance strategy.
   a. Collateral Management
   c. Hard money loan
   b. Debenture
   d. Debt

23. A _____ is the transfer of wealth from one party (such as a person or company) to another. A _____ is usually made in exchange for the provision of goods, services or both, or to fulfill a legal obligation.

The simplest and oldest form of _____ is barter, the exchange of one good or service for another.

   a. Going concern
   c. Social gravity
   b. Soft count
   d. Payment

24. The _____ is a logical argument by David Hume against the Mercantilist (1700-1776) idea that a nation should strive for a positive balance of trade, or net exports. The argument considers the effects of international transactions in a gold standard, a system in which gold is the official means of international payments and each natione;s currency is in the form of gold itself or of paper currency fully convertible into gold.

Hume argued that when a country with a gold standard had a positive balance of trade, gold would flow into the country in the amount that the value of exports exceeds the value of imports.

   a. Price-specie-flow mechanism
   c. Bank rescue package
   b. Hicks-optimal outcome
   d. Human Rights Act 1993

Chapter 18. The International Monetary System, 1870-1973

25. A _____ is:

- Rewrite _____, in generative grammar and computer science
- Standardization, a formal and widely-accepted statement, fact, definition, or qualification
- Operation, a determinate _____ for performing a mathematical operation and obtaining a certain result (Mathematics, Logic)
    - Unary operation
    - Binary operation
- _____ of inference, a function from sets of formulae to formulae (Mathematics, Logic)
- _____ of thumb, principle with broad application that is not intended to be strictly accurate or reliable for every situation. Also often simply referred to as a _____
- Moral, an atomic element of a moral code for guiding choices in human behavior
- Heuristic, a quantized '_____' which shows a tendency or probability for successful function
- A regulation, as in sports
- A Production _____, as in computer science
- Procedural law, a _____ set governing the application of laws to cases
    - A law, which may informally be called a '_____'
    - A court ruling, a decision by a court
- In the U.S. Government, a regulation mandated by Congress, but written or expanded upon by the Executive Branch.
- Norm (sociology), an informal but widely accepted _____, concept, truth, definition, or qualification (social norms, legal norms, coding norms)
- Norm (philosophy), a kind of sentence or a reason to act, feel or believe
- 'Rulership' is the concept of governance by a government:
    - Military _____, governance by a military body
    - Monastic _____, a collection of precepts that guides the life of monks or nuns in a religious order where the superior holds the place of Christ
- Slide _____

- '_____,' a song by Ayumi Hamasaki
- '_____,' a song by rapper Nas
- '_____s,' an album by the band The Whitest Boy Alive
- _____s: Pyaar Ka Superhit Formula, a 2003 Bollywood film
- ruler, an instrument for measuring lengths
- _____, a component of an astrolabe, circumferator or similar instrument
- The _____s, a bestselling self-help book
- _____ Project (Run Up-to-date Linux Everywhere), a project that aims to use up-to-date Linux software on old PCs
- _____ engine, a software system that helps managing business _____s
- Ja _____, a hip hop artist
    - R.U.L.E., a 2005 greatest hits album by rapper Ja _____
- '_____s,' a KMFDM song

a. Rule
c. Demand
b. Procter ' Gamble
d. Technocracy

26. _____ was an English writer on economics who has been called the last of the early mercantilists. He was among the first to recognize the exportation of service, or invisible items, as valuable trade, and made early statements strongly in support of capitalism.

Mun began his career by engaging in Mediterranean trade, and afterwards settled in London, amassing a large fortune.

- a. Henry Ford
- b. George Cabot Lodge II
- c. Werner Sombart
- d. Thomas Mun

27. _____ the Great War, and the War to End All Wars, was a global military conflict which involved the majority of the world's great powers, organized into two opposing military alliances: the Entente Powers and the Central Powers. Over 70 million military personnel were mobilized in one of the largest wars in history. In a state of total war, the major combatants fully placed their scientific and industrial capabilities at the service of the war effort.
- a. 130-30 fund
- b. 1921 recession
- c. World War I
- d. 100-year flood

28. _____ is a common concept in economics, and gives rise to derived concepts such as consumer debt. Generally _____ is defined by opposition to production. But the precise definition can vary because different schools of economists define production quite differently.
- a. Foreclosure data providers
- b. Consumption
- c. Cash or share options
- d. Federal Reserve Bank Notes

29. In microeconomics, _____ is quite simply the conversion of inputs into outputs. It is an economic process that uses resources to create a good or service that is suitable for exchange. This can include manufacturing, storing, shipping, and packaging.
- a. Solved
- b. MET
- c. Red Guards
- d. Production

30. The _____ is the way a country manages its currency in respect to foreign currencies and the foreign exchange market. It is closely related to monetary policy and the two are generally dependent on many of the same factors.

The basic types are a floating exchange rate, where the market dictates the movements of the exchange rate, a pegged float, where the central bank keeps the rate from deviating too far from a target band or value, and the fixed exchange rate, which ties the currency to another currency, mostly more widespread currencies such as the U.S. dollar or the euro.

- a. ACEA agreement
- b. Interbank market
- c. ACCRA Cost of Living Index
- d. Exchange rate regime

31. _____, Jr. (January 29, 1843 - September 14, 1901) was the 25th President of the United States, and the last veteran of the American Civil War to be elected.

By the 1880s, McKinley was a national Republican leader; his signature issue was high tariffs on imports as a formula for prosperity, as typified by his McKinley Tariff of 1890.

Chapter 18. The International Monetary System, 1870-1973

a. Adam Smith
b. William McKinley
c. Adolph Fischer
d. Adolf Hitler

32. _____ originally was the term for studying production, buying and selling, and their relations with law, custom, and government. _____ originated in moral philosophy. It developed in the 18th century as the study of the economies of states -- polities, hence _____.
   a. Political economy
   b. Dirigisme
   c. Productive and unproductive labour
   d. Geoeconomics

33. The _____ was held in Genoa, Italy in 1922 from April 10 to May 19. At this conference, the representatives of 34 countries convened to speak about monetary economics in the wake of World War I. The purpose was to formulate strategies to rebuild central and eastern Europe after the war, and also to negotiate a relationship between European capitalist economies, and the new Russian Communist economy .

Among the propositions formulated at the conference was the proposal that central banks make a partial return to the Gold Standard.

   a. 1921 recession
   b. Genoa Conference
   c. 100-year flood
   d. 130-30 fund

34. The _____ of the United States was passed in 1900 (ratified on March 14) and established gold as the only standard for redeeming paper money, stopping bimetallism (which had allowed silver in exchange for gold.) It was signed by President William McKinley.
   a. Flex dollars
   b. Gold Standard Act
   c. Remonetisation
   d. Fed Shreds

35. The _____ was a period of financial crisis that gripped much of Asia beginning in July 1997, and raised fears of a worldwide economic meltdown (financial contagion.)

The crisis started in Thailand with the financial collapse of the Thai baht caused by the decision of the Thai government to float the baht, cutting its peg to the USD, after exhaustive efforts to support it in the face of a severe financial overextension that was in part real estate driven. At the time, Thailand had acquired a burden of foreign debt that made the country effectively bankrupt even before the collapse of its currency.

   a. Asian financial crisis
   b. ACEA agreement
   c. AD-IA Model
   d. ACCRA Cost of Living Index

36. Preparing to rebuild the international economic system as World War II was still raging, 730 delegates from all 44 Allied nations gathered at the Mount Washington Hotel in Bretton Woods, New Hampshire, United States, for the United Nations Monetary and Financial Conference. The delegates deliberated upon and signed the _____ during the first three weeks of July 1944.

Setting up a system of rules, institutions, and procedures to regulate the international monetary system, the planners at Bretton Woods established the International Monetary Fund (IMF) and the International Bank for Reconstruction and Development (IBRD), which today is part of the World Bank Group.

a. Dromography
b. Land reform
c. Heavy-Chemical Industry Drive
d. Bretton Woods Agreements

37. A _____, sometimes called a pegged exchange rate, is a type of exchange rate regime wherein a currency's value is matched to the value of another single currency or to a basket of other currencies such as gold.

A _____ is usually used to stabilize the value of a currency, vis-a-vis the currency it is pegged to. This facilitates trade and investments between the two countries, and is especially useful for small economies where external trade forms a large part of their GDP.

a. Leading indicators
b. Monetary economics
c. Law of supply
d. Fixed exchange rate

38. _____ is exchange of capital, goods, and services across international borders or territories. In most countries, it represents a significant share of gross domestic product (GDP.) While _____ has been present throughout much of history, its economic, social, and political importance has been on the rise in recent centuries.

a. Intra-industry trade
b. International trade
c. Import license
d. Incoterms

39. The _____ was an act signed into law on June 17, 1930, that raised U.S. tariffs on over 20,000 imported goods to record levels. In the United States 1,028 economists signed a petition against this legislation, and after it was passed, many countries retaliated with their own increased tariffs on U.S. goods, and American exports and imports were reduced by more than half.

Although rated capacity had increased tremendously, actual output, income, and expenditure had not.

a. Judgment summons
b. Loss of use
c. Smoot-Hawley Tariff Act
d. Patent Law Treaty

40. A _____ is a general term that describes any government policy or regulation that restricts international trade. The barriers can take many forms, including the following terms that include many restrictions in international trade within multiple countries that import and export any items of trade.

- Import duty
- Import licenses
- Export licenses
- Import quotas
- Tariffs
- Subsidies
- Non-tariff barriers to trade
- Voluntary Export Restraints
- Local Content Requirements
- Embargo

Most _____s work on the same principle: the imposition of some sort of cost on trade that raises the price of the traded products. If two or more nations repeatedly use _____s against each other, then a trade war results.

a. National Foreign Trade Council
b. Certificate of origin
c. Global financial system
d. Trade barrier

41. The term _____ is applied broadly to a variety of situations in which some financial institutions or assets suddenly lose a large part of their value. In the 19th and early 20th centuries, many financial crises were associated with banking panics, and many recessions coincided with these panics. Other situations that are often called financial crises include stock market crashes and the bursting of other financial bubbles, currency crises, and sovereign defaults.

a. Macroeconomics
b. Co-operative economics
c. Market failure
d. Financial crisis

42. _____ is the price of a commodity such as a good or service in terms of another; ie, the ratio of two prices. A _____ may be expressed in terms of a ratio between any two prices or the ratio between the price of one particular good and a weighted average of all other goods available in the market. A _____ is an opportunity cost.

a. False economy
b. False shortage
c. Food cooperative
d. Relative price

43. A _____ occurs when a bank is unable to meet its obligations to its depositors or other creditors. More specifically, a bank fails economically when the market value of its assets declines to a value that is less than the market value of its liabilities. As such, the bank is unable to fulfill the demands of all of its depositors on time.

a. Concentration account
b. Bank failure
c. Transactional account
d. Lombard Club

44. The _____ was a worldwide economic downturn starting in most places in 1929 and ending at different times in the 1930s or early 1940s for different countries. It was the largest and most important economic depression in the 20th century, and is used in the 21st century as an example of how far the world's economy can fall. The _____ originated in the United States; historians most often use as a starting date the stock market crash on October 29, 1929, known as Black Tuesday.

a. Great Depression
b. Wall Street Crash of 1929
c. British Empire Economic Conference
d. Jarrow March

45. A _____ is a public market for the trading of company stock and derivatives at an agreed price; these are securities listed on a stock exchange as well as those only traded privately.

The size of the world _____ was estimated at about $36.6 trillion US at the beginning of October 2008 . The total world derivatives market has been estimated at about $791 trillion face or nominal value, 11 times the size of the entire world economy.

a. Stock market
b. Adam Smith
c. Adolph Fischer
d. Adolf Hitler

46. A _____ is a sudden dramatic decline of stock prices across a significant cross-section of a stock market. Crashes are driven by panic as much as by underlying economic factors. They often follow speculative stock market bubbles.
   a. Stock market crash
   b. 100-year flood
   c. 1921 recession
   d. 130-30 fund

47. The _____ is an international organization that oversees the global financial system by following the macroeconomic policies of its member countries, in particular those with an impact on exchange rates and the balance of payments. It is an organization formed to stabilize international exchange rates and facilitate development. It also offers financial and technical assistance to its members, making it an international lender of last resort.
   a. Office of Thrift Supervision
   b. ACEA agreement
   c. ACCRA Cost of Living Index
   d. International Monetary Fund

48. In business and accounting, _____ are everything of value that is owned by a person or company. It is a claim on the property your income of a borrower. The balance sheet of a firm records the monetary value of the _____ owned by the firm.
   a. ACEA agreement
   b. ACCRA Cost of Living Index
   c. Amortization schedule
   d. Assets

49. _____ is money accepted for exchange of goods in an economy. The prevalence of one money over another arises, usually, when a government designates through decrees that the government shall accept only particular notes and coins in payment for taxes. Typically, money of _____ consists of stamped coins and minted paper bills.
   a. Local currency
   b. Security thread
   c. Currency
   d. Totnes pound

50. The _____ is the official currency of 16 of the 27 member states of the European Union (EU.) The states, known collectively as the Eurozone, are Austria, Belgium, Cyprus, Finland, France, Germany, Greece, Ireland, Italy, Luxembourg, Malta, the Netherlands, Portugal, Slovakia, Slovenia, and Spain. The currency is also used in a further five European countries, with and without formal agreements and is consequently used daily by some 327 million Europeans.
   a. Equity capital market
   b. Import and Export Price Indices
   c. IRS Code 3401
   d. Euro

51. The term _____ refers to government debt, expenditures and revenues, or to finance (particularly financial revenue) in general.

   - _____ deficit is the budget deficit of federal or local government
   - _____ policy is the discretionary spending of governments. Contrasts with monetary policy.
   - _____ year and _____ quarter are reporting periods for firms and other agencies.

   a. Bucket shop
   b. Drawdown
   c. Procter ' Gamble
   d. Fiscal

52. In economics, _____ is the use of government spending and revenue collection to influence the economy.

Chapter 18. The International Monetary System, 1870-1973

_____ can be contrasted with the other main type of economic policy, monetary policy, which attempts to stabilize the economy by controlling interest rates and the supply of money. The two main instruments of _____ are government spending and taxation.

a. Sustainable investment rule
b. 100-year flood
c. Fiscalism
d. Fiscal policy

53. _____ is the quality of paper money substitutes which entitles the holder to redeem them on demand into money proper.

Historically, the banknote has followed a common or very similar pattern in the western nations. Originally decentralized and issued from various independent banks, it was gradually brought under state control and became a monopoly privilege of the central banks.

a. Convertibility
b. Dollarization
c. Currency board
d. Devaluation

54. _____, in economics, occurs when assets and/or money rapidly flow out of a country, due to an economic event that disturbs investors and causes them to lower their valuation of the assets in that country, or otherwise to lose confidence in its economic strength. This leads to a disappearance of wealth and is usually accompanied by a sharp drop in the exchange rate of the affected country (depreciation in a variable exchange rate regime, or a forced devaluation in a fixed exchange rate regime.)

This fall is particularly damaging when the capital belongs to the people of the affected country, because not only are the citizens now burdened by the loss of faith in the economy and devaluation of their currency, but probably also their assets have lost much of their nominal value.

a. Liquid capital
b. Firm-specific infrastructure
c. Capital formation
d. Capital flight

55. _____ is a reduction in the value of a currency with respect to other monetary units. In common modern usage, it specifically implies an official lowering of the value of a country's currency within a fixed exchange rate system, by which the monetary authority formally sets a new fixed rate with respect to a foreign reference currency. In contrast, (currency) depreciation is used for the unofficial decrease in the exchange rate in a floating exchange rate system.

a. Texas redbacks
b. Reserve currency
c. Petrodollar recycling
d. Devaluation

56. _____s is the social science that studies the production, distribution, and consumption of goods and services. The term _____s comes from the Ancient Greek οἰκονομῖα from οἶκος (oikos, 'house') + νόμος (nomos, 'custom' or 'law'), hence 'rules of the house(hold)'. Current _____ models developed out of the broader field of political economy in the late 19th century, owing to a desire to use an empirical approach more akin to the physical sciences.

a. Energy economics
b. Inflation
c. Opportunity cost
d. Economic

Chapter 18. The International Monetary System, 1870-1973

57. In economics, _____ is a rise in the general level of prices of goods and services in an economy over a period of time. When the general price level rises, each unit of currency buys fewer goods and services; consequently, _____ is also a decline in the real value of money--a loss of purchasing power in the medium of exchange which is also the monetary unit of account in the economy. A chief measure of general price-level _____ is the general _____ rate, which is the percentage change in a general price index (normally the Consumer Price Index) over time.
   a. Energy economics
   b. Economic
   c. Opportunity cost
   d. Inflation

58. An _____ is the price a borrower pays for the use of money they do not own, for instance a small company might borrow from a bank to kick start their business, and the return a lender receives for deferring the use of funds, by lending it to the borrower. _____s are normally expressed as a percentage rate over the period of one year.

   _____s targets are also a vital tool of monetary policy and are used to control variables like investment, inflation, and unemployment.

   a. Arrow-Debreu model
   b. Enterprise value
   c. ACCRA Cost of Living Index
   d. Interest rate

59. In economics, _____ is the total amount of money available in an economy at a particular point in time. There are several ways to define 'money', but standard measures usually include currency in circulation and demand deposits.

   _____ data are recorded and published, usually by the government or the central bank of the country.

   a. Money supply
   b. Velocity of money
   c. Veil of money
   d. Neutrality of money

60. _____ means a rise of a price of goods or products. This term is specially used as _____ of a currency, where it means a rise of currency to the relation with a foreign currency in a fixed exchange rate. In floating exchange rate correct term would be appreciation.
   a. Deglobalization
   b. Death spiral financing
   c. Revaluation
   d. Legal monopoly

61. _____ is an economic concept with commonplace familiarity. It is the price that a good or service is offered at, or will fetch, in the marketplace. It is of interest mainly in the study of microeconomics.
   a. Paper trading
   b. Market price
   c. Noisy market hypothesis
   d. Market anomaly

62. _____ is a term used in accounting, economics and finance to spread the cost of an asset over the span of several years.

In simple words we can say that _____ is the reduction in the value of an asset due to usage, passage of time, wear and tear, technological outdating or obsolescence, depletion, inadequacy, rot, rust, decay or other such factors.

In accounting, _____ is a term used to describe any method of attributing the historical or purchase cost of an asset across its useful life, roughly corresponding to normal wear and tear.

Chapter 18. The International Monetary System, 1870-1973

a. Salvage value
b. Net income per employee
c. Historical cost
d. Depreciation

63. _____ is the process by which the government, central bank (ii) availability of money, and (iii) cost of money or rate of interest, in order to attain a set of objectives oriented towards the growth and stability of the economy. Monetary theory provides insight into how to craft optimal _____.

_____ is referred to as either being an expansionary policy where an expansionary policy increases the total supply of money in the economy, and a contractionary policy decreases the total money supply.

a. 130-30 fund
b. 1921 recession
c. 100-year flood
d. Monetary policy

64. In finance, _____ is a financial action that does not promise safety of the initial investment along with the return on the principal sum. _____ typically involves the lending of money or the purchase of assets, equity or debt but in a manner that has not been given thorough analysis or is deemed to have low margin of safety or a significant risk of the loss of the principal investment. The term, '_____,' which is formally defined as above in Graham and Dodd's 1934 text, Security Analysis, contrasts with the term 'investment,' which is a financial operation that, upon thorough analysis, promises safety of principal and a satisfactory return.

a. Global Financial Centres Index
b. Municipal Bond Arbitrage
c. Hybrid market
d. Speculation

65. The _____ is where currency trading takes place. It is where banks and other official institutions facilitate the buying and selling of foreign currencies. FX transactions typically involve one party purchasing a quantity of one currency in exchange for paying a quantity of another.

a. Currency swap
b. Foreign exchange market
c. Floating currency
d. Covered interest arbitrage

66. The _____ was a December 1971 agreement that ended the fixed exchange rates established at the Bretton Woods Conference of 1944.

The Bretton Woods Conference of 1944 established an international fixed exchange rate regime in which currencies were pegged to the United States dollar, which was based on the gold standard.

By 1970, however, it was clear that the exchange rate regime was under threat, as the United States dollar was greatly overvalued because of heavy American spending on Lyndon B. Johnson's Great Society and the Vietnam War.

a. Hanseatic League
b. Commercial Revolution
c. History of capitalism
d. Smithsonian agreement

67. _____ is a decrease in the rate of inflation. This phase of the business cycle, in which retailers can no longer pass on higher prices to their customers, often occurs during a recession. In contrast, deflation occurs when prices are actually dropping.

a. Reflation
b. Mundell-Tobin effect
c. Stealth inflation
d. Disinflation

Chapter 19. Macroeconomic Policy and Coordination Under Floating Exchange Rates

1. In finance, the _____s between two currencies specifies how much one currency is worth in terms of the other. It is the value of a foreign natione;s currency in terms of the home natione;s currency. For example an _____ of 102 Japanese yen to the United States dollar means that JPY 102 is worth the same as USD 1.
   a. Exchange rate
   b. Interbank market
   c. ACEA agreement
   d. ACCRA Cost of Living Index

2. A _____ or a flexible exchange rate is a type of exchange rate regime wherein a currency's value is allowed to fluctuate according to the foreign exchange market. A currency that uses a _____ is known as a floating currency. The opposite of a _____ is a fixed exchange rate.
   a. Trade Weighted US dollar Index
   b. Foreign exchange market
   c. Floating currency
   d. Floating exchange rate

3. _____ is a concept found in moral, political, and bioethical philosophy. Within these contexts, it refers to the capacity of a rational individual to make an informed, un-coerced decision. In moral and political philosophy, _____ is often used as the basis for determining moral responsibility for one's actions.
   a. AD-IA Model
   b. Autonomy
   c. ACCRA Cost of Living Index
   d. ACEA agreement

4. Preparing to rebuild the international economic system as World War II was still raging, 730 delegates from all 44 Allied nations gathered at the Mount Washington Hotel in Bretton Woods, New Hampshire, United States, for the United Nations Monetary and Financial Conference. The delegates deliberated upon and signed the _____ during the first three weeks of July 1944.

Setting up a system of rules, institutions, and procedures to regulate the international monetary system, the planners at Bretton Woods established the International Monetary Fund (IMF) and the International Bank for Reconstruction and Development (IBRD), which today is part of the World Bank Group.

   a. Land reform
   b. Dromography
   c. Heavy-Chemical Industry Drive
   d. Bretton Woods Agreements

5. A _____, sometimes called a pegged exchange rate, is a type of exchange rate regime wherein a currency's value is matched to the value of another single currency or to a basket of other currencies such as gold.

A _____ is usually used to stabilize the value of a currency, vis-a-vis the currency it is pegged to. This facilitates trade and investments between the two countries, and is especially useful for small economies where external trade forms a large part of their GDP.

   a. Monetary economics
   b. Law of supply
   c. Fixed exchange rate
   d. Leading indicators

6. The _____ is a monetary system in which a region's common medium of exchange are paper notes that are normally freely convertible into pre-set, fixed quantities of gold. The _____ is not currently used by any government, having been replaced completely by fiat currency. Gold certificates were used as paper currency in the United States from 1882 to 1933, these certificates were freely convertable into gold coins.

In the 1790s Britain suffered a massive shortage of silver coinage and ceased to mint larger silver coins.

Chapter 19. Macroeconomic Policy and Coordination Under Floating Exchange Rates

    a. 130-30 fund
    b. 1921 recession
    c. Gold standard
    d. 100-year flood

7. _____ is the process by which the government, central bank (ii) availability of money, and (iii) cost of money or rate of interest, in order to attain a set of objectives oriented towards the growth and stability of the economy. Monetary theory provides insight into how to craft optimal _____.

_____ is referred to as either being an expansionary policy where an expansionary policy increases the total supply of money in the economy, and a contractionary policy decreases the total money supply.

    a. 100-year flood
    b. 1921 recession
    c. 130-30 fund
    d. Monetary policy

8. In business and accounting, _____ are everything of value that is owned by a person or company. It is a claim on the property your income of a borrower. The balance sheet of a firm records the monetary value of the _____ owned by the firm.

    a. ACCRA Cost of Living Index
    b. ACEA agreement
    c. Amortization schedule
    d. Assets

9. The term _____ refers to government debt, expenditures and revenues, or to finance (particularly financial revenue) in general.

- _____ deficit is the budget deficit of federal or local government
- _____ policy is the discretionary spending of governments. Contrasts with monetary policy.
- _____ year and _____ quarter are reporting periods for firms and other agencies.

    a. Drawdown
    b. Bucket shop
    c. Fiscal
    d. Procter ' Gamble

10. In economics, _____ is the use of government spending and revenue collection to influence the economy.

_____ can be contrasted with the other main type of economic policy, monetary policy, which attempts to stabilize the economy by controlling interest rates and the supply of money. The two main instruments of _____ are government spending and taxation.

    a. Fiscalism
    b. 100-year flood
    c. Sustainable investment rule
    d. Fiscal policy

11. In economics, _____ is a rise in the general level of prices of goods and services in an economy over a period of time. When the general price level rises, each unit of currency buys fewer goods and services; consequently, _____ is also a decline in the real value of money--a loss of purchasing power in the medium of exchange which is also the monetary unit of account in the economy. A chief measure of general price-level _____ is the general _____ rate, which is the percentage change in a general price index (normally the Consumer Price Index) over time.

Chapter 19. Macroeconomic Policy and Coordination Under Floating Exchange Rates

a. Economic
b. Energy economics
c. Opportunity cost
d. Inflation

12. Economics:

- _____ ,the desire to own something and the ability to pay for it
- _____ curve, a graphic representation of a _____ schedule
- _____ deposit, the money in checking accounts
- _____ pull theory, the theory that inflation occurs when _____ for goods and services exceeds existing supplies
- _____ schedule, a table that lists the quantity of a good a person will buy it each different price
- _____ side economics, the school of economics at believes government spending and tax cuts open economy by raising _____

a. McKesson ' Robbins scandal
b. Demand
c. Production
d. Variability

13. In economics, an _____ is any good or commodity, transported from one country to another country in a legitimate fashion, typically for use in trade. _____ goods or services are provided to foreign consumers by domestic producers. _____ is an important part of international trade.
   a. AD-IA Model
   b. ACCRA Cost of Living Index
   c. ACEA agreement
   d. Export

14. _____ is exchange of capital, goods, and services across international borders or territories. In most countries, it represents a significant share of gross domestic product (GDP.) While _____ has been present throughout much of history, its economic, social, and political importance has been on the rise in recent centuries.
   a. Incoterms
   b. Import license
   c. Intra-industry trade
   d. International trade

15. In finance, the _____ is the global financial market for short-term borrowing and lending. It provides short-term liquidity funding for the global financial system. The _____ is where short-term obligations such as Treasury bills, commercial paper and bankers' acceptances are bought and sold.
   a. Money market
   b. Consignment stock
   c. Deferred compensation
   d. T-Model

16. In finance, _____ is a financial action that does not promise safety of the initial investment along with the return on the principal sum. _____ typically involves the lending of money or the purchase of assets, equity or debt but in a manner that has not been given thorough analysis or is deemed to have low margin of safety or a significant risk of the loss of the principal investment. The term, '_____,' which is formally defined as above in Graham and Dodd's 1934 text, Security Analysis, contrasts with the term 'investment,' which is a financial operation that, upon thorough analysis, promises safety of principal and a satisfactory return.
   a. Speculation
   b. Global Financial Centres Index
   c. Municipal Bond Arbitrage
   d. Hybrid market

Chapter 19. Macroeconomic Policy and Coordination Under Floating Exchange Rates

17. _____ is a type of trade policy that allows traders to act and transact without interference from government. Thus, the policy permits trading partners mutual gains from trade, with goods and services produced according to the theory of comparative advantage.

Under a _____ policy, prices are a reflection of true supply and demand, and are the sole determinant of resource allocation.

a. 100-year flood
b. 1921 recession
c. 130-30 fund
d. Free trade

18. In finance, _____ is investment originating from other countries. See Foreign direct investment.
a. Preclusive purchasing
b. Demand side economics
c. Horizontal merger
d. Foreign investment

19. In economic models, the _____ time frame assumes no fixed factors of production. Firms can enter or leave the marketplace, and the cost (and availability) of land, labor, raw materials, and capital goods can be assumed to vary. In contrast, in the short-run time frame, certain factors are assumed to be fixed, because there is not sufficient time for them to change.
a. Long-run
b. Diseconomies of scale
c. Price/performance ratio
d. Productivity world

20. In economics, economic equilibrium is simply a state of the world where economic forces are balanced and in the absence of external influences the (equilibrium) values of economic variables will not change. It is the point at which quantity demanded and quantity supplied are equal. _____, for example, refers to a condition where a market price is established through competition such that the amount of goods or services sought by buyers is equal to the amount of goods or services produced by sellers.
a. Regulated market
b. Market equilibrium
c. Product-Market Growth Matrix
d. Marketization

21. _____s is the social science that studies the production, distribution, and consumption of goods and services. The term _____s comes from the Ancient Greek oá¼°κονομῐα from oá¼¶κος (oikos, 'house') + vÏŒμος (nomos, 'custom' or 'law'), hence 'rules of the house(hold)'. Current _____ models developed out of the broader field of political economy in the late 19th century, owing to a desire to use an empirical approach more akin to the physical sciences.
a. Energy economics
b. Opportunity cost
c. Inflation
d. Economic

22. _____ refers to the actions that governments take in the economic field. It covers the systems for setting interest rates and government deficit as well as the labour market, national ownership, and many other areas of government.

Such policies are often influenced by international institutions like the International Monetary Fund or World Bank as well as political beliefs and the consequent policies of parties.

a. ACCRA Cost of Living Index
b. Economic policy
c. ACEA agreement
d. AD-IA Model

Chapter 19. Macroeconomic Policy and Coordination Under Floating Exchange Rates

23. The _____ is the official currency of 16 of the 27 member states of the European Union (EU.) The states, known collectively as the Eurozone, are Austria, Belgium, Cyprus, Finland, France, Germany, Greece, Ireland, Italy, Luxembourg, Malta, the Netherlands, Portugal, Slovakia, Slovenia, and Spain. The currency is also used in a further five European countries, with and without formal agreements and is consequently used daily by some 327 million Europeans.
   a. Equity capital market
   b. Import and Export Price Indices
   c. IRS Code 3401
   d. Euro

24. _____ is an economic situation in which inflation and economic stagnation occur simultaneously and remain unchecked for a period of time. The portmanteau _____ is generally attributed to British politician Iain Macleod, who coined the term in a speech to Parliament in 1965. The concept is notable partly because, in postwar macroeconomic theory, inflation and recession were regarded as mutually exclusive, and also because _____ has generally proven to be difficult and costly to eradicate once it gets started.
   a. Stagflation
   b. Real interest rate
   c. Price/wage spiral
   d. Chronic inflation

25. A _____ is something for which there is demand, but which is supplied without qualitative differentiation across a market. It is a product that is the same no matter who produces it, such as petroleum, notebook paper, or milk. In other words, copper is copper.
   a. 100-year flood
   b. Hard commodity
   c. Soft commodity
   d. Commodity

26. In economics, the _____ is one of the two primary components of the balance of payments, the other being the capital account. It is the sum of the balance of trade (exports minus imports of goods and services), net factor income (such as interest and dividends) and net transfer payments (such as foreign aid.)

$$\text{Current account} = \text{Balance of trade} \\ + \text{Net factor income from abroad} \\ + \text{Net unilateral transfers from abroad}$$

The _____ balance is one of two major metrics of the nature of a country's foreign trade (the other being the net capital outflow.)

   a. Gross private domestic investment
   b. National Income and Product Accounts
   c. Compensation of employees
   d. Current account

27. In economics, _____ is the total amount of money available in an economy at a particular point in time. There are several ways to define 'money', but standard measures usually include currency in circulation and demand deposits.

_____ data are recorded and published, usually by the government or the central bank of the country.

   a. Velocity of money
   b. Veil of money
   c. Neutrality of money
   d. Money supply

28. The term '_____' refers to the concept of collecting information and attempting to spot a pattern in the information. In some fields of study, the term '_____' has more formally-defined meanings.

Chapter 19. Macroeconomic Policy and Coordination Under Floating Exchange Rates

In project management _____ is a mathematical technique that uses historical results to predict future outcome.

a. Trend analysis
c. Quantile regression
b. Probit model
d. Coefficient of determination

29. _____, in economics, is the period of time required for economic agents to reallocate resources, and generally reestablish equilibrium.

The actual length of this period, usually numbered in years or decades, varies widely depending on circumstantial context. During the _____, all factors are variable.

a. Government surplus
c. Temporary equilibrium method
b. Producer surplus
d. Long Term

30. A variety of measures of _____ and output are used in economics to estimate total economic activity in a country or region, including gross domestic product (GDP), gross national product (GNP), and net _____

There are three main ways of calculating these numbers; the output approach, the income approach and the expenditure approach. In theory, the three must yield the same, because total expenditures on goods and services must equal the total income paid to the producers (Gnational income), and that must also equal the total value of the output of goods and services (GNP.)

a. Volume index
c. Gross world product
b. GNI per capita
d. National income

31. _____ is a decrease in the rate of inflation. This phase of the business cycle, in which retailers can no longer pass on higher prices to their customers, often occurs during a recession. In contrast, deflation occurs when prices are actually dropping.

a. Stealth inflation
c. Disinflation
b. Reflation
d. Mundell-Tobin effect

32. _____ is the increase in the amount of the goods and services produced by an economy over time. It is conventionally measured as the percent rate of increase in real gross domestic product, or real GDP. Growth is usually calculated in real terms, i.e. inflation-adjusted terms, in order to net out the effect of inflation on the price of the goods and services produced.

a. ACEA agreement
c. ACCRA Cost of Living Index
b. AD-IA Model
d. Economic growth

33. In economics, a _____ is a general slowdown in economic activity over a sustained period of time, or a business cycle contraction. During _____s, many macroeconomic indicators vary in a similar way. Production as measured by Gross Domestic Product (GDP), employment, investment spending, capacity utilization, household incomes and business profits all fall during _____s.

Chapter 19. Macroeconomic Policy and Coordination Under Floating Exchange Rates

a. Monetary economics
c. Leading indicators
b. Treasury View
d. Recession

34. In algebra, a _____ is a function depending on n that associates a scalar, det(A), to an n×n square matrix A. The fundamental geometric meaning of a _____ is a scale factor for measure when A is regarded as a linear transformation. _____s are important both in calculus, where they enter the substitution rule for several variables, and in multilinear algebra.

For a fixed nonnegative integer n, there is a unique _____ function for the n×n matrices over any commutative ring R. In particular, this function exists when R is the field of real or complex numbers.

a. 1921 recession
c. Determinant
b. 100-year flood
d. 130-30 fund

35. _____ is the economic policy of restraining trade between states, through methods such as tariffs on imported goods, restrictive quotas, and a variety of other restrictive government regulations designed to discourage imports, and prevent foreign take-over of local markets and companies. This policy is closely aligned with anti-globalization, and contrasts with free trade, where government barriers to trade are kept to a minimum. The term is mostly used in the context of economics, where _____ refers to policies or doctrines which 'protect' businesses and workers within a country by restricting or regulating trade with foreign nations.

a. Google economy
c. Knowledge economy
b. Digital economy
d. Protectionism

36. In economics, _____ is how a natione;s total economy is distributed among its population. . _____ has always been a central concern of economic theory and economic policy. Classical economists such as Adam Smith, Thomas Malthus and David Ricardo were mainly concerned with factor _____, that is, the distribution of income between the main factors of production, land, labour and capital.

a. Eco commerce
c. Income distribution
b. Authorised capital
d. Equipment trust certificate

37. _____ is a fee paid on borrowed assets. It is the price paid for the use of borrowed money , or, money earned by deposited funds . Assets that are sometimes lent with _____ include money, shares, consumer goods through hire purchase, major assets such as aircraft, and even entire factories in finance lease arrangements.

a. Internal debt
c. Asset protection
b. Insolvency
d. Interest

38. An _____ is the price a borrower pays for the use of money they do not own, for instance a small company might borrow from a bank to kick start their business, and the return a lender receives for deferring the use of funds, by lending it to the borrower. _____s are normally expressed as a percentage rate over the period of one year.

_____s targets are also a vital tool of monetary policy and are used to control variables like investment, inflation, and unemployment.

a. Arrow-Debreu model
c. Enterprise value
b. ACCRA Cost of Living Index
d. Interest rate

Chapter 19. Macroeconomic Policy and Coordination Under Floating Exchange Rates

39. The term financial crisis is applied broadly to a variety of situations in which some financial institutions or assets suddenly lose a large part of their value. In the 19th and early 20th centuries, many _____ were associated with banking panics, and many recessions coincided with these panics. Other situations that are often called _____ include stock market crashes and the bursting of other financial bubbles, currency crises, and sovereign defaults.
   a. Microeconomics
   b. General equilibrium
   c. Georgism
   d. Financial crises

40. _____ is that which is owed; usually referencing assets owed, but the term can also cover moral obligations and other interactions not requiring money. In the case of assets, _____ is a means of using future purchasing power in the present before a summation has been earned. Some companies and corporations use _____ as a part of their overall corporate finance strategy.
   a. Hard money loan
   b. Debenture
   c. Collateral Management
   d. Debt

41. In calculus, a function f defined on a subset of the real numbers with real values is called _____, if for all x and y such that x >≤ y one has f(x) >≤ f(y), so f preserves the order. In layman's terms, the sign of the slope is always positive (the curve tending upwards) or zero (i.e., non-decreasing, or asymptotic, or depicted as a horizontal, flat line) Likewise, a function is called monotonically decreasing (non-increasing) if, whenever x >≤ y, then f(x) >≥ f(y), so it reverses the order.
   a. 130-30 fund
   b. Monotonic
   c. 1921 recession
   d. 100-year flood

42. _____ is a term used in accounting, economics and finance to spread the cost of an asset over the span of several years.

    In simple words we can say that _____ is the reduction in the value of an asset due to usage, passage of time, wear and tear, technological outdating or obsolescence, depletion, inadequacy, rot, rust, decay or other such factors.

    In accounting, _____ is a term used to describe any method of attributing the historical or purchase cost of an asset across its useful life, roughly corresponding to normal wear and tear.

   a. Net income per employee
   b. Depreciation
   c. Salvage value
   d. Historical cost

43. The term _____ is applied broadly to a variety of situations in which some financial institutions or assets suddenly lose a large part of their value. In the 19th and early 20th centuries, many financial crises were associated with banking panics, and many recessions coincided with these panics. Other situations that are often called financial crises include stock market crashes and the bursting of other financial bubbles, currency crises, and sovereign defaults.
   a. Financial crisis
   b. Co-operative economics
   c. Macroeconomics
   d. Market failure

44. A variety of measures of national income and output are used in economics to estimate total economic activity in a country or region, including gross domestic product (GDP), _____ , and net national income (NNI.)

Chapter 19. Macroeconomic Policy and Coordination Under Floating Exchange Rates

There are three main ways of calculating these numbers; the output approach, the income approach and the expenditure approach. In theory, the three must yield the same, because total expenditures on goods and services must equal the total income paid to the producers (GNI), and that must also equal the total value of the output of goods and services (_____.)

a. Gross world product
b. Purchasing power parity
c. Household final consumption expenditure
d. Gross national product

45. A _____ secures the proper functioning of money by regulating economic agents, transaction types, and money supply.

_____s are traditionally formed by the policy decisions of individual governments and administrated as a domestic economic issue.

The current trend, however, is to use international trade and investment to alter the policy and legislation of individual governments.

a. Financial rand
b. Consumer basket
c. Netting
d. Monetary system

46. _____ is money accepted for exchange of goods in an economy. The prevalence of one money over another arises, usually, when a government designates through decrees that the government shall accept only particular notes and coins in payment for taxes. Typically, money of _____ consists of stamped coins and minted paper bills.

a. Security thread
b. Currency
c. Local currency
d. Totnes pound

47. _____ is the electoral problem resulting from competition between two or more candidates or political parties from the same or approximate location in the political ideological spectrum or space against an opposing candidate or political party from the other side of the political ideological spectrum or space. The resulting fragmentation of political support may result in electoral defeat. _____s, and thus political calculations attempting to avoid them, appear most frequently in elections involving executives and representatives from single member districts.

a. 130-30 fund
b. Coordination failure
c. 1921 recession
d. 100-year flood

Chapter 20. Optimum Currency Areas and the European Experience

1. _____ describes a set of laws relating to domestic agriculture and imports of foreign agricultural products. Governments usually implement agricultural policies with the goal of achieving a specific outcome in the domestic agricultural product markets. Outcomes can involve, for example, a guaranteed supply level, price stability, product quality, product selection, land use or employment.
   a. ACEA agreement
   b. ACCRA Cost of Living Index
   c. Intercropping
   d. Agricultural Policy

2. _____ is money accepted for exchange of goods in an economy. The prevalence of one money over another arises, usually, when a government designates through decrees that the government shall accept only particular notes and coins in payment for taxes. Typically, money of _____ consists of stamped coins and minted paper bills.
   a. Security thread
   b. Currency
   c. Local currency
   d. Totnes pound

3. The _____ is the official currency of 16 of the 27 member states of the European Union (EU.) The states, known collectively as the Eurozone, are Austria, Belgium, Cyprus, Finland, France, Germany, Greece, Ireland, Italy, Luxembourg, Malta, the Netherlands, Portugal, Slovakia, Slovenia, and Spain. The currency is also used in a further five European countries, with and without formal agreements and is consequently used daily by some 327 million Europeans.
   a. IRS Code 3401
   b. Equity capital market
   c. Euro
   d. Import and Export Price Indices

4. _____ is sometimes referred to as _____, actually it means Economic Monetary Union.

First ideas of an economic and monetary union in Europe were raised well before establishing the European Communities. For example, already in the League of Nations, Gustav Stresemann asked in 1929 for a European currency (Link) against the background of an increased economic division due to a number of new nation states in Europe after WWI.

   a. European Monetary Union
   b. Euro Interbank Offered Rate
   c. Exchange rate mechanism
   d. European Monetary System

5. _____ is a Regional Trade Agreement among Argentina, Brazil, Paraguay and Uruguay founded in 1991 by the Treaty of Asunci>ón, which was later amended and updated by the 1994 Treaty of Ouro Preto. Its purpose is to promote free trade and the fluid movement of goods, people, and currency.

_____ origins trace back to 1985 when Presidents Ra>úl Alfons>ín of Argentina and Jos>é Sarney of Brazil signed the Argentina-Brazil Integration and Economics Cooperation Program or PICE .

   a. Free trade area
   b. 100-year flood
   c. 130-30 fund
   d. Mercosur

6. An economic and _____ is a single market with a common currency. It is to be distinguished from a mere currency union , which does not involve a single market. This is the fifth stage of economic integration.
   a. Customs union
   b. Monetary Union
   c. Free trade zone
   d. Commercial invoice

Chapter 20. Optimum Currency Areas and the European Experience

7. In economics, _____ is a rise in the general level of prices of goods and services in an economy over a period of time. When the general price level rises, each unit of currency buys fewer goods and services; consequently, _____ is also a decline in the real value of money--a loss of purchasing power in the medium of exchange which is also the monetary unit of account in the economy. A chief measure of general price-level _____ is the general _____ rate, which is the percentage change in a general price index (normally the Consumer Price Index) over time.
   a. Energy economics
   b. Inflation
   c. Economic
   d. Opportunity cost

8. Preparing to rebuild the international economic system as World War II was still raging, 730 delegates from all 44 Allied nations gathered at the Mount Washington Hotel in Bretton Woods, New Hampshire, United States, for the United Nations Monetary and Financial Conference. The delegates deliberated upon and signed the _____ during the first three weeks of July 1944.

   Setting up a system of rules, institutions, and procedures to regulate the international monetary system, the planners at Bretton Woods established the International Monetary Fund (IMF) and the International Bank for Reconstruction and Development (IBRD), which today is part of the World Bank Group.

   a. Dromography
   b. Land reform
   c. Heavy-Chemical Industry Drive
   d. Bretton Woods Agreements

9. A _____, sometimes called a pegged exchange rate, is a type of exchange rate regime wherein a currency's value is matched to the value of another single currency or to a basket of other currencies such as gold.

   A _____ is usually used to stabilize the value of a currency, vis-a-vis the currency it is pegged to. This facilitates trade and investments between the two countries, and is especially useful for small economies where external trade forms a large part of their GDP.

   a. Leading indicators
   b. Fixed exchange rate
   c. Monetary economics
   d. Law of supply

10. A _____ or a flexible exchange rate is a type of exchange rate regime wherein a currency's value is allowed to fluctuate according to the foreign exchange market. A currency that uses a _____ is known as a floating currency. The opposite of a _____ is a fixed exchange rate.
    a. Foreign exchange market
    b. Floating exchange rate
    c. Trade Weighted US dollar Index
    d. Floating currency

11. In finance, the _____s between two currencies specifies how much one currency is worth in terms of the other. It is the value of a foreign natione;s currency in terms of the home natione;s currency. For example an _____ of 102 Japanese yen to the United States dollar means that JPY 102 is worth the same as USD 1.
    a. Interbank market
    b. ACCRA Cost of Living Index
    c. ACEA agreement
    d. Exchange rate

12. A _____, reserve bank, or monetary authority is the entity responsible for the monetary policy of a country or of a group of member states. It is a bank that can lend money to other banks in times of need. Its primary responsibility is to maintain the stability of the national currency and money supply, but more active duties include controlling subsidized-loan interest rates, and acting as a lender of last resort to the banking sector during times of financial crisis (private banks often being integral to the national financial system.)

a. 100-year flood
b. 130-30 fund
c. 1921 recession
d. Central Bank

13. The _____ is composed of the European Central Bank (ECB) and the national central banks (NCBs) of all 27 European Union (EU) Member States.

Since not all the EU states have joined the Euro, the ESCB could not be used as the monetary authority of the eurozone. For this reason the Eurosystem (which excludes all the NCBs which have not adopted the Euro) became the institution in charge of those tasks which in principle had to be managed by the ESCB.

a. European System of Central Banks
b. AD-IA Model
c. ACCRA Cost of Living Index
d. ACEA agreement

14. A variety of measures of national income and output are used in economics to estimate total economic activity in a country or region, including gross domestic product (GDP), _____ , and net national income (NNI.)

There are three main ways of calculating these numbers; the output approach, the income approach and the expenditure approach. In theory, the three must yield the same, because total expenditures on goods and services must equal the total income paid to the producers (GNI), and that must also equal the total value of the output of goods and services (_____.)

a. Gross national product
b. Gross world product
c. Household final consumption expenditure
d. Purchasing power parity

15. _____ is the process by which the government, central bank (ii) availability of money, and (iii) cost of money or rate of interest, in order to attain a set of objectives oriented towards the growth and stability of the economy. Monetary theory provides insight into how to craft optimal _____.

_____ is referred to as either being an expansionary policy where an expansionary policy increases the total supply of money in the economy, and a contractionary policy decreases the total money supply.

a. 130-30 fund
b. 100-year flood
c. 1921 recession
d. Monetary policy

16. In economics, _____ is the monetary policy device that a country's government (i.e., sovereign power) uses to regulate the flows into and out of a country's capital account, i.e., the flows of investment-oriented money into and out of a country or currency. _____s have become more prominent in the years since the Clinton administration blessed the efforts of the world community to create the World Trade Organization (WTO), primarily because globalization has increased the acceleration of currency domain strength, in other words, giving some currencies utility far beyond their physical geographic boundaries.

Chapter 20. Optimum Currency Areas and the European Experience

One characteristic of developed economies is liquid debt markets.

a. Shadow Open Market Committee
b. Second-round effect
c. Money creation
d. Capital control

17. The European _____, was a system introduced by the European Community in March 1979, as part of the European Monetary System (EMS), to reduce exchange rate variability and achieve monetary stability in Europe, in preparation for Economic and Monetary Union and the introduction of a single currency, the euro, which took place on 1 January 1999. Subsequent exchange rate agreements made with countries wishing to join the Eurozone are known as _____ II.

The _____ is based on the concept of fixed currency exchange rate margins, but with exchange rates variable within those margins.

a. European Monetary System
b. European Monetary Union
c. Euro Interbank Offered Rate
d. Exchange rate mechanism

18. _____ refers to the objective and subjective components of the believability of a source or message.

Traditionally, _____ has two key components: trustworthiness and expertise, which both have objective and subjective components. Trustworthiness is a based more on subjective factors, but can include objective measurements such as established reliability.

a. Credibility
b. 100-year flood
c. 130-30 fund
d. 1921 recession

19. _____ is a measure of the strength of a brand, product, service relative to competitive offerings. There is often a geographic element to the competitive landscape. In defining _____, you must see to what extent a product, brand, or firm controls a product category in a given geographic area.

a. Horizontal territorial allocation
b. Demand shaping
c. Price elasticity of supply
d. Market dominance

20. A _____ is a duty imposed on goods when they are moved across a political boundary. They are usually associated with protectionism, the economic policy of restraining trade between nations. For political reasons, _____s are usually imposed on imported goods, although they may also be imposed on exported goods.

a. 130-30 fund
b. 100-year flood
c. 1921 recession
d. Tariff

21. The _____ are two of the treaties of the European Union signed on March 25, 1957. Both treaties were signed by The Six: Belgium, France, Italy, Luxembourg, the Netherlands and West Germany.

The first established the European Economic Community and the second established the European Atomic Energy Community (EAEC or Euratom.)

Chapter 20. Optimum Currency Areas and the European Experience

a. Treaties of Rome
c. Treaty of Amsterdam
b. Maastricht Treaty
d. 100-year flood

22. _____s is the social science that studies the production, distribution, and consumption of goods and services. The term _____s comes from the Ancient Greek oἰκονομῐ́α from oἶκος (oikos, 'house') + νόμος (nomos, 'custom' or 'law'), hence 'rules of the house(hold)'. Current _____ models developed out of the broader field of political economy in the late 19th century, owing to a desire to use an empirical approach more akin to the physical sciences.
   a. Inflation
   c. Economic
   b. Opportunity cost
   d. Energy economics

23. An _____ is a single market with a common currency. It is to be distinguished from a mere currency union, which does not involve a single market. This is the fifth stage of economic integration.
   a. Economic and monetary union
   c. Incoterms
   b. ATA Carnet
   d. Import quota

24. The _____ is one of the world's most important central banks, responsible for monetary policy covering the 16 member States of the Eurozone. It was established by the European Union (EU) in 1998 with its headquarters in Frankfurt, Germany.

The predecessor to the _____ was the European Monetary Institute.

   a. ACCRA Cost of Living Index
   c. ACEA agreement
   b. European Central Bank
   d. AD-IA Model

25. The _____ was signed on 7 February 1992 in Maastricht, the Netherlands after final negotiations on 9 December 1991 between the members of the European Community and entered into force on 1 November 1993 during the Delors Commission. It created the European Union and led to the creation of the euro. The _____ has been amended to a degree by later treaties.
   a. Treaty of Amsterdam
   c. 100-year flood
   b. Treaties of Rome
   d. Maastricht Treaty

26. _____ refers to the actions that governments take in the economic field. It covers the systems for setting interest rates and government deficit as well as the labour market, national ownership, and many other areas of government.

Such policies are often influenced by international institutions like the International Monetary Fund or World Bank as well as political beliefs and the consequent policies of parties.

   a. ACCRA Cost of Living Index
   c. AD-IA Model
   b. ACEA agreement
   d. Economic policy

27. In economics, an _____ is a geographical region in which it would maximize economic efficiency to have the entire region share a single currency. It describes the optimal characteristics for the merger of currencies or the creation of a new currency. The theory is used often to argue whether or not a certain region is ready to become a monetary union, one of the final stages in economic integration.

Chapter 20. Optimum Currency Areas and the European Experience

    a. Optimum currency area
    c. Overshooting model
    b. International finance
    d. International investment position

28. _____ is a term used to describe how different aspects between economies are integrated. The basics of this theory were written by the Hungarian Economist Béla Balassa in the 1960s. As _____ increases, the barriers of trade between markets diminishes.
    a. Import
    c. Inward investment
    b. Import license
    d. Economic integration

29. _____ refers to an absence of excessive fluctuations in the macroeconomy. An economy with fairly constant output growth and low and stable inflation would be considered economically stable. An economy with frequent large recessions, a pronounced business cycle, very high or variable inflation, or frequent financial crises would be considered economically unstable.
    a. Export subsidy
    c. Income effect
    b. Export-led growth
    d. Economic stability

30. A fixed exchange rate, sometimes called a _____, is a type of exchange rate regime wherein a currency's value is matched to the value of another single currency or to a basket of other currencies such as gold.

A fixed exchange rate is usually used to stabilize the value of a currency, vis-a-vis the currency it is pegged to. This facilitates trade and investments between the two countries, and is especially useful for small economies where external trade forms a large part of their GDP.
    a. Leading indicators
    c. Mainstream economics
    b. Recession
    d. Pegged exchange rate

31. Economics:

- _____,the desire to own something and the ability to pay for it
- _____ curve,a graphic representation of a _____ schedule
- _____ deposit, the money in checking accounts
- _____ pull theory,the theory that inflation occurs when _____ for goods and services exceeds existing supplies
- _____ schedule,a table that lists the quantity of a good a person will buy it each different price
- _____ side economics,the school of economics at believes government spending and tax cuts open economy by raising _____

    a. Production
    c. Demand
    b. McKesson ' Robbins scandal
    d. Variability

32. The _____ was a period of financial crisis that gripped much of Asia beginning in July 1997, and raised fears of a worldwide economic meltdown (financial contagion.)

Chapter 20. Optimum Currency Areas and the European Experience

The crisis started in Thailand with the financial collapse of the Thai baht caused by the decision of the Thai government to float the baht, cutting its peg to the USD, after exhaustive efforts to support it in the face of a severe financial overextension that was in part real estate driven. At the time, Thailand had acquired a burden of foreign debt that made the country effectively bankrupt even before the collapse of its currency.

   a. ACEA agreement
   b. ACCRA Cost of Living Index
   c. AD-IA Model
   d. Asian financial crisis

33. _____ was an arrangement established in 1979 under the Jenkins European Commission where most nations of the European Economic Community (EEC) linked their currencies to prevent large fluctuations relative to one another.

After the collapse of the Bretton Woods system in 1971, most of the EEC countries agreed in 1972 to maintain stable exchange rates by preventing exchange fluctuations of more than 2.25% (the European 'currency snake'.) In March 1979, this system was replaced by the _____, and the European Currency Unit (ECU) was defined.

   a. Euro Interbank Offered Rate
   b. Exchange rate mechanism
   c. European Monetary Union
   d. European Monetary System

34. In macroeconomics, _____ is a condition of the national economy, where all or nearly all persons willing and able to work at the prevailing wages and working conditions are able to do so. It is defined either as 0% unemployment, literally, no unemployment (the rate of unemployment is the fraction of the work force unable to find work), as by James Tobin, or as the level of employment rates when there is no cyclical unemployment. It is defined by the majority of mainstream economists as being an acceptable level of natural unemployment above 0%, the discrepancy from 0% being due to non-cyclical types of unemployment.
   a. Full employment
   b. Harrod-Johnson diagram
   c. Marginal propensity to consume
   d. Demand shock

35. A _____ secures the proper functioning of money by regulating economic agents, transaction types, and money supply.

_____s are traditionally formed by the policy decisions of individual governments and administrated as a domestic economic issue.

The current trend, however, is to use international trade and investment to alter the policy and legislation of individual governments.

   a. Netting
   b. Monetary System
   c. Consumer basket
   d. Financial rand

36. The term _____ is applied broadly to a variety of situations in which some financial institutions or assets suddenly lose a large part of their value. In the 19th and early 20th centuries, many financial crises were associated with banking panics, and many recessions coincided with these panics. Other situations that are often called financial crises include stock market crashes and the bursting of other financial bubbles, currency crises, and sovereign defaults.

Chapter 20. Optimum Currency Areas and the European Experience

a. Market failure
b. Co-operative economics
c. Macroeconomics
d. Financial crisis

37. In economics, _____ is the total amount of money available in an economy at a particular point in time. There are several ways to define 'money', but standard measures usually include currency in circulation and demand deposits.

_____ data are recorded and published, usually by the government or the central bank of the country.

a. Money supply
b. Neutrality of money
c. Velocity of money
d. Veil of money

38. _____ or worker mobility is the socioeconomic ease with which an individual or groups of individuals who are currently receiving remuneration in the form of wages can take advantage of various economic opportunities.

Worker mobility is best gauged by the lack of impediments to such mobility. Impediments to mobility are easily divided into two distinct classes with one being personal and the other being systemic.

a. Physical quality-of-life index
b. Labor mobility
c. Genuine progress indicator
d. Purchasing power

39. _____ is a type of trade policy that allows traders to act and transact without interference from government. Thus, the policy permits trading partners mutual gains from trade, with goods and services produced according to the theory of comparative advantage.

Under a _____ policy, prices are a reflection of true supply and demand, and are the sole determinant of resource allocation.

a. Free trade
b. 100-year flood
c. 1921 recession
d. 130-30 fund

40. _____ is exchange of capital, goods, and services across international borders or territories. In most countries, it represents a significant share of gross domestic product (GDP.) While _____ has been present throughout much of history, its economic, social, and political importance has been on the rise in recent centuries.

a. Import license
b. Incoterms
c. Intra-industry trade
d. International trade

41. _____ is a common concept in economics, and gives rise to derived concepts such as consumer debt. Generally _____ is defined by opposition to production. But the precise definition can vary because different schools of economists define production quite differently.

a. Federal Reserve Bank Notes
b. Cash or share options
c. Consumption
d. Foreclosure data providers

Chapter 20. Optimum Currency Areas and the European Experience

42. A _____ or labor union is an organization of workers who have banded together to achieve common goals in key areas and working conditions. The _____, through its leadership, bargains with the employer on behalf of union members (rank and file members) and negotiates labor contracts (Collective bargaining) with employers. This may include the negotiation of wages, work rules, complaint procedures, rules governing hiring, firing and promotion of workers, benefits, workplace safety and policies.

   a. Case-Shiller Home Price Indices
   b. Guaranteed investment contracts
   c. Consumer goods
   d. Trade union

43. The term _____ refers to government debt, expenditures and revenues, or to finance (particularly financial revenue) in general.

   - _____ deficit is the budget deficit of federal or local government
   - _____ policy is the discretionary spending of governments. Contrasts with monetary policy.
   - _____ year and _____ quarter are reporting periods for firms and other agencies.

   a. Bucket shop
   b. Procter ' Gamble
   c. Drawdown
   d. Fiscal

44. As a subfield of public economics, _____ is concerned with 'understanding which functions and instruments are best centralized and which are best placed in the sphere of decentralized levels of government' (Oates, 1999.) In other words, it is the study of how competencies (expenditure side) and fiscal instruments (revenue side) are allocated across different (vertical) layers of the administration.

   An important part of its subject matter is the system of transfer payments or grants by which a central government shares its revenues with lower levels of government.

   a. 100-year flood
   b. 130-30 fund
   c. 1921 recession
   d. Fiscal federalism

Chapter 21. The Global Capital Market: Performance and Policy Problems

1. The _____ is the market for securities, where companies and governments can raise longterm funds. It is a market in which money is lent for periods longer than a year. The _____ includes the stock market and the bond market.
   a. Multi-family office
   b. Performance attribution
   c. Financial instrument
   d. Capital market

2. In finance, the _____s between two currencies specifies how much one currency is worth in terms of the other. It is the value of a foreign natione;s currency in terms of the home natione;s currency. For example an _____ of 102 Japanese yen to the United States dollar means that JPY 102 is worth the same as USD 1.
   a. ACCRA Cost of Living Index
   b. Exchange rate
   c. ACEA agreement
   d. Interbank market

3. _____ is a concept in economics, finance, and psychology related to the behaviour of consumers and investors under uncertainty. _____ is the reluctance of a person to accept a bargain with an uncertain payoff rather than another bargain with a more certain, but possibly lower, expected payoff. For example, a risk-averse investor might choose to put his or her money into a bank account with a low but guaranteed interest rate, rather than into a stock that is likely to have high returns, but also has a chance of becoming worthless.
   a. Risk theory
   b. Compound annual growth rate
   c. Reinsurance
   d. Risk aversion

4. _____ is a type of trade policy that allows traders to act and transact without interference from government. Thus, the policy permits trading partners mutual gains from trade, with goods and services produced according to the theory of comparative advantage.

   Under a _____ policy, prices are a reflection of true supply and demand, and are the sole determinant of resource allocation.

   a. 130-30 fund
   b. 100-year flood
   c. 1921 recession
   d. Free trade

5. _____ is exchange of capital, goods, and services across international borders or territories. In most countries, it represents a significant share of gross domestic product (GDP.) While _____ has been present throughout much of history , its economic, social, and political importance has been on the rise in recent centuries.
   a. International trade
   b. Incoterms
   c. Import license
   d. Intra-industry trade

6. In business and accounting, _____ are everything of value that is owned by a person or company. It is a claim on the property your income of a borrower. The balance sheet of a firm records the monetary value of the _____ owned by the firm.
   a. ACEA agreement
   b. Amortization schedule
   c. ACCRA Cost of Living Index
   d. Assets

7. The _____ was a period of financial crisis that gripped much of Asia beginning in July 1997, and raised fears of a worldwide economic meltdown (financial contagion.)

The crisis started in Thailand with the financial collapse of the Thai baht caused by the decision of the Thai government to float the baht, cutting its peg to the USD, after exhaustive efforts to support it in the face of a severe financial overextension that was in part real estate driven. At the time, Thailand had acquired a burden of foreign debt that made the country effectively bankrupt even before the collapse of its currency.

a. ACEA agreement
c. ACCRA Cost of Living Index
b. AD-IA Model
d. Asian financial crisis

8. _____ is that which is owed; usually referencing assets owed, but the term can also cover moral obligations and other interactions not requiring money. In the case of assets, _____ is a means of using future purchasing power in the present before a summation has been earned. Some companies and corporations use _____ as a part of their overall corporate finance strategy.
   a. Debt
   c. Hard money loan
   b. Debenture
   d. Collateral Management

9. _____ is the concept or idea of fairness in economics, particularly as to taxation or welfare economics.

In welfare economics, _____ may be distinguished from economic efficiency in overall evaluation of social welfare. Although '_____' has broader uses, it may be posed as a counterpart to economic inequality in yielding a 'good' distribution of welfare.

a. ACCRA Cost of Living Index
c. ACEA agreement
b. AD-IA Model
d. Equity

10. The term _____ is applied broadly to a variety of situations in which some financial institutions or assets suddenly lose a large part of their value. In the 19th and early 20th centuries, many financial crises were associated with banking panics, and many recessions coincided with these panics. Other situations that are often called financial crises include stock market crashes and the bursting of other financial bubbles, currency crises, and sovereign defaults.
    a. Macroeconomics
    c. Co-operative economics
    b. Market failure
    d. Financial crisis

11. A _____, reserve bank, or monetary authority is the entity responsible for the monetary policy of a country or of a group of member states. It is a bank that can lend money to other banks in times of need. Its primary responsibility is to maintain the stability of the national currency and money supply, but more active duties include controlling subsidized-loan interest rates, and acting as a lender of last resort to the banking sector during times of financial crisis (private banks often being integral to the national financial system.)
    a. 130-30 fund
    c. 100-year flood
    b. 1921 recession
    d. Central bank

12.

A _____ is a type of financial intermediary and a type of bank. Commercial banking is also known as business banking. It is a bank that provides checking accounts, savings accounts, and money market accounts and that accepts time deposits.

a. Commercial bank
b. Daylight overdraft
c. Bought deal
d. Lombard banking

13. The _____ consists of a number of economic theories which describe the nature of the firm, company including its existence, its behaviour, and its relationship with the market.

In simplified terms, the _____ aims to answer these questions:

1. Existence - why do firms emerge, why are not all transactions in the economy mediated over the market?
2. Boundaries - why the boundary between firms and the market is located exactly there? Which transactions are performed internally and which are negotiated on the market?
3. Organization - why are firms structured in such specific way? What is the interplay of formal and informal relationships?

Despite looking simple, these questions are not answered by the established economic theory, which usually views firms as given, and treats them as black boxes without any internal structure.

The First World War period saw a change of emphasis in economic theory away from industry-level analysis which mainly included analysing markets to analysis at the level of the firm, as it became increasingly clear that perfect competition was no longer an adequate model of how firms behaved. Economic theory till then had focussed on trying to understand markets alone and there had been little study on understanding why firms or organisations exist.

a. Policy Ineffectiveness Proposition
b. Theory of the firm
c. Khazzoom-Brookes postulate
d. Technology gap

14. An _____ is a financial institution that raises capital, trades in securities and manages corporate mergers and acquisitions. _____s profit from companies and governments by raising money through issuing and selling securities in the capital markets (both equity, bond) and insuring bonds (selling credit default swaps), as well as providing advice on transactions such as mergers and acquisitions. To perform these services in the United States, an adviser must be a licensed broker-dealer, and is subject to SEC (FINRA) regulation see SEC.

a. Annual percentage rate
b. Anonymous internet banking
c. Interbanca
d. Investment bank

15. A _____ association is a financial institution that specializes in accepting savings deposits and making mortgage and other loans. The S'L or thrift term is mainly used in the United States; similar institutions in the United Kingdom, Ireland and some Commonwealth countries include building societies and trustee savings banks.

They are often mutually held, meaning that the depositors and borrowers are members with voting rights, and have the ability to direct the financial and managerial goals of the organization, similar to the policyholders of a mutual insurance company.

a. Collective investment scheme
b. Participating policy
c. Fonds commun de placement
d. Savings and loan

16. In economics, _____ describes the state of a market with respect to competition.

- Perfect competition, in which the market consists of a very large number of firms producing a homogeneous product.
- Monopolistic competition where there are a large number of independent firms which have a very small proportion of the market share.
- Oligopoly, in which a market is dominated by a small number of firms which own more than 40% of the market share.
- Oligopsony, a market dominated by many sellers and a few buyers.
- Monopoly, where there is only one provider of a product or service.
- Natural monopoly, a monopoly in which economies of scale cause efficiency to increase continuously with the size of the firm. A firm is a natural monopoly if it is able to serve the entire market demand at a lower cost than any combination of two or more smaller, more specialized firms.
- Monopsony, when there is only one buyer in a market.

The imperfectly competitive structure is quite identical to the realistic market conditions where some monopolistic competitors, monopolists, oligopolists, and duopolists exist and dominate the market conditions. The elements of _____ include the number and size distribution of firms, entry conditions, and the extent of differentiation.

These somewhat abstract concerns tend to determine some but not all details of a specific concrete market system where buyers and sellers actually meet and commit to trade.

a. Monopolistic competition
b. Human capital
c. Labour economics
d. Market structure

17. _____ is money accepted for exchange of goods in an economy. The prevalence of one money over another arises, usually, when a government designates through decrees that the government shall accept only particular notes and coins in payment for taxes. Typically, money of _____ consists of stamped coins and minted paper bills.
a. Security thread
b. Totnes pound
c. Local currency
d. Currency

18. The _____ is the official currency of 16 of the 27 member states of the European Union (EU.) The states, known collectively as the Eurozone, are Austria, Belgium, Cyprus, Finland, France, Germany, Greece, Ireland, Italy, Luxembourg, Malta, the Netherlands, Portugal, Slovakia, Slovenia, and Spain. The currency is also used in a further five European countries, with and without formal agreements and is consequently used daily by some 327 million Europeans.
a. Equity capital market
b. IRS Code 3401
c. Import and Export Price Indices
d. Euro

19. An offshore bank is a bank located outside the country of residence of the depositor, typically in a low tax jurisdiction (or tax haven) that provides financial and legal advantages. These advantages typically include:

- greater privacy
- low or no taxation (i.e. tax havens)
- easy access to deposits (at least in terms of regulation)
- protection against local political or financial instability

While the term originates from the Channel Islands being 'offshore' from the United Kingdom, and most offshore banks are located in island nations to this day, the term is used figuratively to refer to such banks regardless of location, including Swiss banks and those of other landlocked nations such as Luxembourg and Andorra.

_____ has often been associated with the underground economy and organized crime, via tax evasion and money laundering; however, legally, _____ does not prevent assets from being subject to personal income tax on interest. Except for certain persons who meet fairly complex requirements, the personal income tax of many countries makes no distinction between interest earned in local banks and those earned abroad.

   a. ACCRA Cost of Living Index
   b. Offshore banking
   c. Offshore bank
   d. Exchange of information

20. The _____ was the continuing state of conflict, tension, and competition that existed after World War II between the Soviet Union and its satellites and the powers of the Western world under the leadership of the United States from the mid-1940s to the early 1990s. Throughout this period, the conflict was expressed through military coalitions, espionage, weapons development, invasions, propaganda, and competitive technological development, which included the space race. The conflict included costly defense spending, a massive conventional and nuclear arms race, and numerous proxy wars; the two superpowers never fought one another directly.
   a. Reagan Doctrine
   b. Mutual assured destruction
   c. Sino-Soviet split
   d. Cold War

21. _____s are deposits denominated in US dollars at banks outside the United States, and thus are not under the jurisdiction of the Federal Reserve. Consequently, such deposits are subject to much less regulation than similar deposits within the United States, allowing for higher margins. There is nothing 'European' about _____ deposits; a US dollar-denominated deposit in Tokyo or Caracas would likewise be deemed _____ deposits.
   a. ACEA agreement
   b. AD-IA Model
   c. Eurodollar
   d. ACCRA Cost of Living Index

22. The _____ is a bank regulation that sets the minimum reserves each bank must hold to customer deposits and notes. It would normally be in the form of fiat currency stored in a bank vault (vault cash), or with a central bank.

The reserve ratio is sometimes used as a tool in the monetary policy, influencing the country's economy, borrowing, and interest rates.

   a. Probability of default
   b. Fractional-reserve banking
   c. Reserve requirement
   d. Private money

23. A _____ or a flexible exchange rate is a type of exchange rate regime wherein a currency's value is allowed to fluctuate according to the foreign exchange market. A currency that uses a _____ is known as a floating currency. The opposite of a _____ is a fixed exchange rate.
   a. Foreign exchange market
   b. Floating currency
   c. Trade Weighted US dollar Index
   d. Floating exchange rate

24. A _____ occurs when a bank is unable to meet its obligations to its depositors or other creditors. More specifically, a bank fails economically when the market value of its assets declines to a value that is less than the market value of its liabilities. As such, the bank is unable to fulfill the demands of all of its depositors on time.
   a. Bank failure
   b. Lombard Club
   c. Transactional account
   d. Concentration account

25. _____s are a form of government regulation which subject banks to certain requirements, restrictions and guidelines.

The objectives of _____, and the emphasis, varies between jurisdiction. The most common objectives are:

   1. Prudential -- to reduce the level of risk bank creditors are exposed to (i.e. to protect depositors)
   2. Systemic risk reduction -- to reduce the risk of disruption resulting from adverse trading conditions for banks causing multiple or major bank failures
   3. Avoid misuse of banks -- to reduce the risk of banks being used for criminal purposes, e.g. laundering the proceeds of crime
   4. To protect banking confidentiality
   5. Credit allocation -- to direct credit to favored sectors

Banking regulations can vary widely across nations and jurisdictions

   a. Patent portfolio
   b. Property right
   c. Bank regulation
   d. Buydown

26. The _____ is a bank regulation, which sets a framework on how banks and depository institutions must handle their capital. The categorization of assets and capital is highly standardized so that it can be risk weighted. Internationally, the Basel Committee on Banking Supervision housed at the Bank for International Settlements influence each country's banking _____s.
   a. Banking agent
   b. Time deposit
   c. Bank run
   d. Capital requirement

27. Discounting is a financial mechanism in which a debtor obtains the right to delay payments to a creditor, for a defined period of time, in exchange for a charge or fee. Essentially, the party that owes money in the present purchases the right to delay the payment until some future date. The _____, or charge, is simply the difference between the original amount owed in the present and the amount that has to be paid in the future to settle the debt.
   a. Certified Risk Manager
   b. Reliability theory
   c. Discount
   d. Reinsurance

28. The _____ is an instrument of monetary policy (usually controlled by central banks) that allows eligible institutions to borrow money from the central bank, usually on a short-term basis, to meet temporary shortages of liquidity caused by internal or external disruptions. The term originated with the practice of sending a bank representative to a reserve bank teller window when a bank needed to borrow money.

The interest rate charged on such loans by a central bank is called the discount rate, base rate, repo rate, or primary rate.

Chapter 21. The Global Capital Market: Performance and Policy Problems 169

    a. Capital requirement
    b. Private money
    c. Prime rate
    d. Discount window

29. The _____ is a United States government corporation created by the Glass-Steagall Act of 1933. It provides deposit insurance, which guarantees the safety of deposits in member banks, currently up to $250,000 per depositor per bank. Funds in non-interest bearing transaction accounts are fully insured, with no limit, under the temporary Transaction Account Guarantee Program.
    a. Foreign direct investment
    b. Luxembourg Income Study
    c. Great Leap Forward
    d. Federal Deposit Insurance Corporation

30. _____, in law and economics, is a form of risk management primarily used to hedge against the risk of a contingent loss. _____ is defined as the equitable transfer of the risk of a loss, from one entity to another, in exchange for a premium, and can be thought of as a guaranteed small loss to prevent a large, possibly devastating loss. An insurer is a company selling the _____; an insured or policyholder is the person or entity buying the _____.
    a. ACEA agreement
    b. ACCRA Cost of Living Index
    c. Insurance
    d. AD-IA Model

31. A _____ is an institution willing to extend credit when no one else will.

Originally the term referred to a reserve financial institution that secured other banks or eligible institutions, as a last resort; most often the central bank of a country. The purpose of this loan and lender is to prevent the collapse of institutions that are experiencing financial difficulty, most often near collapse.

    a. Capital requirement
    b. Lender of last resort
    c. Transactional account
    d. Time deposit

32. In economics, the _____ measures the payments that flow between any individual country and all other countries. It is used to summarize all international economic transactions for that country during a specific time period, usually a year. The _____ is determined by the country's exports and imports of goods, services, and financial capital, as well as financial transfers.
    a. Gross domestic product per barrel
    b. Skyscraper Index
    c. Gross world product
    d. Balance of payments

33. A _____ is the transfer of wealth from one party (such as a person or company) to another. A _____ is usually made in exchange for the provision of goods, services or both, or to fulfill a legal obligation.

The simplest and oldest form of _____ is barter, the exchange of one good or service for another.

    a. Soft count
    b. Social gravity
    c. Going concern
    d. Payment

34. _____ is the removal or simplification of government rules and regulations that constrain the operation of market forces. _____ does not mean elimination of laws against fraud, but eliminating or reducing government control of how business is done, thereby moving toward a more free market.

The stated rationale for '_____' is often that fewer and simpler regulations will lead to a raised level of competitiveness, therefore higher productivity, more efficiency and lower prices overall.

a. Fundamental psychological law
b. Macroeconomic policy instruments
c. Secular basis
d. Deregulation

35. _____ is a fee paid on borrowed assets. It is the price paid for the use of borrowed money, or, money earned by deposited funds. Assets that are sometimes lent with _____ include money, shares, consumer goods through hire purchase, major assets such as aircraft, and even entire factories in finance lease arrangements.

a. Internal debt
b. Asset protection
c. Interest
d. Insolvency

36. An _____ is the price a borrower pays for the use of money they do not own, for instance a small company might borrow from a bank to kick start their business, and the return a lender receives for deferring the use of funds, by lending it to the borrower. _____s are normally expressed as a percentage rate over the period of one year.

_____s targets are also a vital tool of monetary policy and are used to control variables like investment, inflation, and unemployment.

a. Arrow-Debreu model
b. Enterprise value
c. ACCRA Cost of Living Index
d. Interest rate

37. The _____ of monetary management established the rules for commercial and financial relations among the world's major industrial states in the mid 20th Century. The _____ was the first example of a fully negotiated monetary order intended to govern monetary relations among independent nation-states.

Preparing to rebuild the international economic system as World War II was still raging, 730 delegates from all 44 Allied nations gathered at the Mount Washington Hotel in Bretton Woods, New Hampshire, United States, for the United Nations Monetary and Financial Conference.

a. Bretton Woods system
b. 130-30 fund
c. 1921 recession
d. 100-year flood

38. The term financial crisis is applied broadly to a variety of situations in which some financial institutions or assets suddenly lose a large part of their value. In the 19th and early 20th centuries, many _____ were associated with banking panics, and many recessions coincided with these panics. Other situations that are often called _____ include stock market crashes and the bursting of other financial bubbles, currency crises, and sovereign defaults.

a. General equilibrium
b. Microeconomics
c. Georgism
d. Financial crises

39. _____, in economics, is the period of time required for economic agents to reallocate resources, and generally reestablish equilibrium.

The actual length of this period, usually numbered in years or decades, varies widely depending on circumstantial context. During the _____, all factors are variable.

a. Producer surplus
c. Government surplus
b. Temporary equilibrium method
d. Long Term

40. _____ is the prospect that a party insulated from risk may behave differently from the way it would behave if it were fully exposed to the risk. In insurance, _____ that occurs without conscious or malicious action is called morale hazard.

_____ is related to information asymmetry, a situation in which one party in a transaction has more information than another.

a. 1921 recession
c. 100-year flood
b. 130-30 fund
d. Moral hazard

41. The _____ is where currency trading takes place. It is where banks and other official institutions facilitate the buying and selling of foreign currencies. FX transactions typically involve one party purchasing a quantity of one currency in exchange for paying a quantity of another.
a. Foreign exchange market
c. Currency swap
b. Covered interest arbitrage
d. Floating currency

42. _____ is a concept with somewhat disparate meanings in several fields. It also has a common meaning which has a loose connection with some of those more definite meanings.

Casually, it is typically used to denote a lack of order, or purpose, or cause.

a. 100-year flood
c. 1921 recession
b. 130-30 fund
d. Randomness

43. A _____, sometimes denoted _____, is a mathematical formalization of a trajectory that consists of taking successive random steps. The results of _____ analysis have been applied to computer science, physics, ecology, economics, and a number of other fields as a fundamental model for random processes in time. For example, the path traced by a molecule as it travels in a liquid or a gas, the search path of a foraging animal, the price of a fluctuating stock and the financial status of a gambler can all be modeled as _____s.
a. Random walk
c. 100-year flood
b. 1921 recession
d. 130-30 fund

44. A _____ is the minimum difference a person requires to be willing to take an uncertain bet, between the expected value of the bet and the certain value that he is indifferent to.

The certainty equivalent is the guaranteed payoff at which a person is 'indifferent' between accepting the guaranteed payoff and a higher but uncertain payoff. (It is the amount of the higher payout minus the _____.)

a. Ruin theory
c. Risk premium
b. Workers compensation
d. Linear model

Chapter 22. Developing Countries: Growth, Crisis, and Reform

1. _____ is that which is owed; usually referencing assets owed, but the term can also cover moral obligations and other interactions not requiring money. In the case of assets, _____ is a means of using future purchasing power in the present before a summation has been earned. Some companies and corporations use _____ as a part of their overall corporate finance strategy.
   a. Debt
   b. Debenture
   c. Collateral Management
   d. Hard money loan

2. A _____ product is a product designed for cheapness and short-term convenience rather than medium to long-term durability, with most products only intended for single use. The term is also sometimes used for products that may last several months (ex. _____ air filters) to distinguish from similar products that last indefinitely (ex.
   a. 100-year flood
   b. 130-30 fund
   c. 1921 recession
   d. Disposable

3. _____ is a type of trade policy that allows traders to act and transact without interference from government. Thus, the policy permits trading partners mutual gains from trade, with goods and services produced according to the theory of comparative advantage.

   Under a _____ policy, prices are a reflection of true supply and demand, and are the sole determinant of resource allocation.

   a. 100-year flood
   b. 130-30 fund
   c. 1921 recession
   d. Free trade

4. In calculus, a function f defined on a subset of the real numbers with real values is called _____, if for all x and y such that x >≤ y one has f(x) >≤ f(y), so f preserves the order. In layman's terms, the sign of the slope is always positive (the curve tending upwards) or zero (i.e., non-decreasing, or asymptotic, or depicted as a horizontal, flat line) Likewise, a function is called monotonically decreasing (non-increasing) if, whenever x >≤ y, then f(x) >≥ f(y), so it reverses the order.
   a. Monotonic
   b. 100-year flood
   c. 1921 recession
   d. 130-30 fund

5. A _____ is an expression that compares quantities relative to each other. The most common examples involve two quantities, but any number of quantities can be compared. _____s are represented mathematically by separating each quantity with a colon, for example the _____ 2:3, which is read as the _____ 'two to three'.
   a. Y-intercept
   b. 100-year flood
   c. 130-30 fund
   d. Ratio

6. _____ is the net revenue derived from the issuing of currency.

   _____ derived from specie - metal coins - arises from the difference between the face value of a coin and the cost of producing, distributing and retiring it from circulation.

   _____ derived from notes is more indirect, being the difference between interest earned on securities acquired in exchange for bank notes and the costs of producing and distributing those notes.

   a. 130-30 fund
   b. 100-year flood
   c. Money Tracker
   d. Seigniorage

Chapter 22. Developing Countries: Growth, Crisis, and Reform

7. In finance, a _____ is a debt security, in which the authorized issuer owes the holders a debt and, depending on the terms of the _____, is obliged to pay interest (the coupon) and/or to repay the principal at a later date, termed maturity. A _____ is a formal contract to repay borrowed money with interest at fixed intervals.

Thus a _____ is like a loan: the issuer is the borrower (debtor), the holder is the lender (creditor), and the coupon is the interest.

a. Prize Bond
b. Zero-coupon
c. Callable
d. Bond

8. _____ is the concept or idea of fairness in economics, particularly as to taxation or welfare economics.

In welfare economics, _____ may be distinguished from economic efficiency in overall evaluation of social welfare. Although '_____' has broader uses, it may be posed as a counterpart to economic inequality in yielding a 'good' distribution of welfare.

a. AD-IA Model
b. ACEA agreement
c. ACCRA Cost of Living Index
d. Equity

9. In economics and finance, _____ represents passive holdings of securities such as foreign stocks, bonds none of which entails active management or control of the securities' issuer by the investor; where such control exists, it is known as foreign direct investment. Generally, this means the investor holds less than 10% of the total shares or less than the amount needed to hold the majority vote.

Some examples of _____ are:

- purchase of shares in a foreign company.
- purchase of bonds issued by a foreign government.
- acquisition of assets in a foreign country.

Factors affecting international _____:

- tax rates on interest or dividends (investors will normally prefer countries where the tax rates are relatively low)
- interest rates (money tends to flow to countries with high interest rates)
- exchange rates (foreign investors may be attracted if the local currency is expected to strengthen)

_____ is part of the capital account on the balance of payments statistics.

a. Fund administration
b. Retirement Compensation Arrangements
c. CAN SLIM
d. Portfolio investment

10. _____ is the incidence or process of transferring ownership of a business, enterprise, agency or public service from the public sector (government) to the private sector (business.) In a broader sense, _____ refers to transfer of any government function to the private sector including governmental functions like revenue collection and law enforcement.

The term '_____' also has been used to describe two unrelated transactions.

a. Ricardian equivalence
b. Compound empowerment
c. Performance reports
d. Privatization

11. The _____ was a period of financial crisis that gripped much of Asia beginning in July 1997, and raised fears of a worldwide economic meltdown (financial contagion.)

The crisis started in Thailand with the financial collapse of the Thai baht caused by the decision of the Thai government to float the baht, cutting its peg to the USD, after exhaustive efforts to support it in the face of a severe financial overextension that was in part real estate driven. At the time, Thailand had acquired a burden of foreign debt that made the country effectively bankrupt even before the collapse of its currency.

a. ACEA agreement
b. Asian financial crisis
c. ACCRA Cost of Living Index
d. AD-IA Model

12. The _____ of monetary management established the rules for commercial and financial relations among the world's major industrial states in the mid 20th Century. The _____ was the first example of a fully negotiated monetary order intended to govern monetary relations among independent nation-states.

Preparing to rebuild the international economic system as World War II was still raging, 730 delegates from all 44 Allied nations gathered at the Mount Washington Hotel in Bretton Woods, New Hampshire, United States, for the United Nations Monetary and Financial Conference.

a. 1921 recession
b. 130-30 fund
c. Bretton Woods System
d. 100-year flood

13. _____, in economics, occurs when assets and/or money rapidly flow out of a country, due to an economic event that disturbs investors and causes them to lower their valuation of the assets in that country, or otherwise to lose confidence in its economic strength. This leads to a disappearance of wealth and is usually accompanied by a sharp drop in the exchange rate of the affected country (depreciation in a variable exchange rate regime, or a forced devaluation in a fixed exchange rate regime.)

This fall is particularly damaging when the capital belongs to the people of the affected country, because not only are the citizens now burdened by the loss of faith in the economy and devaluation of their currency, but probably also their assets have lost much of their nominal value.

a. Firm-specific infrastructure
b. Capital formation
c. Liquid capital
d. Capital flight

Chapter 22. Developing Countries: Growth, Crisis, and Reform 175

14. The _____ is the central banking system of the United States. Created in 1913 by the enactment of the Federal Reserve Act (signed by Woodrow Wilson), it is a quasi-public and quasi-private (government entity with private components) banking system that comprises (1) the presidentially appointed Board of Governors of the _____ in Washington, D.C.; (2) the Federal Open Market Committee; (3) twelve regional Federal Reserve Banks located in major cities throughout the nation acting as fiscal agents for the U.S. Treasury, each with its own nine-member board of directors; (4) numerous other private U.S. member banks, which subscribe to required amounts of non-transferable stock in their regional Federal Reserve Banks; and (5) various advisory councils. Since February 2006, Ben Bernanke has served as the Chairman of the Board of Governors of the _____.
   a. Federal Reserve System Open Market Account
   b. Monetary Policy Report to the Congress
   c. Term auction facility
   d. Federal Reserve System

15. _____ is a fee paid on borrowed assets. It is the price paid for the use of borrowed money, or, money earned by deposited funds. Assets that are sometimes lent with _____ include money, shares, consumer goods through hire purchase, major assets such as aircraft, and even entire factories in finance lease arrangements.
   a. Asset protection
   b. Insolvency
   c. Internal debt
   d. Interest

16. An _____ is the price a borrower pays for the use of money they do not own, for instance a small company might borrow from a bank to kick start their business, and the return a lender receives for deferring the use of funds, by lending it to the borrower. _____s are normally expressed as a percentage rate over the period of one year.

   _____s targets are also a vital tool of monetary policy and are used to control variables like investment, inflation, and unemployment.
   a. Interest rate
   b. Arrow-Debreu model
   c. Enterprise value
   d. ACCRA Cost of Living Index

17. In economics, the _____ measures the payments that flow between any individual country and all other countries. It is used to summarize all international economic transactions for that country during a specific time period, usually a year. The _____ is determined by the country's exports and imports of goods, services, and financial capital, as well as financial transfers.
   a. Gross world product
   b. Balance of payments
   c. Gross domestic product per barrel
   d. Skyscraper Index

18. The term _____ is applied broadly to a variety of situations in which some financial institutions or assets suddenly lose a large part of their value. In the 19th and early 20th centuries, many financial crises were associated with banking panics, and many recessions coincided with these panics. Other situations that are often called financial crises include stock market crashes and the bursting of other financial bubbles, currency crises, and sovereign defaults.
   a. Macroeconomics
   b. Market failure
   c. Financial crisis
   d. Co-operative economics

19. In economics, _____ is the total amount of money available in an economy at a particular point in time. There are several ways to define 'money', but standard measures usually include currency in circulation and demand deposits.

   _____ data are recorded and published, usually by the government or the central bank of the country.

Chapter 22. Developing Countries: Growth, Crisis, and Reform

a. Neutrality of money
c. Velocity of money
b. Veil of money
d. Money supply

20. A _____ is the transfer of wealth from one party (such as a person or company) to another. A _____ is usually made in exchange for the provision of goods, services or both, or to fulfill a legal obligation.

The simplest and oldest form of _____ is barter, the exchange of one good or service for another.

a. Soft count
c. Social gravity
b. Going concern
d. Payment

21. _____ is the quality of paper money substitutes which entitles the holder to redeem them on demand into money proper.

Historically, the banknote has followed a common or very similar pattern in the western nations. Originally decentralized and issued from various independent banks, it was gradually brought under state control and became a monopoly privilege of the central banks.

a. Dollarization
c. Currency board
b. Convertibility
d. Devaluation

22. _____ is a decrease in the rate of inflation. This phase of the business cycle, in which retailers can no longer pass on higher prices to their customers, often occurs during a recession. In contrast, deflation occurs when prices are actually dropping.

a. Reflation
c. Mundell-Tobin effect
b. Stealth inflation
d. Disinflation

23. _____ is money accepted for exchange of goods in an economy. The prevalence of one money over another arises, usually, when a government designates through decrees that the government shall accept only particular notes and coins in payment for taxes. Typically, money of _____ consists of stamped coins and minted paper bills.

a. Local currency
c. Totnes pound
b. Currency
d. Security thread

24. The _____ is the official currency of 16 of the 27 member states of the European Union (EU.) The states, known collectively as the Eurozone, are Austria, Belgium, Cyprus, Finland, France, Germany, Greece, Ireland, Italy, Luxembourg, Malta, the Netherlands, Portugal, Slovakia, Slovenia, and Spain. The currency is also used in a further five European countries, with and without formal agreements and is consequently used daily by some 327 million Europeans.

a. IRS Code 3401
c. Import and Export Price Indices
b. Equity capital market
d. Euro

25. The _____ is a monetary system in which a region's common medium of exchange are paper notes that are normally freely convertible into pre-set, fixed quantities of gold. The _____ is not currently used by any government, having been replaced completely by fiat currency. Gold certificates were used as paper currency in the United States from 1882 to 1933, these certificates were freely convertable into gold coins.

In the 1790s Britain suffered a massive shortage of silver coinage and ceased to mint larger silver coins.

a. 130-30 fund
c. 1921 recession
b. Gold standard
d. 100-year flood

26. _____ is the prospect that a party insulated from risk may behave differently from the way it would behave if it were fully exposed to the risk. In insurance, _____ that occurs without conscious or malicious action is called morale hazard.

_____ is related to information asymmetry, a situation in which one party in a transaction has more information than another.

a. 1921 recession
c. 130-30 fund
b. Moral hazard
d. 100-year flood

27. _____s is the social science that studies the production, distribution, and consumption of goods and services. The term _____s comes from the Ancient Greek oá¼°κονομῖα from oá¼¶κος (oikos, 'house') + vÏŒμος (nomos, 'custom' or 'law'), hence 'rules of the house(hold)'. Current _____ models developed out of the broader field of political economy in the late 19th century, owing to a desire to use an empirical approach more akin to the physical sciences.

a. Opportunity cost
c. Energy economics
b. Inflation
d. Economic

28. The terms '_____,' 'tiger economy' or simply 'miracle' have come to refer to great periods of change, particularly periods of dramatic economic growth, in the recent histories of a number of countries:

- Baltic Tiger (Estonia, Latvia, Lithuania, c. 2000-present)
- Brazilian miracle (1968-1973)
- Celtic Tiger (Ireland, c. 1990s-2001, 2003-2006)
- Four Asian Tigers (Taiwan, South Korea, Hong Kong, Singapore, c. 1960s-1990s)
    - Miracle on the Han River (South Korea, c. 1950-1997)
    - Taiwan Miracle
- Il Boom (the Italian _____, 1955-1972)
- Greek _____
- Japanese post-war _____
- Massachusetts Miracle (1980s)
- Miracle of Chile (c. 1970's-present)
- Spanish miracle
- Wirtschaftswunder - Post-World War II economic growth in Austria and West Germany
- Trente Glorieuses - Post World War II economic growth in France (c. 1945-1975)

a. Augmentation
c. Economic miracle
b. Appropriation
d. Oslo Agreements

29. In economics, the _____ is one of the two primary components of the balance of payments, the other being the capital account. It is the sum of the balance of trade (exports minus imports of goods and services), net factor income (such as interest and dividends) and net transfer payments (such as foreign aid.)

Chapter 22. Developing Countries: Growth, Crisis, and Reform

$$\text{Current account} = \text{Balance of trade} \\ + \text{Net factor income from abroad} \\ + \text{Net unilateral transfers from abroad}$$

The _____ balance is one of two major metrics of the nature of a country's foreign trade (the other being the net capital outflow.)

a. Current account
b. Gross private domestic investment
c. National Income and Product Accounts
d. Compensation of employees

30. _____ in economics refers to metrics and measures of output from production processes, per unit of input. Labor _____, for example, is typically measured as a ratio of output per labor-hour, an input. _____ may be conceived of as a metrics of the technical or engineering efficiency of production.

a. Fordism
b. Productivity
c. Production-possibility frontier
d. Piece work

31. _____ is a comparative concept of the ability and performance of a firm, sub-sector or country to sell and supply goods and/or services in a given market. Although widely used in economics and business management, the usefulness of the concept, particularly in the context of national _____, is vigorously disputed by economists, such as Paul Krugman.

The term may also be applied to markets, where it is used to refer to the extent to which the market structure may be regarded as perfectly competitive.

a. Quota share
b. Countervailing duties
c. Debt moratorium
d. Competitiveness

32. The term financial crisis is applied broadly to a variety of situations in which some financial institutions or assets suddenly lose a large part of their value. In the 19th and early 20th centuries, many _____ were associated with banking panics, and many recessions coincided with these panics. Other situations that are often called _____ include stock market crashes and the bursting of other financial bubbles, currency crises, and sovereign defaults.

a. Microeconomics
b. General equilibrium
c. Georgism
d. Financial crises

33. In finance, the _____s between two currencies specifies how much one currency is worth in terms of the other. It is the value of a foreign natione;s currency in terms of the home natione;s currency. For example an _____ of 102 Japanese yen to the United States dollar means that JPY 102 is worth the same as USD 1.

a. Interbank market
b. Exchange rate
c. ACEA agreement
d. ACCRA Cost of Living Index

34. _____ is a term used in accounting, economics and finance to spread the cost of an asset over the span of several years.

Chapter 22. Developing Countries: Growth, Crisis, and Reform

In simple words we can say that _____ is the reduction in the value of an asset due to usage, passage of time, wear and tear, technological outdating or obsolescence, depletion, inadequacy, rot, rust, decay or other such factors.

In accounting, _____ is a term used to describe any method of attributing the historical or purchase cost of an asset across its useful life, roughly corresponding to normal wear and tear.

a. Salvage value
b. Historical cost
c. Depreciation
d. Net income per employee

35. A _____ is a duty imposed on goods when they are moved across a political boundary. They are usually associated with protectionism, the economic policy of restraining trade between nations. For political reasons, _____s are usually imposed on imported goods, although they may also be imposed on exported goods.

a. 100-year flood
b. 130-30 fund
c. 1921 recession
d. Tariff

36. A _____ is a monetary authority which is required to maintain a fixed exchange rate with a foreign currency. This policy objective requires the conventional objectives of a central bank to be subordinated to the exchange rate target.

The main qualities of an orthodox _____ are:

- A _____'s foreign currency reserves must be sufficient to ensure that all holders of its notes and coins (and all banks creditor of a Reserve Account at the _____) can convert them into the reserve currency (usually 110-115% of the monetary base M0.)
- A _____ maintains absolute, unlimited convertibility between its notes and coins and the currency against which they are pegged (the anchor currency), at a fixed rate of exchange, with no restrictions on current-account or capital-account transactions.
- A _____ only earns profit from interests on foreign reserves (less the expense of note-issuing), and does not engage in forward-exchange transactions. These foreign reserves exist (1) because local notes have been issued in exchange, or (2) because commercial banks must by regulation deposit a minimum reserve at the _____. (1) generates a seignorage revenue. (2) is the revenue on minimum reserves (revenue of investment activities less cost of minimum reserves remuneration)
- A _____ has no discretionary powers to effect monetary policy and does not lend to the government. Governments cannot print money, and can only tax or borrow to meet their spending commitments.
- A _____ does not act as a lender of last resort to commercial banks, and does not regulate reserve requirements.
- A _____ does not attempt to manipulate interest rates by establishing a discount rate like a central bank. The peg with the foreign currency tends to keep interest rates and inflation very closely aligned to those in the country against whose currency the peg is fixed.

The _____ in question will no longer issue fiat money but instead will only issue one unit of local currency for each unit (or decided amount) of foreign currency it has in its vault (often a hard currency such as the U.S. dollar or the euro.) The surplus on the balance of payments of that country is reflected by higher deposits local banks hold at the central bank as well as (initially) higher deposits of the (net) exporting firms at their local banks.

a. Petrodollar
b. Currency competition
c. Reserve currency
d. Currency board

37. In economics, an _____ is any good or commodity, transported from one country to another country in a legitimate fashion, typically for use in trade. _____ goods or services are provided to foreign consumers by domestic producers. _____ is an important part of international trade.
   a. ACEA agreement
   b. AD-IA Model
   c. ACCRA Cost of Living Index
   d. Export

38. _____ is the process by which the government, central bank (ii) availability of money, and (iii) cost of money or rate of interest, in order to attain a set of objectives oriented towards the growth and stability of the economy. Monetary theory provides insight into how to craft optimal _____.

_____ is referred to as either being an expansionary policy where an expansionary policy increases the total supply of money in the economy, and a contractionary policy decreases the total money supply.

   a. Monetary policy
   b. 130-30 fund
   c. 1921 recession
   d. 100-year flood

39. _____ occurs when the inhabitants of a country use foreign currency in parallel to or instead of the domestic currency.

_____ can occur

- unofficially, when private agents prefer the foreign currency over the domestic currency. They hold for example deposits in the foreign currency because of a bad track record of the local currency.

- semiofficially (or officially bimonetary systems), where foreign currency is legal tender, but plays a secondary role to domestic currency
- officially, when a country ceases to issue the domestic currency and uses only foreign currency. It adopts the foreign currency as legal tender.

The term _____ is not only applied to usage of the United States dollar, but also generally to the use of any foreign currency as the national currency.

   a. Dollarization
   b. Commodity money
   c. Currency board
   d. World currency

40. _____ is a common concept in economics, and gives rise to derived concepts such as consumer debt. Generally _____ is defined by opposition to production. But the precise definition can vary because different schools of economists define production quite differently.
   a. Consumption
   b. Foreclosure data providers
   c. Federal Reserve Bank Notes
   d. Cash or share options

Chapter 22. Developing Countries: Growth, Crisis, and Reform

41. In economics, _____ is inflation that is very high or 'out of control', a condition in which prices increase rapidly as a currency loses its value. Definitions used by the media vary from a cumulative inflation rate over three years approaching 100% to 'inflation exceeding 50% a month.' In informal usage the term is often applied to much lower rates. As a rule of thumb, normal inflation is reported per year, but _____ is often reported for much shorter intervals, often per month.
   a. 1921 recession
   b. 130-30 fund
   c. 100-year flood
   d. Hyperinflation

42. In economics, _____ is a rise in the general level of prices of goods and services in an economy over a period of time. When the general price level rises, each unit of currency buys fewer goods and services; consequently, _____ is also a decline in the real value of money--a loss of purchasing power in the medium of exchange which is also the monetary unit of account in the economy. A chief measure of general price-level _____ is the general _____ rate, which is the percentage change in a general price index (normally the Consumer Price Index) over time.
   a. Opportunity cost
   b. Inflation
   c. Energy economics
   d. Economic

43. The _____ is the way a country manages its currency in respect to foreign currencies and the foreign exchange market. It is closely related to monetary policy and the two are generally dependent on many of the same factors.

The basic types are a floating exchange rate, where the market dictates the movements of the exchange rate, a pegged float, where the central bank keeps the rate from deviating too far from a target band or value, and the fixed exchange rate, which ties the currency to another currency, mostly more widespread currencies such as the U.S. dollar or the euro.

   a. ACEA agreement
   b. ACCRA Cost of Living Index
   c. Exchange rate regime
   d. Interbank market

44. A _____ refers to any type debt instrument, such as a loan, bond, mortgage that does not have a fixed rate of interest over the life of the instrument. Such debt typically uses an index or other base rate for establishing the interest rate for each relevant period. One of the most common rates to use as the basis for applying interest rates is the London Inter-bank Offered Rate, or LIBOR
   a. Money market
   b. Moneylender
   c. Floating interest rate
   d. Disposal tax effect

45. In economics, _____ is how a natione;s total economy is distributed among its population. ._____ has always been a central concern of economic theory and economic policy. Classical economists such as Adam Smith, Thomas Malthus and David Ricardo were mainly concerned with factor _____, that is, the distribution of income between the main factors of production, land, labour and capital.
   a. Eco commerce
   b. Equipment trust certificate
   c. Authorised capital
   d. Income distribution

46. _____ is an economic system in which wealth, and the means of producing wealth, are privately owned. Through _____, the land, labor, and capital are owned, operated, and traded for the purpose of generating profits, without force or fraud, by private individuals either singly or jointly, and investments, distribution, income, production, pricing and supply of goods, commodities and services are determined by voluntary private decision in a market economy. A distinguishing feature of _____ is that each person owns his or her own labor and therefore is allowed to sell the use of it to employers.

Chapter 22. Developing Countries: Growth, Crisis, and Reform

a. Capitalism
b. Socialism for the rich and capitalism for the poor
c. Creative capitalism
d. Late capitalism

47. _____ is the increase in the amount of the goods and services produced by an economy over time. It is conventionally measured as the percent rate of increase in real gross domestic product, or real GDP. Growth is usually calculated in real terms, i.e. inflation-adjusted terms, in order to net out the effect of inflation on the price of the goods and services produced.

a. ACCRA Cost of Living Index
b. ACEA agreement
c. AD-IA Model
d. Economic growth

48. A variety of measures of national income and output are used in economics to estimate total economic activity in a country or region, including gross domestic product (GDP), _____ , and net national income (NNI.)

There are three main ways of calculating these numbers; the output approach, the income approach and the expenditure approach. In theory, the three must yield the same, because total expenditures on goods and services must equal the total income paid to the producers (GNI), and that must also equal the total value of the output of goods and services (_____.)

a. Purchasing power parity
b. Gross world product
c. Household final consumption expenditure
d. Gross national product

49. _____ is exchange of capital, goods, and services across international borders or territories. In most countries, it represents a significant share of gross domestic product (GDP.) While _____ has been present throughout much of history , its economic, social, and political importance has been on the rise in recent centuries.

a. Intra-industry trade
b. Import license
c. Incoterms
d. International trade

50. A _____ is the exclusive authority to determine how a resource is used, whether that resource is owned by government or by individuals. All economic goods have a _____s attribute. This attribute has three broad components

1. The right to use the good
2. The right to earn income from the good
3. The right to transfer the good to others

The concept of _____s as used by economists and legal scholars are related but distinct. The distinction is largely seen in the economists' focus on the ability of an individual or collective to control the use of the good.

a. Property right
b. Post-sale restraint
c. High-reeve
d. Holder in due course

51. In economics, _____ is the active redirecting resources from being consumed today so that they may create benefits in the future; the use of assets to earn income or profit. _____ is the process of making an investment in order to earn a profit, for example equity investment either through a fund, a 401k plan, or individually. People often invest in order to build up their estate or to accumulate funds for retirement.

Chapter 22. Developing Countries: Growth, Crisis, and Reform

To try to predict good stocks to invest in, two main schools of thought exist: technical analysis and fundamentals analysis.

a. AD-IA Model
b. ACEA agreement
c. Investing
d. ACCRA Cost of Living Index

52. In statistics, econometrics, epidemiology and related disciplines, the method of _____ is used to estimate causal relationships when controlled experiments are not feasible.

Statistically, _____ methods allow consistent estimation when the explanatory variables (covariates) are correlated with the error terms. Such correlation may occur when the dependent variable causes at least one of the of covariates ('reverse' causation), when there are relevant explanatory variables which are omitted from the model, or when the covariates are subject to measurement error.

a. Iteratively reweighted least squares
b. Instrumental variables
c. Unit-weighted regression
d. Omitted-variable bias

53. _____ is a measure of the number of deaths (in general scaled to the size of that population, per unit time. _____ is typically expressed in units of deaths per 1000 individuals per year; thus, a _____ of 9.5 in a population of 100,000 would mean 950 deaths per year in that entire population. It is distinct from morbidity rate, which refers to the number of individuals in poor health during a given time period (the prevalence rate) or the number who currently have that disease (the incidence rate), scaled to the size of the population.

a. 100-year flood
b. 1921 recession
c. 130-30 fund
d. Mortality rate

Chapter 1
1. d 2. d 3. d 4. d 5. c 6. a 7. c 8. b 9. b 10. d
11. c 12. c 13. d 14. b 15. d 16. a 17. d 18. a 19. d 20. b
21. d 22. d 23. d 24. d 25. a 26. d 27. a 28. d

Chapter 2
1. d 2. c 3. c 4. d 5. d 6. d 7. c 8. d 9. a 10. b
11. d 12. b 13. a 14. b 15. c 16. d 17. d 18. d

Chapter 3
1. d 2. d 3. a 4. b 5. d 6. d 7. d 8. c 9. b 10. d
11. b 12. b 13. a 14. d 15. d 16. b 17. d 18. c 19. d 20. a
21. d 22. d 23. d 24. a 25. a 26. d 27. b 28. c 29. d 30. a
31. b 32. c 33. d

Chapter 4
1. d 2. d 3. a 4. d 5. d 6. d 7. d 8. d 9. d 10. b
11. d 12. d 13. c 14. c 15. a 16. a 17. d 18. c 19. d 20. c
21. a 22. c 23. d 24. b 25. a 26. a 27. d 28. a 29. b 30. d
31. b 32. d 33. c 34. c 35. c 36. d

Chapter 5
1. c 2. d 3. b 4. c 5. d 6. d 7. a 8. c 9. d 10. d
11. c 12. d 13. c 14. c 15. d 16. d 17. a 18. a 19. d 20. d
21. d 22. b 23. d 24. d 25. a 26. c 27. a 28. d 29. b 30. d
31. d 32. d 33. d 34. d 35. d 36. a 37. b 38. b 39. d 40. d
41. c

Chapter 6
1. d 2. a 3. d 4. b 5. b 6. a 7. d 8. c 9. b 10. d
11. c 12. d 13. b 14. b 15. c 16. d 17. d 18. d 19. d 20. d
21. d 22. a 23. b 24. d 25. a 26. d 27. d 28. a 29. c 30. d
31. d 32. d 33. d 34. d 35. d 36. c 37. d 38. a 39. d 40. b
41. a 42. a

Chapter 7
1. a 2. d 3. a 4. a 5. c 6. d 7. b 8. d 9. a 10. d
11. c 12. a 13. a 14. d 15. d 16. c 17. d 18. d 19. d 20. d
21. d 22. d 23. d 24. d 25. b 26. d 27. b 28. b 29. a

Chapter 8
1. d 2. d 3. b 4. d 5. d 6. d 7. d 8. d 9. a 10. d
11. c 12. a 13. d 14. d 15. c 16. d 17. d 18. d 19. d 20. b
21. a 22. a 23. b 24. d 25. b 26. c 27. b 28. a 29. c 30. d
31. d 32. d

ANSWER KEY

Chapter 9
1. c 2. c 3. b 4. b 5. b 6. b 7. b 8. d 9. d 10. d
11. c 12. a 13. b 14. a 15. d 16. d 17. d 18. d 19. b 20. c
21. a 22. d 23. d 24. b 25. c 26. d 27. b 28. c 29. d 30. d
31. d 32. d 33. b 34. d 35. a 36. a 37. b 38. a 39. d 40. d
41. d 42. d 43. d 44. d

Chapter 10
1. d 2. c 3. c 4. d 5. a 6. c 7. a 8. d 9. d 10. d
11. b 12. d 13. d 14. c 15. d 16. d 17. d 18. a

Chapter 11
1. d 2. c 3. d 4. c 5. c 6. b 7. c 8. a 9. d 10. d
11. d 12. d 13. d 14. d 15. a 16. d 17. d 18. c 19. d 20. d
21. b

Chapter 12
1. d 2. d 3. a 4. d 5. d 6. c 7. d 8. b 9. b 10. d
11. d 12. d 13. d 14. a 15. a 16. b 17. d 18. b 19. d 20. d
21. a 22. d 23. b 24. c 25. d 26. d 27. a 28. d 29. b 30. d
31. d 32. c 33. d 34. d 35. d 36. b 37. b 38. d 39. b 40. b
41. c 42. a 43. c 44. d 45. a 46. c 47. d 48. d 49. d

Chapter 13
1. d 2. d 3. b 4. c 5. a 6. b 7. d 8. c 9. d 10. d
11. a 12. d 13. b 14. c 15. d 16. d 17. c 18. b 19. d 20. b
21. a 22. c 23. d 24. d 25. d 26. b 27. a 28. b 29. d 30. a
31. d 32. d 33. b 34. c 35. a 36. d 37. c 38. d 39. d 40. c
41. d 42. b 43. b 44. b

Chapter 14
1. b 2. b 3. d 4. b 5. b 6. c 7. b 8. d 9. c 10. b
11. a 12. a 13. d 14. d 15. d 16. b 17. c 18. d 19. d 20. d
21. b 22. c 23. d 24. d 25. b 26. d 27. d 28. b 29. a 30. d
31. d 32. d 33. d 34. a 35. c 36. d 37. b 38. d 39. b 40. d
41. d 42. a 43. d 44. a 45. d 46. d 47. d 48. c 49. d 50. d
51. d 52. d 53. d 54. d 55. d 56. a 57. a 58. b

Chapter 15
1. a 2. c 3. a 4. d 5. c 6. d 7. b 8. b 9. b 10. b
11. d 12. d 13. a 14. a 15. d 16. d 17. d 18. c 19. d 20. a
21. d 22. d 23. c 24. c 25. d 26. d 27. c 28. b 29. d 30. d
31. a 32. c 33. c 34. b 35. d 36. d 37. d 38. d 39. b 40. d
41. d

Chapter 16

1. b	2. b	3. b	4. d	5. d	6. d	7. c	8. d	9. d	10. d
11. d	12. c	13. a	14. d	15. b	16. d	17. b	18. c	19. d	20. d
21. c	22. c	23. d	24. b	25. d	26. d	27. a	28. d	29. b	30. c
31. b	32. c	33. c	34. a	35. d	36. d	37. d	38. c	39. d	40. a
41. b	42. d								

Chapter 17

1. d	2. d	3. b	4. a	5. d	6. a	7. c	8. b	9. b	10. d
11. a	12. b	13. b	14. d	15. d	16. d	17. d	18. a	19. b	20. d
21. a	22. d	23. b	24. d	25. d	26. b	27. d	28. d	29. d	30. b
31. a	32. b	33. a	34. a	35. d	36. a	37. a	38. c	39. a	40. d
41. d	42. b	43. d	44. d	45. a	46. d				

Chapter 18

1. d	2. d	3. b	4. a	5. b	6. d	7. d	8. c	9. d	10. b
11. d	12. d	13. a	14. d	15. b	16. d	17. c	18. d	19. d	20. d
21. a	22. d	23. d	24. a	25. a	26. d	27. c	28. b	29. d	30. d
31. b	32. a	33. b	34. b	35. a	36. d	37. d	38. b	39. c	40. d
41. d	42. d	43. b	44. a	45. a	46. a	47. d	48. d	49. c	50. d
51. d	52. d	53. a	54. d	55. d	56. d	57. d	58. d	59. a	60. c
61. b	62. d	63. d	64. d	65. b	66. d	67. d			

Chapter 19

1. a	2. d	3. b	4. d	5. c	6. c	7. d	8. d	9. c	10. d
11. d	12. b	13. d	14. d	15. a	16. a	17. d	18. d	19. a	20. b
21. d	22. b	23. d	24. a	25. d	26. d	27. d	28. a	29. d	30. d
31. c	32. d	33. d	34. c	35. d	36. c	37. d	38. d	39. d	40. d
41. b	42. b	43. a	44. d	45. d	46. b	47. b			

Chapter 20

1. d	2. b	3. c	4. a	5. d	6. b	7. b	8. d	9. b	10. b
11. d	12. d	13. a	14. a	15. d	16. d	17. d	18. a	19. d	20. d
21. a	22. c	23. a	24. b	25. d	26. d	27. a	28. d	29. d	30. d
31. c	32. d	33. d	34. a	35. b	36. d	37. a	38. b	39. a	40. d
41. c	42. d	43. d	44. d						

Chapter 21

1. d	2. b	3. d	4. d	5. a	6. d	7. d	8. a	9. d	10. d
11. d	12. a	13. b	14. d	15. d	16. d	17. d	18. d	19. b	20. d
21. c	22. c	23. d	24. a	25. c	26. d	27. c	28. d	29. d	30. c
31. b	32. d	33. d	34. d	35. c	36. d	37. a	38. d	39. d	40. d
41. a	42. d	43. a	44. c						

ANSWER KEY

Chapter 22

1. a	2. d	3. d	4. a	5. d	6. d	7. d	8. d	9. d	10. d
11. b	12. c	13. d	14. d	15. d	16. a	17. b	18. c	19. d	20. d
21. b	22. d	23. b	24. d	25. b	26. b	27. d	28. c	29. a	30. b
31. d	32. d	33. b	34. c	35. d	36. d	37. d	38. a	39. a	40. a
41. d	42. b	43. c	44. c	45. d	46. a	47. d	48. d	49. d	50. a
51. c	52. b	53. d							

www.ingramcontent.com/pod-product-compliance
Lightning Source LLC
Chambersburg PA
CBHW082147230426
43672CB00015B/2861